D0231509

LINK

INES DE CASTRO ■ JOHN CLIFFORD

'A sombre, beautiful play about the political martyrdom of a Portuguese prince's Spanish mistress. Based on historical events, the story has the sober majesty of a Schiller tragedy (*Mary Stuart* comes to mind) and the graceful condensed wit of Clifford at his non-whimsical best'. Michael Coveney.

BACK STREET MAMMY ■ TRISH COOKE

'Dynette is a black schoolgirl whose high academic potential is suddenly undermined by her burgeoning sexuality and an unwanted pregnancy . . . *Time Out.* 'Cooke's play is pro-abortion and sceptical about marriage, but resoundingly on the side of life . . , It has wit, passion and narrative agility'. Jim Hiley, *Listener.*

SLEEPING NIGHTIE ■ VICTORIA HARDIE

'A very special piece of theatre which successfully dramatises the internal emotional landscape of its characters while also addressing critical social issues like child abuse head on'. Lyn Gardner, *City Limits.*

UNA POOKA ■ MICHAEL HARDING

'Even in a large field, *Una Pooka* would stand out as a major work . . . For the weekend of the Pope's visit in 1979, a young childless couple put up in their council house the husband's family from down the country'. *Irish Press.* 'One of the most fascinating new Irish plays in at least a decade'. *Irish Times.*

LOOSE ENDS ■ STUART HEPBURN

'This encounter between an (apparently) streetwise Glasgow wide boy and a young Highlander . . . contains some of the sharpest and most perceptive writing I've come across'. *Guardian.*

VALUED FRIENDS ■ STEPHEN JEFFREYS

Winner of the 1989 *Evening Standard*'s Most Promising Playwright Award: 'About a group of friends sharing an Earl's Court basement flat in the recent property boom, *Valued Friends* is at first glance an enjoyable comedy, at second glance a perceptive, bitter-sweet study of a relationship askew, at third glance a statement about human insecurity'. *Financial Times.*

in the same series

First Run
Selected and introduced by Kate Harwood
  Prickly Heat by Simon Donald
  Inventing a New Colour by Paul Godfrey
  Low Level Panic by Clare McIntyre
  Leave Taking by Winsome Pinnock
  A Handful of Stars by Billy Roche

Stars in the Morning Sky
Introduced by Michael Glenny
  Heart of a Dog by Alexander Chervinsky
  Stars in the Morning Sky by Alexander Galin
  A Man with Connections by Alexander Gelman
  Forget Herostratus! by Grigory Gorin
  Three Girls in Blue by Ludmila Petrushevskaya

Australia Plays
Introduced by Katharine Brisbane
  Travelling North by David Williamson
  The Golden Age by Louis Nowra
  No Sugar by Jack Davis
  Away by Michael Gow
  The Rivers of China by Alma De Groen

Scot-Free
Introduced by Alasdair Cameron
  Writer's Cramp by John Byrne
  Losing Venice by John Clifford
  The Letter-box by Ann Marie Di Mambro
  Elizabeth Gordon Quinn by Chris Hannan
  Dead Dad Dog by John McKay
  Saturday at the Commodore by Rona Munro
  The Steamie by Tony Roper

FIRST RUN 2

■ NEW PLAYS BY NEW WRITERS

INES DE CASTRO ■ JOHN CLIFFORD

BACK STREET MAMMY ■ TRISH COOKE

SLEEPING NIGHTIE ■ VICTORIA HARDIE

UNA POOKA ■ MICHAEL HARDING

LOOSE ENDS ■ STUART HEPBURN

VALUED FRIENDS ■ STEPHEN JEFFREYS

SELECTED AND INTRODUCED BY
■ KATE HARWOOD

N
H
B

NICK HERN BOOKS

■ A Division of Walker Books Limited

A Nick Hern Book

First Run 2 first published in 1990 as an original paperback by
Nick Hern Books, a division of Walker Books Limited,
87 Vauxhall Walk, London SE11 5HJ

Set in Baskerville by Book Ens, Saffron Walden, Essex
Printed by Richard Clay Ltd, Bungay, Suffolk

British Cataloguing in Publication Data
First run 2.
  1. Drama in English – Anthologies
  I. Harwood, Kate
  822′.914′08

  ISBN 1-85459-002-2

Contents

Introduction

British Theatre is often accused of being too literary. Our critics say that in our productions language leads and that our directors are only interested in exploring what is said; that our actors speak their characters' thoughts beautifully but are physically repressed. It is often said too that our directors and designers lack visual flare and fail to make design visually active. On the other hand there is a great deal of respect for a number of foreign directors who are perceived as exploring and exploiting text in a way that British directors don't. It is also true that the most acclaimed of our young directing talents seem to be working hard to incorporate a variety of influences and to shift the central focus away from a reliance on language towards the totality of theatrical experience. However the history of the British theatre is the history of the British playwrights and any innovator in today's theatre is simply missing a trick if he or she does not look into the pool of resources that exists in contemporary theatre writing.

Much of the fresh energy of the past few years has come from new companies, such as Theatre de Complicité, Cheek by Jowl, Communicado, dereck dereck and Gloria. These companies have had great popular success, either with renovating classics, adapting novels or with devised work that uses language as only one component in the overall experience. Writers are credited as translators, adapters or contributors to the process but it is unusual that a writer initiates a project. The results are frequently invigorating and challenging, but ultimately limited. It's a bit like trying to hack a way out of the jungle with your stronger arm tied behind your back. How far can theatrical movement progress without new writers? Is playwriting no longer fashionable or, more alarming, no longer at the cutting edge of experiment in British Theatre? Is it possible to have a Theatre of Ideas without writers?

Innovation is one thing, but borrowing from other cultures and traditions can be a sterile exercise. True experimentation should be an organic experience, conducted with a knowledge and understanding of our own achievements. If only more of these companies would look for writers to complement their new-found styles, they would extend their range and might effect more permanent change in British theatre. Without new content new styles risk repetitiveness.

And the playwright needs to be included in the process. It is hard to write for the theatre from the outside; the best plays are written from within. Theatre is a craft with techniques that must be learnt and then made use of. The best playwrights are freed by its restrictions. It is not surprising that some of our most notable writers started their careers as actors. Rehearsing and performing quickly teaches a sense of what works theatrically, this knowledge becomes second nature and when applied by the actor/playwright makes for exciting and efficient work. Actors turned playwrights range from Shakespeare to Pinter, and the tradition continues with many of the current newer writers. But for those young playwrights who have never acted nor wanted to act, direct exposure to actors and the rehearsal process can offer similar liberation. It is no accident that the explosion of new writing talent in the sixties coincided with the formation and development of a number of new companies, such as Monstrous Regiment and Joint Stock, in which writers were strongly involved from the outset, while Portable Theatre was actually created by writers. In some cases, this involvement with a company could release and change the direction of a writer's work. Caryl Churchill's early plays, such as *Owners* and *Objections to Sex and Violence*, were often cerebral and, although filled with dramatic strength, would have relegated her to the margins of theatre history if her total output had been plays of that kind. But her exposure to performers and to the process of jointly creating a play with Joint Stock and Monstrous Regiment both deepened her writing and seemed to make it more accessible. Why can't the new contemporary companies find the writers that would speak for them? It could be that they don't see the attraction of working with new plays or playwrights, but they may feel that the writer who would suit their company's style of work doesn't exist. The playwrights *are* there, but won't appear until they are sought out and invited to join the process. Of course this isn't the only thing that is militating against new writing today but, as the freshest impulse has come from these newer style-based companies, it is calamitous that they aren't involving the writers. I urge them to do so.

Writing in autumn 1989, I find it hard to spot any growth area for new writing. The output of the theatres devoted to it is dwindling, and the past year has seen the closure (for the most part) of both the Royal Court's Theatre Upstairs and the Bristol Old Vic Studio. One response has been for many of the new writing venues and repertory theatres to try to find plays that they can co-produce, but this doubles the difficulties: it is hard enough to get *one* theatre interested in a play but now *two* managements have to fall for it, and what brings a gleam to the metropolitan eye may empty the theatre in Leeds. Another result is that playreadings have mushroomed, in the genuine belief that this is the best way in the current climate to encourage and develop writers. In reality the playreading is becoming an end in itself. We talk encouragingly of 'showcases', but the young writers bitterly lament the way their work is restricted and misrepresented in the one-off, hit-or-miscast static playreading. These are often the same type of plays that ten years ago would have been rehearsed and given a three-week run in a studio theatre. Although the play may have gone no further, at least the work would have been thoroughly tested and explored and the writer would have benefited from the valuable experience of seeing the work actually rehearsed, staged and exposed to a real audience. There would then be the possibility of real development.

Can the generation whose plays feature in this anthology produce writers of the weight and durability of Pinter, Hare or Churchill? I have no doubt that there are several young writers who have the potential of becoming dramatists of real and lasting stature, but I fear that our theatre is not providing the environment in which they can mature. The previous generation would have seen their work through several studio productions before moving on to a main stage. Now a young playwright will deliver a poorly-paid commission and be forced to wait for up to two years before the money can be scraped together to put the play on. This has a number of effects. Loyalty to a single theatre begins to break down, which is not wholly bad for the writer, but which does lead to an increased homogeneity in the output of the new writing theatres as the same half-dozen playwrights circulate from one to the other. Secondly that vital practical experience takes much longer to accumulate. And thirdly the writer cannot earn enough from the theatre and so is swiftly tempted by film and television. And financial success there is hard to forego. Very soon we find that the young writer, after only one or two studio successes, has no time to write another stage play, yet hasn't really perfected the craft before being 'lost' to screenwriting.

If, as I suspect, there is no real substitute for having several plays produced in order for a writer fully to develop, then we are already failing this generation of playwrights. But other areas could and should be opening up, not only within the new companies but also in our huge network of regional theatres, which must remain alive to working with both new and emerged playwrights. British theatre will not nor cannot move forward without its playwrights.

In the face of all this gloom, there have been advances that should not be overlooked. The most significant movement of the last two decades has been popular feminism, and this has been well reflected in the theatre. At the beginning of the year (1989), it was noted without surprise but with interest that the Royal Court was presenting consecutively six plays by women. However a cursory glance at some statistics also from the Royal Court (the only files to which I have access) shows that the great majority of women writers are still waiting at the door rather than filling the theatres with their work as they should be by now. Between 1956 and 1980 the Royal Court produced approximately 475 plays on its two stages or as one-off Sunday night 'plays without decor'. Only 39 of these were written or even co-written by women and twelve of the 39 were either by Ann Jellicoe or Caryl Churchill. From 1980 to the present the overall figure improves to 52 out of 176, and, though a breakdown of the productions since 1985 shows an astonishing 32 out of 40 playreadings to have been by women and likewise eleven out of 26 plays staged in the Theatre Upstairs, the Royal Court main stage still saw only six plays out of 29 produced to have been by women. The next move must be to take these women writers on to the larger stages. It would be interesting to know the comparable statistics for the other new writing theatres.

A growing body of work now exists from Black and Asian writers, and a great deal of energy from this source is still generated by the independent companies. In fact, the biggest black hit in London this year was an extraordinary piece of community theatre, a Reggae musical called *Ragamuffin*, written and directed by V Amani Naphtali for Double Edge Theatre Company. This played to packed houses in the Albany Empire, Deptford, and then in the Hackney Empire. The other touring ethnic companies still seem keen to promote new writing: indeed, Temba produced one of the plays in this volume. And I hope that the decision by Tara Arts to concentrate on classics for the time being won't permanently exclude new plays.

But new writing isn't only about innovation and new discoveries, and it is worrying that the theatre profession as a whole is in danger of being regarded as the 'nursery' to the film and television industries. Writers, actors and directors of talent seem to emerge in theatre and make their names only shortly before 'retiring' to the screen. This is alarming. Theatre is a serious and established art form and must be funded as such; it can't be allowed to decline into a testing ground. Besides, as television loses its interest in providing for minority voices as well as being under terrifying new commercial pressures, it is in our theatre that a forum exists that is comparatively free of censorship and with an ability to address its audience directly and immediately.

For the overall health of our profession, therefore, a flourishing commercial theatre is as important as the subsidised sector. Surveying the year as a whole from autumn 1988 to 1989, it was good to see a variety of new plays opening in the West End. Alan Ayckbourn's latest, *Henceforward*, was a bleak and at times barely comic view of futuristic Britain. *A Madhouse in Goa* by Martin Sherman and Iris Murdoch's *The Black Prince* were both unusual plays that lasted well in the West End. I saw three American imports: *M. Butterfly*, which repeated its Broadway success, and *Frankie and Johnny in the Clair de Lune* and *Steel Magnolias*, both lightweight comedies with lachrymose and sentimental endings. Later in the year Ronald Harwood's *Another Time* found favour for its strong performances and apparently serious theme.

Another American import that didn't go to the West End despite Broadway success was David Mamet's powerful Hollywood fable, *Speed the Plow*, which was only one of three new dramas on the main stages of the National Theatre. Deceptively light, the final act made dramatic and universal the murky moral choices faced in the film industry. David Storey's first play for some time, *A March on Russia*, covered rather familiar territory at the Lyttelton, while Joshua Sobol's *Ghetto*, in a version by David Lan, found huge audiences for a bravura theatrical portrait of life and death in the Jewish Ghetto at Vilna. The National's smallest theatre, the Cottesloe, staged one of the *three* Jim Cartwright plays that I saw this year. This play, *Bed*, a tremendously original concept, seemed to lack the drive of his first play, *Road*. Bolton's Octagon Theatre commissioned and produced his two-hander, *To*, with great success, and it was good to see a regional company making use of a local writer. The National Studio generously enabled the Royal Court to workshop Cartwright's new commissioned musical, *On*. It is hoped to mount a full production next year.

Caryl Churchill's eleventh play for the Royal Court was

produced in the spring. *Icecream* was a deceptively spare 'road-play' about contemporary Anglo/American attitudes. Less attention-grabbing than some of her earlier plays, it nonetheless proved mesmeric and unforgettable.

The Royal Shakespeare Company created a fringe to its fringe by producing two new plays for only a few performances at the Almeida by writers who should have been exposed to wider audiences in the RSC's own studio theatre, the Pit. In *H.I.D. (Hess is Dead)*, Howard Brenton produced some fine dramatic writing in a play that was largely influenced by the fact that it had been commissioned by the experimental Dutch theatre, The Mickery. There was video and choreography in a piece that challenged the accepted story of the death of Rudolf Hess. Nick Darke's play about Nicaragua, *Kissing the Pope*, had an extraordinary narrative drive with a story of localised skirmishes between the Contras and Sandinistas which gradually acquired wider political punch. At the Pit itself, there were two productions of new plays. The first was American playwright Richard Nelson's hugely entertaining *Some Americans Abroad*. Supposedly about America's attitude to British culture, it was really a campus novel on legs. The second, *Mary and Lizzie* by Frank McGuinness, was a satirical – fantasy about Marx and Engels during their sojourn in the North of England. Only one new play opened at Stratford this year following the sad closure of the Other Place, but for me it was unquestionably one of the best of the year. Vibrantly theatrical and savagely entertaining, Peter Flannery's *Singer* explored the pressure of the past on present individual and social behaviour in ambitious epic form.

Elsewhere, Leicester Haymarket mounted a welcome season of new writing with plays from Dick Edwards, David Drane, Graham Alborough and Gregory Motton. Dick Edwards's play, *Low People*, told a sad story of industrial slavery in a style reminiscent of German writers such as Kroetz. Gregory Motton's new play, *Looking at You (Revived) Again*, showed a man caught in a metaphoric wilderness between an old and a new love; passionate and lonely writing, it was good to see it transfer to the Bush Theatre. Earlier in the year Leicester had a huge hit with a bilingual English-Gujerati play, *Kirti, Sona and Ba* by Jezz Simons and Jyoti Patel, which struck a chord locally with its story of pressures on contemporary Indian families living in the city.

Liverpool Playhouse Studio invited several writers to contribute to a vision of Britain today entitled *Fear and Misery of the Third Term*, to be played as part of a double-bill with Brecht's *Fear and Misery of the Third Reich*. In the end, nine different writers obliged and still found something new to say about the effects of Thatcherism. The two playlets that have most remained with me were *You're a Nuisance Aren't You* by Charlotte Keatley, in which an Iron Lady showed a group of school children round a 'Heritage' museum, and *Means Test* by Nick Darke, in which an average Briton seemed doomed to deserve nothing from the State.

At least some small-scale companies were employing new playwrights. Some have that as their central policy and I enjoyed Paines Plough's adaptation of *Germinal* by William Gaminara. *Frida and Diego*, Greg Cullen's portrait (for Red Shift) of the tortured marriage of Diego Rivera and his wife Frida, was a poetic and painful play. Made in Wales, who are an important touring company for new Welsh drama, produced Peter Lloyd's tight little play, *The Scam*, about two urban kids trying to make it on the apple farms in the Welsh border country. And the company called 'I Cymri' brought us the explosive and ambitious family drama, *House of America* by Edward Thomas. The Women's Playhouse Trust produced Winsome Pinnock's second play, *A Hero's Welcome*, a moving account of three young Jamaican girls' dreams of escape in the fifties, and their relationships with their men, including the sad 'hero' of the title.

Other highlights of the year included *Iranian Nights*, Tariq Ali and Howard Brenton's short, sharp response to the Rushdie affair; Harwant Bains's ambitious and powerful second play, *Blood*, about the tragic aftermath of the events of Partition and its lasting effect on two cousins attempting to make good in contemporary London. Martin Crimp's new work for the Orange Tree, Richmond, *Play with Repeats*, was a strange, haunting piece about a man's failure to connect with modern society. Catherine Johnson's *Boys Mean Business* at the Bush – a striking follow-up to her award-winning, first play, *Rag Doll* – was a witty and sharply written picture of disaffected youth in a decaying seaside resort. Kevin Hood's *The Astronomer's Garden* for Croydon Warehouse, looked at passion beneath the stars with a play set in the life of the seventeenth-century astronomer, Halley. The actor Jack Shepherd also wrote a biographical play in which Tom Paine and William Blake battled it out in a garden *In Lambeth*.

Which brings me to my choice of plays for this volume. John Clifford's *Inés de Castro* was an oasis of good writing at this year's Edinburgh Festival. The play is based on a sixteenth-century Portuguese story of a tragic love affair. Clearly the writer's many translations of Spanish Golden Age drama have given him a feel for both the time and place, because this partly felt like a newly discovered classic, although shot through with a painful modernity. Simply told and immensely moving, it was a study of a mature couple trying to preserve an honest love in the face of appalling and overwhelming adversity.

I saw Trish Cooke's *Back Street Mammy* at the Lyric Studio, Hammersmith, in Temba Theatre Company's production. Trish's own performing career informed much of the play's lively immediacy, but its story of a young British-born West Indian girl's decision to have an abortion has a strong moral complexity that enriches the simplicity of its style. Equally effective is the use she makes of the older generation in the play, who are still trying to resolve their own tangled love affairs. A bold and promising debut.

I have known Victoria Hardie's *Sleeping Nightie* for some time, as it had been commissioned by the Royal Court, but I am relieved that through co-operation with Croydon Warehouse it hasn't had to wait too long for a production. A stylish look at a mother's fears for her newly born son in the light of her own blighted childhood, the play confronts the contemporary world and its problems head on, and if it finds it can't resolve them it is honest enough to identify some of them.

Michael Harding's *Una Pooka* is the only one of the six plays here that I didn't see, but I loved it when I read it. It was a huge success at the Peacock Theatre, Dublin, in the summer of this year. A grimly funny look at religion and superstition in the Irish character, it is also superbly written and theatrically inventive.

Stuart Hepburn's short two-hander was my only other delight in Edinburgh. *Loose Ends* is packed with dramatic action which is concentrated simply on the relationship between two young men adrift in Glasgow. In performance at the Traverse, it was very funny and very moving, no mean feat at 10 o'clock on a Festival morning.

Stephen Jeffreys's *Valued Friends* was seen at Hampstead Theatre early in the year, and as this volume goes to press there is news that it has won its author the 1989 Evening Standard Most Promising Playwright Award. Its story of the determination of a group of friends to resist the development of their rented flat and of their own subsequent decision to buy and exploit it is a microcosm of contemporary acquisitiveness. The play never sacrifices its characters to its idea, however, and it was a richly satisfying evening in the theatre.

Six very individual plays then, and their very individuality probably the major cause for celebration all year. The British theatre is lucky that so many writers still wish to write for it with such challenging and varied choices. I hope it remains flexible and open enough to accommodate them.

Kate Harwood
October 1989

INES DE CASTRO ■ JOHN CLIFFORD

John Clifford was born in North Staffordshire in 1950 but has lived in Scotland since 1968. He began his playwriting career by translating two plays by Calderon, *The House with Two Doors* and *The Doctor of Honour*. His first original plays were written for radio: *Desert Places* (BBC Radio Scotland, 1983) and *Ending Time* (BBC Radio 3, 1984). Between 1985 and 1987 he wrote three plays for Jenny Killick at the Traverse Theatre, Edinburgh: *Losing Venice* (also staged at the Almeida Theatre, London, at the Perth Festival, Australia, at the Hong Kong Arts Festival, on tour in Sweden, and in Los Angeles), *Lucy's Play* (also seen in Los Angeles) and *Playing with Fire*. Clifford has also translated and adapted Tirso de Molina's *Heaven Bent, Hell Bound* (Actors' Touring Company, 1987), Calderon's *Schism in England* (National Theatre and Edinburgh Festival, 1989) and *Celestina* by Fernando de Rojas (scheduled for the National Theatre in autumn 1990). At the time of going to press, Clifford is working on *Santiago*, a drama documentary for Channel 4.

Before directing *Inés de Castro*, Ian Brown previously directed Clifford's adaptations of *Romeo and Juliet* (his first piece of work for the professional theatre) and of *Great Expectations* (which toured the Near and Far East in the autumn of 1989). They plan to work together again on a new play set in the Third World.

Note

This story was first dramatised by Antonio Ferreira (1528–69).

It is based on a historical incident that supposedly occurred almost two centuries before, at a time of tension between Spain and Portugal, when the Spanish mistress of the then Crown Prince was murdered because she was considered a threat to the security of the state.

Ferreira was taught by the Scottish humanist, George Buchanan, at the University of Coimbra. Buchanan had dramatised incidents from classical mythology; he wrote tragedies in Latin verse, which he had his students act in class, to teach them the principles of the Greek tragic form.

Ferreira conceived what was then the revolutionary idea of taking an incident in Portuguese history, and turning it into a tragedy written in Portuguese. He did this because he wanted to assert the dignity of Portuguese language and culture.

The play was first published soon after the Spaniards invaded Portugal, and for very much the same reasons.

The great poet Luis de Camoens re-told the story in part of his poem *As Lusiadas*, an epic in which he wanted to give to Portuguese history the stature that the *Aeneid* gave to the history and people of Rome.

In what follows, I have re-invented history; I have taken nothing from the play, and have not attempted to dramatise the poem. But I would be happy if what I have written somehow reflects the spirit of both these works.

Characters

INÉS DE CASTRO
PRINCE PEDRO/CHORUS 1
PACHECO/CHORUS 2
BLANCA/CHORUS 3
NURSE/OLD WOMAN/CHORUS 4
KING/CHORUS 5

The Chorus do not speak as a mass. They are a succession of different individual voices of very ordinary people whose identity, when it matters, will be very apparent from what they say. They could be given more conventional labels like: Neighbour, Jewish Villager, Mother, Stallholder, Workman, Young Girl . . . but these seemed clumsy and cumbersome in the script.

There will be two areas to the set: an inner area where the action takes place, and an outer area, where the actors sit or stand when out of character. The stage directions 'Enter' and 'Exit' refer to the actor's relationship to the area of action. The actors remain on the stage throughout.

It would be good to have the four elements on the stage: earth, water, fire and air.

Also it might be useful to remember that tragedy began as a ritual, and it happened in a sacred place.

There is absolutely no need for the stage to look medieval. The story may happen in another place and time, but its concerns are very much from here and now.

Inés de Castro was first staged at the Traverse Theatre, Edinburgh on 8 July 1989 with the following cast:

INÉS DE CASTRO	Alison Peebles
PRINCE PEDRO/CHORUS 1	Stewart McQuarrie
PACHECHO/CHORUS 2	Alexander West
BLANCA/CHORUS 3	Hilary Maclean
NURSE/OLD WOMAN/CHORUS 4	Una McLean
KING/CHORUS 5	Stewart Preston

Directed by Ian Brown
Designed by Paul Brown
Lighting Design by Ace McCarron
Music by Richard Sisson

The play was commissioned by the Traverse Theatre with financial assistance from the Scottish Arts Council and the Calouste Gulbenkian Foundation (Lisbon) whose support is gratefully acknowledged.

Enter INÉS.

INÉS. I don't want to be shut in by the sky.
I don't want it pressing down on my head like a gravestone.
I don't want to be imprisoned by the heat.
I want everything to be open. I want flowers.
Flowers everywhere, and wind to blow them.
I want them to change, and shimmer, and give off the most
amazing scent.
I want the air to feel like silk.
And when I open my eyes in the morning
I want to see these things always as if for the very first time.
I don't want their colours to be dulled by habit
Or their scent to fade with the passing of time.
And when I turn from this beauty
To the faces of the people around me
I want to see it all reflected in their eyes.
I don't want deadness, habit, vacancy.
I want to walk down a street and see people greet each other.
See everyone always greet each other.
Meet with extravagant embraces and cries of delighted surprise.
And when they walk, I want to see purpose in their stride,
And energy and strength and fierce, fulfilled joy.
What I don't want, what I never want to see,
Is what I see now. What I see every day.
What I see in every face in every street at every moment.
What I'm told is the way things are
And the way things have to be.
For as I walk, when I look,
All I see is dead unhappy blankness and it drives me to despair.

Enter CHORUS.

CHORUS 1. You shouldn't want impossible things.

INÉS. Why not?

CHORUS 2. You'll be unhappy.

INÉS. Boring!

CHORUS 3. It's true.

INÉS. Rubbish!

CHORUS 2. You'll just make yourself miserable.

INÉS. Why do people always say such things?

CHORUS 5. Because they're true.

INÉS. They're not. They're not!

CHORUS 1. True for us, anyway.

CHORUS 2. We're ordinary people.

CHORUS 3. We do our jobs.

CHORUS 5. We don't have the leisure to reflect.

INÉS. You want me to be ordinary too?

CHORUS 1. We don't want to see you sad.

CHORUS 2. Tormenting yourself with impossible dreams.

CHORUS 3. And then, when they don't turn out to be true,
scourging yourself with disappointment.

CHORUS 5. We don't want to see you dead.

INÉS. No one's talking of death just now.

CHORUS 2. Not yet.

INÉS. What do you mean?

CHORUS 2. Nothing.

CHORUS 3. It's all far above our heads.

  Exit CHORUS. *Enter* NURSE.

INÉS. Nurse.

NURSE. I'm busy.

INÉS. Nurse!

NURSE. What?

INÉS. I'm frightened.

NURSE. Don't be frightened love.

INÉS. Why not?
  Why not?

NURSE. I've got my work to do.

INÉS. You used to care for me. You'd tell me stories. Wonderful
  stories.

NURSE. That was work dear.

INÉS. They were stories!

NURSE. None of them were true.

INÉS. They should be!

NURSE. Nothing is how it should be.

INÉS. Why won't Pedro come?

NURSE. He's been sent away.

INÉS. I sit and wait for him.
  I sit and curse myself for cowardice.

NURSE. He'll be back when he can.

INÉS. They say he's at the border
  Preparing for the war. A war against my people.

NURSE. It'll pass.

INÉS. It'll pass. It'll pass. That's what we always tell ourselves,
  As the clouds gather. As they mass above our heads.
  They'll go away, we imagine, they'll spare us.
  They'll spare our children. But don't we know,
  Deep inside, don't we know it's all a lie?
  There's too much poison in the world. It'll never go away.

NURSE. You think too much. Help me with the floor.

INÉS. I used to love the one about the princess
  Who was made to scrub the floors
  Because nobody knew who she was.
  Until the prince came by and knew her at once.
  I made that happen. The prince came.
  Came because I wanted him. And I escaped.
  Escaped from that dreary little town.
  That dead town I had to call my home.
  Perched on its clifftop and turning its back on the sea.
  Where all that ever happened was people going to church
  on Sunday.

Where they tore you to pieces if you didn't wear your scarf
just so,
Or left a speck of dust on your buckled shoes.
Where the only other thing that anyone ever spoke about
was death.

NURSE. It wasn't like that at all.

INÉS. It was. Nothing ever happened.

NURSE. Each day the men would harness the oxen to the boats
  and take them down the sands to the sea.
  Eight of them. Eight men to a boat.
  Each day. Each day except Sunday.
  No matter how wild the weather,
  Or how threatening the waves.
  They'd push the boats out.
  You'd look at the water and you'd think, how can anyone live,
  How can anyone go out in such sea and live.
  But the men didn't look. They'd stow their gear
  And get out their oars, and begin to row.
  And the surf would thunder in, as if nothing in the world could
  possibly resist it.
  But the men would push out the boats
  And row row against it,
  Row right through the heart of it
  And you'd stand and you'd watch
  And you'd think will they get through will they get through
  And the surf crashing in all around them.
  And then they'd be through and getting smaller and smaller
  And you'd say they'll be back before evening
  And you'd turn away.
  But once in a while, and no one could ever tell when,
  One week, perhaps, not a special week,
  One apparently ordinary day.
  That evening you'd go down with the oxen to the shore
  And you'd think: the wind's got up,
  And you could feel the cold, you could feel the coldness
  coming.
  But it had been calm that morning, you'd remember,
  The waves had been smaller, you remember,
  And you'd thought, today at least,
  You'd thought, today at least they'll be safe.
  And then you'd stand with your oxen
  And your feet in the shifting sand

And you'd count them returning.
And then you'd stand and you'd stand
And the others would all turn away.
For that day, that very ordinary day,
Was the day they never came back.

INÉS. I'm sorry.

NURSE. And you tell me nothing ever happened.

INÉS. I wasn't thinking.

NURSE. You never think!

INÉS. I want to live! That's all I ever wanted. And they all hated me and wanted me dead.

NURSE. You shouldn't say such things. You should be ashamed.

INÉS. It's true.

NURSE. They never did. No one would want such a wicked thing.

INÉS. Will you stop cleaning!

NURSE. The floor's dirty.

INÉS. I don't care!

NURSE. And besides someone's coming.

INÉS. Who?

NURSE. I've forgotten. You got me all upset.

INÉS. I didn't mean to.

NURSE. You weren't to know. It all happened before you were born. I just cleaned for your father then. Until the day your mother died and I found myself holding you. You were so tiny. And I said to myself don't touch her. Don't. Put her down. They'll only take advantage. And they did. But I couldn't. I couldn't put you down. You were so tiny. So helpless. All I wanted was to keep you safe. I swore I'd protect you. A fine mess I've made of it.

INÉS. You have not.

NURSE. I have so. Look at you. Among all these foreigners. These Portuguese. They hate you more than your own folk ever did. I wish we were home.

INÉS. No. I'm glad I left. Glad! We've been happy.

NURSE. It won't last.

INÉS. Why not?

NURSE. Never trust a man. He'll go and die on you. They all do.
   They just go and die on you out of spite.

INÉS. He's not like that.

NURSE. They're in love with death, the lot of them.
   Death is their companion. Death their friend.
   I've watched them. When they pray to the lady in the chapel
   it's not for safety but for strength.
   For the courage to meet death in the eye and never falter.
   That's what they pray for. All of them. Not for life. Not for
   love. But for a good death.
   And they're all the same. You've been happy with yours but
   you'll pay for it.

INÉS. I don't care what it costs.

NURSE. Well you should.

INÉS. How can you say such things. You helped us.

NURSE. You were fretting yourself to pieces. And he had a way
   with him.

INÉS. He looked at me like no one else.
   Not like an object or a piece of meat.
   Not like a jewel or the fulfilment of a dream.
   Not like the men my father always pushed at me. With their
   greedy faces and their groping hands. The ones I was meant to
   marry. Marry to conclude some alliance or cement some deal.
     All of them were liars. Brave sometimes with their swords,
   but cowards with their inner selves. Inept useless cowards. He
   wasn't like that at all. Not the one I chose. I knew it, the
   minute I saw him I knew it, and I wanted him.

NURSE. He was married.

INÉS. That's never been a marriage. You know that. It was just
   politics. He never loved her. She never gave him children. They
   were never happy. They've never laughed. Not like us.

NURSE. You used to laugh together the whole night long. I never
   got a wink of sleep.

INÉS. You never wanted to sleep!

NURSE. You'd walk by the sea and the waves would never touch you. But now the tide is lapping at your feet. It had to. It was madness.

INÉS. It was joy. Joy for both of us.

Enter PACHECO.

PACHECO. And now it's over.

INÉS. Pacheco!

PACHECO. Madam.

INÉS. I do not wish to see you.

PACHECO. What you wish is not my concern. I serve the king.

INÉS. They say that kings in ancient times used slaves to clear the road. They walked ahead with wooden brooms so the royal eyes were not insulted by the sight of dirt. That is all your function is. And you are debased enough to take a pride in it. But do not imagine for a moment you can sweep me aside.

PACHECO. You exaggerate your importance.

INÉS. You may be councillor to the king. You may be accustomed to see people grovel at your feet. But I will not. And don't think you can frighten me.

PACHECO. I can smell your sweat.
Shall we go in? We need to talk alone.

INÉS. Go in. I'll follow when I choose.

Exit PACHECO.

INÉS. Where are the children?

NURSE. Safe. I heard he was coming, so I had them hidden.

INÉS. Don't tell me where. Not yet. Tell me how I can thank you.

NURSE. By staying alive. Go into him. And watch your tongue.

Exit INÉS. *Enter* CHORUS 3.

CHORUS 3. I hate having to wait. I hate watching someone with death hanging over them. I hate being helpless. Not knowing what to do. What to do to stop it happening.

NURSE. There's nothing we can do. That's the worst of it. Nothing at all.

CHORUS 3. I was glad at first when they brought her here.

NURSE. After all those years of exile. Years of them trying to shut her out, out of sight, out of mind. Years of them trying to pretend she didn't exist. I thought, at last they've given a place for her. At last they've recognised her right to be in the world.

CHORUS 3. It was work for us. Real work. And good money.

NURSE. The children lost their pinched and frightened faces. They started to laugh and build dams across the streams.

CHORUS 3. The work we had to do on that house. The state it was in. All shuttered and barred. Cobwebs in all the corners. We had to scrub everything. We took down the shutters and threw open the doors.

NURSE. And I thought, she has found a home. At last she has found a home.

CHORUS 3. When we finished it looked lovely. We filled the house with flowers.

NURSE. I hope they spare the children.

Exit CHORUS 3 *and* NURSE. *Enter* PACHECO *and* KING.

KING. Is she there?

PACHECO. Your Majesty.

KING. Is she there?

PACHECO. Where else could she be?

KING. Did she see you?

PACHECO. She had no choice.

KING. Is she prepared?

PACHECO. That is her affair.

KING. What did she say?

PACHECO. She wept. I thought she would be stronger.

KING. When did she weep?

PACHECO. When I mentioned the children.

KING. But they are to be safe.

PACHECO. I think it a mistake.

KING. I did not ask you to think.

PACHECO. They will be found. Someone will use them against you.

KING. They are only children. They have no legitimate rights. They are harmless.

PACHECO. You do not wish to hurt her.

KING. No.

PACHECO. Politics is an ugly business. It is better to do what must be done.

KING. Must it be done?

PACHECO. There's no point in being gentle. You won't get any thanks for it.

KING. It is not a question of thanks. It is a question of what is right.

PACHECO. Of what is right? We know what is right. It is right to kill her.

Enter INÉS.

INÉS. And who gives you that right?

PACHECO. How dare you interrupt!

INÉS. You expect me to sit and weep and then quietly disappear? Is that what you think?
    Do you think me such a coward? Do you so greatly despise me?

KING. We do not despise you, Inés. Nor do we wish to harm you. But you must leave. You are a threat to us.

INÉS. You must be very weak, to be threatened by the likes of me.

KING. We are at war with your country.

INÉS. That has nothing to do with me.

PACHECO. You belong to our enemies and you lie with our prince. Your presence weakens us. You must be removed.

INÉS. You speak of people as if they were abstractions. That I cannot do. I do not understand you. We do not speak each other's language.

KING. But we live in the same world.

I am forced to compromise. I have no choice. Those who sustain me perceive you as a threat. Whether you intend it or not. It makes no difference. They fear you. They fear for their country. For their lives. Can you not understand? They want me to kill you. I beg you. Go back to your father.

INÉS. He hates me more than you.

KING. I do not hate you.

INÉS. Do you know what he will call me? A fallen woman. Apparently I have fallen. Do you know what they do to fallen women? To those with the courage to deserve the name?

They will smear my children with dirt. They will set spies on me to watch my every move until, in the end, they find some pretext to stone me. They always do. Is that what you call humane?

KING. Others wish you worse.

INÉS. What harm have I done them? What harm have I done anyone? Why can't I be left to live in peace?

KING. Inés I am truly sorry. At other times I would embrace you as my child. But our countries are at war. There is nothing to be done. Do not force us to do you harm.

INÉS. Why is it tyrants always blame the victims for their crimes?

PACHECO. Why is it that criminals always protest their innocence?

INÉS. I have done nothing!

PACHECO. Denial is clear evidence of guilt.

KING. Inés there is very little time. I cannot hold him off for any longer. You must leave the country. You have the choice. Life or death. Inés. Believe me. Leave here and you will be safe. Your children will be safe. Life is easily within your grasp. But not for long. It is slipping away from you. You will never get it back.

INÉS. I have lived with your son for many years. In spite of all your efforts to separate us. In spite of everything you have done to tear us apart. We have still been happy. I have born his children. Your grandchildren. My life is bound up with them, as it is with him. We have committed no crime. Why should I leave him?

PACHECO. Because otherwise you'll die.

INÉS. At least give me time.

PACHECO. You have an hour.

Exit KING *and* PACHECO. *Enter* CHORUS 1.

INÉS. What shall I do?

CHORUS 1. There has to be an answer. Don't despair.

INÉS. Always ready with a platitude.

CHORUS 1. I'm a cobbler. I've my little shop. Nothing special.
Nothing fancy, nothing big. But it suits me. On a good site. I
just sit inside, outside when it's fine, sit and mend my shoes.
And I can watch the folk on their way to market. And people
look in sometimes. We have a wee bit chat, pass the time of
day. Then they go again. On Saturdays, I have an extra bottle
of wine. I like a good song. I got no complaints.

INÉS. What use is that to me?

CHORUS 1. I just thought I'd let you know.
Sometimes it's safer to be ordinary.
Always do what's easiest. That's what I'd recommend.

Exit CHORUS 1. *Enter* CHORUS 2, 4, 5.

INÉS. So should I really go to Spain?

CHORUS 2. A man from our village went to Spain. He said he
had to see his cousins. He was in a hurry to go, before they
closed the border. He said he wanted to talk to them. Just the
once, before he died. Just came back the other week. His hair's
turned white. He won't sleep. He walks up and down our
street, making speeches. 'Brother Jews', he shouts, 'Remember
Spain!' He don't make any sense. He says when he went to his
cousin's village it was gone. All of it. Not a building left
standing. Not a stone on a stone. Makes no sense. Who would
destroy a village? No one here has ever heard of such a thing.
He says they'd all been taken to some prison place. A place of
cries and screams and thick choking smoke. All of them. Every
one. Children too. Children. Who would do such a thing? Not
even Spaniards. He says they're all being made to dig their own
graves. And he can't sleep, he can't sleep, because if he rests for
even a moment they'll creep up on him and make him dig his
grave too. And he has to warn us, he must warn us, warn us of

what is to come. So he walks up and down our houses shouting 'Remember Spain! Remember Spain!' We've had to lock him up. He was disturbing everybody.

INÉS. But I'm not a Jew!

CHORUS 2. That's what they all say. Apparently. Doesn't help a bit.

Exit CHORUS. *Enter* BLANCA.

BLANCA. The ovens aren't particular who they burn.

INÉS. Why are you here?

BLANCA. Isn't a wife allowed to see her husband's lover?

INÉS. Have you come to gloat?

BLANCA. I was expecting some great beauty. I feel disappointed. You look quite ordinary. Perhaps because you're under stress.

INÉS. Insulting me is a poor revenge.

BLANCA. The only one I've had for years.

INÉS. I never meant you any harm.

BLANCA. What you meant to do me doesn't matter. What matters is what you did.

INÉS. I did nothing.

BLANCA. You took my husband.

INÉS. We couldn't help ourselves.

BLANCA. Couldn't you. How interesting. I wonder how it feels.

INÉS. You haven't been there, so you wouldn't know.

BLANCA. I wouldn't want to be there. Certainly not where you are now. I've always tried to be correct. You never have. You always did what took your fancy. And so you were such a potent source of fascination. Apparently. Whilst I was insulted and ignored. But all that's over now. I'm very glad.

INÉS. I have an hour. They say that's all that's left for me. I will not spend it with the likes of you.

Exit INÉS. *Enter* PEDRO.

PEDRO. Inés!

BLANCA. It's me.

How typical. The only time my husband ever talks to me is by mistake. And then he turns away. He looks so disappointed.

Do you imagine I don't notice? Look at me. I am human too.

PEDRO. I cannot bear to see you.

BLANCA. What have I done?

PEDRO. You? You've done nothing. I have done you wrong. Each time I see you I have an overwhelming sense of guilt. It rises in my throat. It is a kind of nausea.

BLANCA. Each time you hurt me I feel this urge to apologise. This must stop.

PEDRO. Why are you here?

BLANCA. To see her die.

PEDRO. She is not to die!

BLANCA. Your father does not think so.

PEDRO. He gave me a promise.

BLANCA. Pacheco has the papers in his hand.

PEDRO. Father!

BLANCA. Don't talk to him. Turn back to me! Have I so suddenly ceased to matter?

PEDRO. Yes.

Enter KING. *Exit* BLANCA.

KING. We should embrace.

PEDRO. We cannot.

KING. You should not be here. Inés is safe.

PEDRO. I have just heard otherwise.

KING. Ignore your wife. She's crazed with jealousy.

PEDRO. Do you promise me?

KING. I promise.

PEDRO. You gave me your promise once before. When you sent me to the border. I felt you were lying then. I had to come back. Why should I believe you now?

KING. You're playing into Pacheco's hands. He'll call it treachery if the Spaniards invade.

PEDRO. He can call it what he likes.

KING. I will have to call it treachery too.

PEDRO. You know that is a lie.

KING. This love of yours is a kind of madness. I have told you many times.

PEDRO. I cannot help it.

KING. You must.

PEDRO. Am I simply meant to be a man in armour? Am I not to feel?

KING. You have to do your task. You were sent to organise defence.

PEDRO. What's the use of defending if I cannot love?

KING. What's the use of love without defence? Go. She will not come to any harm.

PEDRO. I don't believe you.

KING. You know me too well.

PEDRO. You taught me to distinguish truth from lies. You showed me the signs. The changed expression in the voice. The involuntary movement of the hands. You taught me all the useful knowledge that I have.

KING. I never thought you'd use it against me.

PEDRO. I was always in such awe of you.
You were everything to me. You were the king.
And when you turned your eyes on me I thrilled in
every part of me.
My heart started to hammer in my chest and I would try
so hard.
I wanted your approval. I'd have done anything.
And when it came, when you gave me some approving
word,
Tossed it to me like a crumb,
I lapped it up and felt so proud.
I felt I surely must have swelled to twice my size.
I felt I surely had at last become a man.

I never dreamed I'd ever have to stand against you.
Because I found you undermining all my happiness.

KING. It makes no difference. It does not matter what you think
or feel. We both of us could wish things to be different, but
now there is no choice. She has to go. If not she'll die. Don't
rail at me. Don't overwhelm me with reproaches. I could not
bear it. Go in and see her. Say your last farewell.

Exit PEDRO. *Enter* PACHECO.

PACHECO. You've let him in to see her.

KING. What else could I do? He is my son.

PACHECO. What's happened to you? We used to get on so well.
We understood each other. We got things done. But in this
affair you've been so weak. You haven't taken up religion? Or
are you simply getting old?

KING. You're very confident.

PACHECO. I have a right to be.
I think you must be tired.

KING. Tired of you perhaps.

PACHECO. You cannot threaten me. I am indispensable.
Remember that. There's been a string of failures. Your life is on
the line.

KING. He has the right to say farewell.

PACHECO. They will strengthen each other. They always do. We
need them vulnerable.

KING. No good will come of killing her.

PACHECO. The harm will come if you let her live. You'll lose
your army and you'll lose your life. You know that. You know
that in your bones. Why you cannot accept it I do not
understand.

KING. It is hateful to have to do what you know is wrong.

PACHECO. It is hateful to die. There's something that's more
hateful still. Remember that. Do what must be done.

Exit KING *and* PACHECO. *Enter* INÉS *and* CHORUS 4.

INÉS. I saw the children. They were very brave. They didn't cry
at all. Felipe swallowed very hard, as if there was a choking in

his throat. He squared his shoulders, or he tried, but they kept hunching down. His voice was shaking, but he tried to steady it. Mario said nothing. He held out his hand. And when I kissed him, he looked away. What have I done to them? What have I done?

CHORUS 4. My daughter's started to paint her toes. Where did she get that from? I told her, I said, whoever's heard of such a thing? And she said, well you haven't obviously. Cheeky thing. I said what's wrong with them the way they are? and she said, they're just boring. I expect they'll all drop off I said and serve you right. And what are you doing it for anyway? She said, boys like it. Honest mum they do. And I said, no they don't and she said, How do you know? Well, I said, your father doesn't like it. She said, so what, he's just like you. Middle-aged. That's brain death, that is, middle age. And I said, middle age? Middle age? And then I thought, she's right. I'm middle-aged. Time does creep up on you. And these days it's a crime just to be old.

INÉS. It's a crime to love, that's all.

Enter CHORUS 5.

INÉS. Now I've gone they'll have buried their heads to sob in the straw. What will become of them?

CHORUS 5. They'll be taken up river, to its source. The nurse has fixed it up. There is a tiny village there. Where my cousins live. A remote and distant place. No one will know them. No one will come. We'll say they're orphans. People will be glad to take them in. They'll have to work, mind, but that won't do them any harm. They'll be fed and sheltered and given care. That's all we can do. What happens to them next isn't our affair.

INÉS. I had such hopes for them. Their lives were to be so much better than ours. Useless hopes. Blighted by this war. Why do people fight? Why can't we live in peace?

CHORUS 4. Don't ask me.

CHORUS 5. I've got a neighbour. Beats his woman black and blue. We can hear it every night. The walls are thin. My wife says we should do something and I say what? He's a big man. I wouldn't fancy a fight with him. And she said, well how do you think she feels? And I said, well if she didn't like it then she'd leave. And she said, well perhaps she can't. I said what's

stopping her? She's a free woman isn't she? Go back to sleep.
But we couldn't sleep for all the screaming. And the next day
she kind of crept about and tried to hide her battered side.
Kept in the shadows where the marks wouldn't show. I said you
should leave him and she said I can't. Why not? I said. She
said, because I love him. In that case, I said, you try and make
less noise. Night after night. You're keeping us awake. I'm tired
of this. And all she did was cry. Some folk have no
consideration.

INÉS. Must we live like this?

CHORUS 4. Find some other way.

INÉS. There isn't any time.

   Exit CHORUS 4 *and* 5. *Enter* PEDRO.

PEDRO. Inés.

INÉS. I never thought you'd come.

PEDRO. I was ordered not to. I disobeyed. I had to come to you.
   I rode along deserted and forgotten paths.
   Some premonition haunted me. The moon was full.
   I passed the ruins of the mountain villages,
   The settlements my father tried to make
   To take the displaced peasants from the towns.
   He took me there when I was a child. He made a speech.
   I remember looking down upon a sea of lined and weary faces
   All looking up at me. And in their eyes there was a kind of
   hope.
   They looked so small, so tiny in front of the mountains.
   I forget his words. Something inspiring I expect. He could
   always make a speech.
   When it was over, they went back and started work.
   Their feet dragged in the dust.
   They walked as though their bodies were enormous weights.
   Yet they were thin as ghosts.
   All the fields were full of stones.
   Women and children stood in a shivering line,
   Passing them from hand to hand.
   And in the distance men with an iron plough
   Would scratch the meagre earth.
   And all that's gone. That weary, endless labour.
   Every trace of it has disappeared.
   The huts have fallen down.

All that's left standing are the walls,
Snaking up and down the empty hills. They stretch for miles.
And I don't understand. I don't understand these walls.
Dividing the earth into tiny, useless plots.
Monuments to wasted energy. Why do we build so many walls?
Why don't we till the ground?
We could make the earth a paradise.

INÉS. Why don't we try?

PEDRO. We did. It brought us here.

INÉS. Must we accept this is the end?

PEDRO. No. No!

INÉS. We've always lived on borrowed time.

PEDRO. Why should it run out now? And here?
We've made love here so many times.

INÉS. We touched like this.

PEDRO. And this.

INÉS. And this!

PEDRO. And we escaped. We got away!
They could put guards on all the gates
They could set spies upon us to watch our every move.
But we got away! We got away!
Here. Lying on the grass and leaves.
Exploring all the different ways of giving pleasure.
Open to each other. Without defence.
And I was free of all the odious tasks
Living puts on me. Free of the divisions
Free of the split between the person that I am
And the person I'm supposed to be.
In a different world. A paradise.

INÉS. We built a city here. Our city.
Beneath these trees. We walked its streets.
We smelt its air. We heard its fountains
Playing in the city squares.
We created it each time we touched.
We laid out its geometry,
We described its avenues
In the intimate sweet language bodies have.

PEDRO. It was beautiful.

I won't believe this world has power over it.
I won't believe it.
It won't ever be destroyed or lost.

They embrace. Enter PACHECO.

PACHECO. Madam.

INÉS. How cruel you are. You saw us together and came to separate us. Can't you leave us be? Is happiness a crime?

PACHECO. Treachery is.

PEDRO. Then we have nothing to fear.

PACHECO. Naturally. Besides, you misjudge me. I did not come to separate you or tear you apart. The king has news for you. That's all. Go in together. He waits for you.

Exit PEDRO *and* INÉS.

PACHECO. The Spaniards have broken through the pass. The one he was entrusted to defend. A runner brought the news. The king's distraught. The army talks of betrayal. I knew they would. And if I know the prince, he'll want to prove them wrong. He'll try. He'll strike a pose. A fine heroic gesture. It won't help him at all. He doesn't stand a chance. They've broken through. They'll march across the plain. They can bring their full strength to bear. He'll arrive exhausted with a tiny force. They'll be ill-equipped, outnumbered ten to one. He'll never stop to make a proper plan. He'll rush upon the Spaniards. He'll be very brave. And they will crush him.

Exit PACHECO. *Enter* PEDRO *and* INÉS.

INÉS. What are you doing?

PEDRO. Getting ready.

INÉS. You're not going?

PEDRO. I must.

INÉS. You're mad.

PEDRO. I am responsible. Don't you understand? It would not have happened if I'd been there.

INÉS. You don't know that.

PEDRO. I must assume it.

INÉS. And you'll leave me here to die?

PEDRO. My father promised.

INÉS. And now you suddenly believe him.

PEDRO. I have no choice.

INÉS. There's a knife at my throat.

PEDRO. What else can I do?

INÉS. Revolt against your father. Refuse to fight the Spaniards.
Use your imagination!

PEDRO. I can imagine very well. I know the Spaniards.
I know what they will do. They'll burn villages and towns.
Kill everyone they find. Rape the women. Make all the children
slaves. And worse. Make us consent to slavery. Destroy our
pride. Make our country a shadow of itself, a mockery. Destroy
our sense of who we are. Of who we could become. We'll come
to pride ourselves on helplessness. We'll make a virtue out of
glorious defeat. We'll serve their purposes and not our own. I
won't suffer that. I'd rather die.
You cannot understand. You're one of them.

INÉS. Must we part as strangers?

PEDRO. It seems we must.

INÉS. You sound just like your father. There's nothing to be
done, he says. And then he lets out a little sigh. Like one of
yours. And with that sigh he has condoned a thousand crimes.

PEDRO. I'm trying to talk of how things are.

INÉS. I think I know. At least I know how men are.
You carry armour and you wear these swords.
And not just them, much greater weapons of
destructiveness.
All the appurtenance of power and strength.
But underneath all that you're just excuses.
Whimpering reasons for helplessness.
And I believed in you. I won't be fooled again.

PEDRO. You're unjust to me.

INÉS. You're leaving your children to be killed!

PEDRO. If the Spaniards catch them, they will kill them too.

INÉS. Where can I take them? Is there nowhere safe?

PEDRO. Nowhere.

INÉS. Is this all the world is? A wilderness?

PEDRO. I don't know.

INÉS. We were talking of a city. Not so long ago, although it seems we were in a different world. A city of our dreams. A place of safety. A place of trust. A place that nurtured people, not sucked them dry. Where they could grow, not be destroyed. And I believed in it. I believed we made it for ourselves. I believed that it was real. More real than that false city over the river. The one the soldiers guard and where the traders ply their wares. More real than the world outside, more real than this bitter country you're called on to defend.

    And now it's all been ruined. Like your father's villages. There's nothing left but broken walls. Walls to surround a dry and barren ground. Something's been broken that's beyond repair.

PEDRO. I won't believe that. I won't. I won't.

INÉS. It's true!

PEDRO. Despair's our enemy. If we give way to it, we shall destroy our happiness.

INÉS. Our happiness! Happiness is such a fragile thing. Everything inside us and around us conspires to break or damage it. Everything in the world we've made. But what else are we here for? What other purpose have our lives?

PEDRO. We do what we can. What we must. That's all. We have to trust all will be well.

They part. Enter KING, PACHECO *and* CHORUS 3 *and* 4. PEDRO *prays.*

PEDRO. Lady of sorrows. Lady of tears.
In time of trouble we have always turned to you.
Protect us now. Save us from our enemies.
Place us in your guard. Guard our country.
Guard all those we love. Guard our children. Keep them safe.
Save them from the fire and from the knife.
Save them from hatred and the loss of innocence.
Lady save us all.
We know we are not worthy.
We have trampled your garden
And poured filth in your streams.

They say that you look down on us and weep.
Dry your tears. Come to our aid.
And if we do not deserve to live
At least give us the courage to accept our death
And to embrace it joyfully.

Exit PEDRO.

CHORUS 4. What'll it do to the meat trade. That's what worries me.

CHORUS 3. War's bad for business.

CHORUS 4. People don't have the cash to spend on luxuries.

CHORUS 3. And labour gets so short. You can never find the slaughtermen.

CHORUS 4. They're all elsewhere engaged.

CHORUS 3. The price will fall. You mark my words.

CHORUS 4. And all kinds of dubious things will start turning up in pies.

PACHECO. He's gone.

KING. He went off so hopefully.

PACHECO. It is the best solution.

KING. I've sent my own son off to die.

PACHECO. It's called strong leadership. It's much admired.

KING. He said he felt certain help would come. He was not afraid of death, he said, because it was better than to live in shame. He said he could not understand it, but he felt a kind of hope. He knew all would be well.

PACHECO. An optimist to the end. Now he's gone, we can rid ourselves of her.

KING. Haven't you had your fill of blood?

PACHECO. It's nothing to do with any thirst for blood. I'm not talking about reasons or desires or appetites. I'm talking about the facts. Why can't you see this? Why have you gone blind?

KING. I gave my promise.

PACHECO. You had to give your promise. Or else he would not have gone. That's all that promises are for.

KING. Must it be done?

PACHECO. We have at most two days. Once they have beaten him, they'll rest. Spaniards always over-estimate their victories. They'll celebrate. They will be slack. And then, precisely then, we'll attack them at the rear. It must be nicely judged. They won't give us a second chance. And you must lead us. It is a crucial time. And the army knows what has brought it all about. Your son's so-called love for the enemy. The army calls it something else. I won't repeat it, I won't offend your ears. But treachery's an ugly word. He is your son. If you condone it, then you too are involved in it. You'll ride in front. Your back is very vulnerable.

KING. But is it just?

PACHECO. Just? We'll have to call it justice, yes.

KING. I've always wanted to be just.

PACHECO. How do they portray justice? With a blancmange?
With a sword. And why a sword?
Because justice must be stern.
Justice cannot flinch. She cannot hesitate.
And she wears a blindfold on her eyes.
She does what must be done.
But she does not have to see the blood.
There is no other way.

KING. I wash my hands of this.

PACHECO. You will know nothing. You can easily deplore it afterwards.

Exit KING *and* PACHECO.

CHORUS 4. There's the prince gone off to war. I'm glad it isn't me.

CHORUS 3. He had to ask the heavens for help. He won't get nothing down on earth.

CHORUS 4. It used to be St James who did the job. Appearing in the sky to frighten off the enemy. But then he turned Spanish so we can't use him now. So mostly we have to make do with St George.

CHORUS 3. He's not bad. Not very reliable. I couldn't claim that you could count on him. But very useful when he comes.

CHORUS 4. Some people say he's English. That would explain his eccentricity. I'm not very partial to the English, speaking personally. Still, at least they live a long way off.

CHORUS 3. Our prince'll have to hedge his bets. If he gets anyone, that is. He'll say it was an angel. Fair enough. He wants to stay clear of foreign saints. Wouldn't do to offend his mistress. They fight enough as it is.

CHORUS 4. What I don't understand is why these saints get mixed up in all this madness.

CHORUS 3. I'd have thought they had more sense.

Exit CHORUS 3.

CHORUS 4. They could do far more for the meat trade. See me, I've all these sausages to clear. Why can't a saint ever come to me? Or to the customers. I'm sure it could easily be arranged. I'm not greedy. I'd be happy with a small one. Hovering in the sky. Just there. Where they wouldn't have to crane their heads too much to see. Warning them to stay clear of the garbage that Maria sells and come to me instead. And they'd get a bargain. I don't cheat. But I know what you're saying, you're saying what a nerve! She's no saint. Well I know that. But neither are they. You ever met a general? Awful people. Very strange. They get angels all the time. So why not me? I'm as good as them. Well? You up there? You listening?

Enter INÉS.

INÉS. He just struts off and goes. He talks of duty. He mutters reassurance. All will be well, he says. I'll not believe him. I won't be such a fool.

CHORUS 4. My man's like that. See him. When he gets wind of a bargain, there's no stopping him. Never mind me. Never mind the children. He's just away. And when I tell him, wait a minute, wait a minute! There's other people in this world. You were going to spend some time with me . . . he just gets so angry. Never mind that the kids go up to strangers in the street 'cause they've forgotten who's their daddy. Never mind anything. If it's not his work it doesn't exist.

Enter BLANCA. *Exit* CHORUS 4.

INÉS. What are they for? Men. Why do we think we need them? What kind of joke is it nature plays on us?

BLANCA. It's not a joke. It's just the way things are. It's called normality.

INÉS. It never seemed that way to me. It struck me as a kind of miracle that we should meet. We, of all the people in the world.

BLANCA. It was arranged. Everything was organised. We never questioned it. It seemed appropriate. Why weren't we happy? We should have been.

INÉS. Did you dream of love?

BLANCA. Of nothing else. It kept me alive, in the long hours of embroidery. I knew what I had to do. My tutor gave me all the treatises. On how to be a dutiful and loving wife. They were in Latin. I read them every day. They spoke of how a wife should be obedient, selfless, kind, should put her husband first, and always should submit.

INÉS. That's monstrous.

BLANCA. I don't see why. I could think of wanting nothing else. Compared to what I had, it seemed a kind of freedom.

INÉS. I thought it would be freedom too. But I was wrong. We've both been betrayed.

BLANCA. I would talk with him and have the strangest feeling: as if I simply wasn't there. Cruelty would have been better than such indifference. At night he lay on me as if I were a log. He stank of wine. His hands were cold. And how it hurt. It tore at me. I could not understand. None of this was ever written in the books. And I could tell no one. I'd been taken from home. I didn't have a friend. People whispered in the corners. I could hear them laugh. They said I was frigid. I didn't understand the word. Barren. That I was failing him.

But what else could I do? The books said submit joyously. I could not bear to. I made excuses and I felt ashamed. But he came anyway. You weren't available. So he came to me. It seemed like a necessity. And how he puffed and groaned.

And when it was over he sighed with relief. As if he'd just discharged a piece of dirt. It lodged in me. I felt unclean. But I could not wash myself.

Then my belly started swelling. How they fussed over me. They said I must be happy. I knew better. And so did they, the third time, and the fourth. Whatever creatures grew in me were dead. They lay in my stomach like lead. They were torn out of me with pincers, cut out of me with knives. One had no head. One no mouth or eyes. Another flapped a little, voiceless, like a fish. Don't look they said, you mustn't see. But I had to look. I had to see my children.

He never looked. He was too afraid. He was afraid of witchcraft, so he had them burnt. I should have kept them in cupboards. I should have pickled them in jars. Then I could take them out and show them you and say: Look. Look. This is what you did to me.

INÉS. It was him. He did it. I never meant you harm.

BLANCA. You said that once before. It doesn't matter. It's what you did. You took him away from me. You destroyed my life.

I found your children. I followed you when you went to say farewell. Don't ask for them. If I can't have them why should you?

Enter PACHECO. *Exit* BLANCA.

INÉS. Pacheco!

There's blood on your hands.

PACHECO. I found two brats behind a stable door. Their heads are in this bag. There was an old woman with them. She got in the way. She's dead too.

INÉS. How could you do this?

PACHECO. With a knife.

INÉS. Have you no feeling?

PACHECO. I feel very well.

INÉS. I can't believe you.

PACHECO. I once knew a boy. His home was taken in a border raid. No one remembers it now. It was an insignificant affair. The Spaniards came at night. They stabbed him and they whipped him and they left him for dead. But he lived. He saw. They found his mother. They tied her to the table and they raped her. They raped her again and again. When they were tired they used their knives. They found his baby sister and they tossed her in the air. They tried to catch her with their blades. And this boy I know of saw it all. He screams inside my mind.

There is nothing worse than being powerless. As you now know.

You have an hour. Arrangements must be made. I
recommend you see a priest.

Exit PACHECO.

INÉS. I've heard it said that if you cut off someone's hand
The sense goes numb. They feel nothing. Not at first.
They sit and stare at the object on the ground
And think: Is that a hand? Did it belong to me?

Certain things I just don't understand.
Why light still shines in the sky
Or grass grows or birds still sing in the tree.
Why life goes on. Why won't it stop,
Why won't it stop and attend to me.

But the world still turns. I try to understand
What I've been told and I try to believe
The ground is still supporting me.
Somehow these things seem contradictory.
And a voice says: It's true. It's happening.
It's happening to you. Not a cruel voice,
Just cold. Indifferent as the sea.

Enter OLD WOMAN.

INÉS. It's there. Just there. Out the corner of my eye. Something
horrible. Calling me. I won't look. I don't want to see.

OLD WOMAN. Inés. Inés.
Open your eyes. You must see me.

INÉS. How did you get in?

OLD WOMAN. Through the door.

INÉS. I thought the place was guarded.

OLD WOMAN. Takes more than guards to keep me out.
More than bolts or bars and doors of steel.
And I can open any lock. I've got a special set of
keys.

INÉS. You're just an old woman.

OLD WOMAN. That's right, my love. That's all I am.

INÉS. What do you want with me?

OLD WOMAN. I'm hungry.

INÉS. I've nothing to give you.

OLD WOMAN. Then I'll wait.
  I've been waiting a long time. People seem to think I'll go
away. They think if they don't look at me or think about me I'll
just disappear. But I never do. I wait. Behind your shoulder.
On the left hand side. I am always with you. I will never leave.

INÉS. Who are you?

OLD WOMAN. A friend.

INÉS. I don't want to know you.

OLD WOMAN. No one does. They're all the same. Go to my
neighbour, they say. Keep away from me. I say, I don't want
your neighbour. Yet. It's you I'm after. They say get away! Get
away from me! But they've got to sleep, haven't they.
Everyone's got to sleep. So I creep in and take away their eyes.
Not all at once, that would be a waste. But bit by bit, so the
world gets darker. You've got to start somewhere.
  And some of them dig in their heels. So I'll take away their
money and their livelihood. Their dignity. Their little pleasures.
I say, come on, you don't need any of these. Not where you're
going. You've got to give them up sometime. So why not now?
And they say not yet. Not yet. Give us a little longer please.
  And I say I'm only an old woman. Come on. Don't you be
scared of me. What are you frightened of? I don't mean you
any harm. And don't think you're special, don't think you're
being singled out. I come to everyone.
  And if they still resist I'll sit on their chest. How their hearts
flutter. Or take away their minds. Or break their bones. Some
turn yellow. Others blue. Some of them do thresh about.
Sometimes I fill their chests with water and they drown in it.
They call that a quiet death. They call it dying in your bed.
People hanker after it, when they live in violent times. More
fool they.
  The harder they hang on, the harder I've to pull, you see. It's
not that I'm vindictive.
  You'll have more sense. I know you will. You worried 'cause
you're young? I think you're better off myself. You don't want
to get old. Believe me. I know old bodies. I creep around
inside. Heaps of rubbish everywhere. And the smell. Of course,
you gets used to it. But you don't want to go through that. You
still smell sweet.

INÉS. Why did you take my children?

OLD WOMAN. I had to dearie. Or else you'd never come.

INÉS. Why come for me?

OLD WOMAN. I must.

INÉS. Will I see them?

OLD WOMAN. Perhaps.

INÉS. I'd like to see them. We never really said goodbye.

OLD WOMAN. They've opened up their eyes. They've stretched
their little arms. They've said, 'That must have been a dream
we had.' And then up comes an old old man with twinkly eyes.
'Come on,' he says, 'I've something for you.' And now St
Peter's giving them a piggy-back and they're laughing in the
sky.

INÉS. That's not true.

OLD WOMAN. It might be. It's a story.

INÉS. Do you tell stories too?

OLD WOMAN. Where else do you think they come from?
    They come from me. Everything does. Everything comes
from me. And then goes back again. Back to me. As you are
going. Now. You cannot stop yourself. For you have longed for
this. All of you. Longed for it. Don't be afraid. I am a friend.

INÉS. I won't be frightened. I won't. I won't be frightened. I
won't. I won't.

Exit OLD WOMAN *with* INÉS. *Enter* CHORUS 5 *and* 3.

CHORUS 5. There wasn't any ceremony. There weren't any
drums. No priests. The mayor wasn't there, nor the head of the
army. It all just happened as if it were routine.

CHORUS 3. I was disappointed. I like a ceremony. I'd have taken
the children. It's an outing. I like the sense of drama and the
roll of drums. And everyone puts on their nicest clothes. It
does the children good, to see the death of a piece of royalty.
Lets them know they're flesh and blood like us.

CHORUS 5. It was very quiet. Everything was still. She sat awhile,
then walked slowly up and down. Perhaps she was drinking in
the air. Perhaps it tasted sweet.

CHORUS 3. Perhaps she was just impatient to be gone.

CHORUS 5. And then he came. An ordinary man. A little frightened. Someone who needed the money.

CHORUS 3. The man Pacheco hired to cut her throat.

Enter PEDRO.

PEDRO. We won. We won! A marvellous victory. A miracle! When we reached their army we knew we stood no chance. Everyone knew. Everyone. But no one faltered. It was dark. We lit our fires. It was raining hard and bitter cold. I went round each group. We talked. Then we embraced. We said farewell. We commended us to God and we waited for the dawn. We knew that death was awaiting us with day. But when it came, it brought a miracle. A gift from God. The streams had risen in the night. Their horses were bogged down. They could not deploy them. We ran at them. An angel guided us. An angel in the sky with drawn and bloody sword! Their hearts were filled with panic. They turned and ran. But we caught up with them. The streams ran red with the enemy's blood!

And I saw them. I saw the streams . . .

Why aren't you glad? What's happening? Why aren't you glad? Haven't you understood? We won! Portugal is saved!

CHORUS 3. You came too late.

Enter KING. *Exit* CHORUS.

PEDRO. Did you do this?

KING. No.

PEDRO. You did.

KING. No. I washed my hands.

PEDRO. Nothing will ever wash them clean.

KING. I could not stop it. I tried.

PEDRO. Liar.

KING. There was nothing I could do.

PEDRO. Liar!

KING. I was helpless.

PEDRO. You are the king!

KING. Helpless. There was nothing I could do.

PEDRO. That's why you gave your promise. To get me away. To buy you time.

KING. You were never meant to see the day.
I never wanted you to know.

PEDRO. I was supposed to die.

KING. I would have avenged you.

PEDRO. You must hate me.

KING. No. I don't hate you. You are my son. I love you.

PEDRO. Love me? You love me?

KING. I never found a way.

PEDRO. I don't think I exist. Not for you. I'm a kind of factor in a plan. A pawn.

KING. My son!

PEDRO. Old men. Tired old men. Desperate for power. That won't let go. That hold on and on and drag the whole world down with them to ruin.
I should kill you. I should kill you with these hands!

KING. I want to die.

PEDRO. Then live!

Exit PEDRO. *Enter* OLD WOMAN.

KING. I keep having dreams. People keep knocking on the door. And I have to open it. I say, it isn't right, I'm the king. I shouldn't have to do this. I'm the king! But they take no notice. They just keep filing in. Hundreds of them. Hundreds. People with their wounds. All festering. Horrible. Horrible. It was a fair fight, I tell them. Entirely fair. Nothing personal. Just go away. Go away! But there's more of them. More. And more. And more.
She never comes. Not Inés. Never. She knows better. It had to happen. I've no regrets. None. None at all.
I'm walking down a passage. It's very long. There are so many doors. I'm trying to open them but I've thrown away the keys. I'm naked and afraid. There's a man further up coming after me. I'm looking for some armour. I try all the doors. But I can't get in. I can't get in. I'm naked. Then I look down. My armour has become my skin.

I'm in a dried-up river bed. My feet raise clouds of dust. A voice says 'Cross' and I start to try. But I don't know the way. I don't know which is forward, which is back. I try to move but my legs don't work. I try to move but I'm getting buried. I'm getting buried in the sand . . .

And then I'm by a canyon, standing by this great enormous hole. It's very deep, and black. Quite black. I know it has no end. And all the river's pouring into it. And I think 'So that's where all the water goes.' And the voice says 'Now walk. Go across.' And then my feet start moving. And then I know. Then I know I've died.

Exit KING *with* OLD WOMAN. *Enter* CHORUS 3 *and* 2.

CHORUS 3. It was a pity they skimped on the funeral. Yes I know there's all the cuts. But they usually know how to look after themselves. And I know there's been disagreements, he might not have exactly wanted to do his father proud. But still. A rickety old carriage. No proper horses. And no black plumes. I like a plume.

CHORUS 2. He spoilt our daughter's wedding. The young prince. The party had just started, the musicians in full swing, when he comes barging in the door. We all fall silent, naturally. The wife nudges me, like, and I go forward, and I say, 'Your Highness, what an honour.' But he never says a word. He just steps forward, starts kicking over tables. Lashing out with a whip. What could we do? Then he says, 'How dare you be happy! How dare you! I lost my love why should you have yours!' And then he starts to cry. The prince. In front of everybody. Embarrassing. Everyone had to go home. We couldn't go on. Not after that. Casts a shadow over things.

CHORUS 3. I missed the dog.

CHORUS 2. What dog?

CHORUS 3. The last king had a dog.

CHORUS 2. That's no excuse.

CHORUS 3. A great black beast it was. It looked ever so sad.

CHORUS 2. There's my daughter with her best dress. Ruined. Wine all down the front. Silk that was. Real silk. Cost me a fortune. And the food all spoilt. Good money. Down the drain. Wicked it is. Wicked. Shouldn't be allowed.

CHORUS 3. They say there's going to be a feast.

CHORUS 2. We'll have to have one. Marry me daughter all over again. More money.

CHORUS 3. And not for the Queen, either. They say she's become a nun.

CHORUS 2. I could make my daughter a nun. But you've to pay for that as well.

Exit CHORUS 2.

CHORUS 3. They say it's for Inés. And she's been dead five years.

Enter CHORUS 5.

CHORUS 5. I had to dig her up.

CHORUS 3. It's morbid.

CHORUS 5. And make her a set of royal robes. And make them fit.

CHORUS 3. I don't approve of it. I don't approve of it at all.

CHORUS 5. We got the boy to do the measurements. But he fainted. I told him. The customer's always right I said. But he took no notice. Young people. I had to do the measurements myself. And I had to dress her up and put her on the throne.
    We had to rig up a set of special wires. And make her festive. We did what we could. We tried. But, dead for years. And festive. Enough to put you off your food.

Enter PEDRO.

PEDRO. Pacheco tried to run. My men caught up with him. They were to tell him not to be afraid. There was to be a banquet. He would be the honoured guest. He came.
    Everyone came. The whole court. Even my wife. She was hiding in a convent. I brought her out of that. I wanted her to see.

Exit PEDRO. *Enter* CHORUS 2.

CHORUS 2. This was the nastiest job I ever did. And I'll make one thing very clear. I'm a family man. I'm not in this for pleasure. It's just a job. The pay's regular, and they treat you right. I just do what I'm told. I'm an ordinary man. I don't ask questions. And this is just what happened.
    The subject, Pacheco, was handed over at 6 pm. On schedule. So we tied him down. And he protests. He said he thought he

was going to be a guest. He'd got a promise. How we laughed.

We shouldn't have done, not really. It wasn't professional. But you have to laugh. We said, he was coming for supper all right. Only they were going to have him. Barbecued. How we laughed. Wasted on him, of course.

Then there was a kind of lull. I made sure all my men looked smart. Then we checked the equipment. We had a special ladle. Hammered into a more precise kind of pouring shape, and lagged so it didn't burn our hands. Nice piece of work. Pass it round.

Of course, we'd lit the fire already, but we stoked it up a bit. I'd bought some special charcoal. The pitch had to be boiling. And he had to see.

We waited till all the guests arrived. There were footmen. They read out all the names. First time I'd seen a banquet. I was most impressed. I tried to remember all the clothes. The wife likes that sort of thing. And I knew she'd want to know the names of all the dishes. But once it started I couldn't really take it in. I had a job to do.

All the guests sat down, and they'd all got started on the soup. Then he gave the signal.

The instructions said: a drop in every orifice. Do it slowly. Make it hot. We started with the ears. Then the eyes. Nostrils. We left the mouth. Instructions said: leave it to the end. So we moved down and did the anus.

It wasn't easy. He had to be on his back. For a while it had us stumped. But where there's a problem, there's always a solution. That's what my father used to say. And he was a craftsman.

So what we did was this. We had the straps very carefully organised. On the upper body, that is. We'd made a kind of framework for the legs. To keep them rigid. Stop them threshing about. We rigged the end up on a block and tackle on a hook. Up there. Right above his head. So it could swing his legs right up and back and bend his body like a hinge. Luis thought of that. A friend of mine. He's a clever man. Ingenious. Saved our skins.

And the subject just screamed and screamed. Screamed something horrible.

And he kept shouting too. Saying he never touched the girl. I swear it, he kept shouting. I swear it. I never harmed her. It was him. He did it. It was him.

And I think he meant me. Gave me quite a turn. I never did that job. Never touched it. Too dangerous.

So I was glad when we got to the mouth. Put a stop to that.
Made me uneasy.
    Put a stop to the screaming too. There were still noises.
Inhuman noises. Inarticulate.
    It all lasted a long long time.
    The smell was terrible. Couldn't get it off my clothes.

Exit CHORUS 2.

Enter PEDRO.

PEDRO. Why aren't you eating?
    Where's your appetite?
    You don't seem to be talking much.
    What's happened to the art of conversation?
    It shouldn't be that hard. Not for you.
    You laughed and joked while she was being killed.
    No one lifted a finger to try and save her.
    And all of you. All of you feast
    While your fellow creatures are tormented.
    All of you gorge yourselves while others starve.
    So what's so different now?
    Where's your habitual indifference?
    Eat. All of you.
    Wife. What's wrong with you?
    Eat. Shall I feed you? Eat. Eat.
    This is a love feast.
    Given in honour of the greatest beauty in the world.
    If we don't love. We die.
    So love her. Kiss her hand.
    You first. Treat her like a queen.
    Like the queen she always truly was.
    I treated her badly while she lived.
    Now I'll make amends.
    She should have ruled with me.
    We were going to build a better world.
    So kiss her now. Accept her as your queen.
    Accept her. Kiss her hand.
    And I'll build her a tomb of stone.
    I'll build it with my hands.
    We'll face each other in our graves
    And when the earth grows weary of us all
    And nature finally turns against us
    When all the poison we have spilled upon the earth
    Returns to us and kills us all

When the sun's light dims and the moon turns to blood
When the heavens open and the dead rise from their
graves
Then we shall see each other and never be apart again.
And remember all of you: this is the work of love.
Love brought all this to be.

Enter GHOST OF INÉS *and* CHORUS 3.

GHOST OF INÉS. That wasn't me. That wasn't me! That wasn't me! It wasn't. It wasn't me.

CHORUS 3. Why are you telling me? I'm just a girl.

GHOST OF INÉS. No one else will listen.

CHORUS 3. I'm on my way home.

GHOST OF INÉS. Can I come with you?

CHORUS 3. You're a ghost.

GHOST OF INÉS. I don't mean you any harm.

CHORUS 3. Haven't you got a home of your own?

GHOST OF INÉS. No.

CHORUS 3. But you must have somewhere.

GHOST OF INÉS. Yes.

CHORUS 3. Is it very cold?

GHOST OF INÉS. No.

CHORUS 3. Hot then?

GHOST OF INÉS. No.

CHORUS 3. Hell's supposed to be very hot.

GHOST OF INÉS. It isn't hot or cold.

CHORUS 3. What sort of place is it then?

GHOST OF INÉS. It's just a place.

CHORUS 3. Where you sort of . . . rest?

GHOST OF INÉS. Yes.

CHORUS 3. So when they say 'Rest in Peace' that's what they mean?

GHOST OF INÉS. I suppose they must.

CHORUS 3. You staying here long?

GHOST OF INÉS. I don't know. Perhaps.

CHORUS 3. What brought you back?

GHOST OF INÉS. Something called me. I don't know what it was. Perhaps when they dug up my body's grave.

CHORUS 3. So you don't live there.

GHOST OF INÉS. In the grave? No. Not in the grave. It's just for a thing, the grave. It's nothing to do with me.

CHORUS 3. So I don't have to be afraid?

GHOST OF INÉS. No. Don't ever be afraid.

CHORUS 3. Was there anything else?

GHOST OF INÉS. Remember me.

CHORUS 3. I won't forget.

GHOST OF INÉS. They'll lie to you. They'll say I had to die. That love is not enough. That we should not allow ourselves to dream. They're wrong. They're very wrong. They'll tell you that they have to kill. That they cannot avoid committing crimes. Don't believe them. Don't believe them for a moment. Remember there's another way.

CHORUS 3. I promise. I won't forget.

GHOST OF INÉS. You're like my child. I wish I'd had a little girl.

CHORUS 3. There's the King.

GHOST OF INÉS. Pedro. Turn back. Turn back! Remember me! Remember me!

PEDRO *does not respond. The child scatters flowers on the grave.*

End of Play

BACK STREET MAMMY ■ TRISH COOKE

Trish Cooke was born in Bradford, West Yorkshire, in 1962. An actress as well as a writer, she has a BA in Performing Arts and has worked in television, film and theatre, both in acting and stage management. She was awarded the Thames Television Writer's Bursary with Liverpool Playhouse for September 1988–89, and *Shoppin' People* was staged there in the spring of 1989. Her play, *Running Dream*, was performed at the Albany Empire in 1989. Her published work includes *Mammy Sugar Falling Down, Grow Up Maxine, Aisha's Brother, Mrs Molly's Shopping Trolley,* and *Looking for Auntie Natal.*

Characters

DYNETTE, a thirty year old language interpreter.
            (*Flashback* at sixteen years old.)

CHORUS 1
JACKIE, DYNETTE's school friend.
MARIA, DYNETTE's mother.
JAN, DYNETTE's sister.

CHORUS 2
EDDIE, DYNETTE's boyfriend.
SKOLAR, DYNETTE's father.

CHORUS 3
JACKO, an old friend of DYNETTE's father and mother.

Back Street Mammy was first staged in London at the Lyric Studio, Hammersmith on 7 September 1989. The cast was as follows:

DYNETTE		Pamela Nomvete
JACKIE		
MARIA	CHORUS 1	Cecilia Noble
JAN		
EDDIE	CHORUS 2	Stephen Persaud
SKOLAR		
JACKO	CHORUS 3	Michael Stewart

Directed by Paulette Randall
Designed by Zara Conway
Lighting by Paul Armstrong

Darkness.

The telephone is ringing. Lights up on an untidy room. Toys fit for a one year old are spread out on the floor. A baby high-chair is on one side of the room with bits of toast and spilled tea on the tray. On the other side of the room is a typewriter, language books, overseas posters.

Enter DYNETTE *through the front door. She is rushing to answer the phone before it stops ringing. She stumbles over a child's toy and curses as she flings it to a safer spot.*

DYNETTE. Kids who'd have them . . . (*She gets to the phone.*) Hello?

JACKIE. Hello it's me . . . Busy?

DYNETTE. Hi ya Jackie. Nah I was gonna have a cup of tea before I started.

JACKIE. Good.

Silence.

DYNETTE. Owt the matter? It's gonna cost yer ringing at this time.

JACKIE. I know . . . felt like ringing.

Silence.

DYNETTE. Aren't yer at work?

Silence.

Come on Jackie what's up?

JACKIE. It's nothing really . . . just that check-up's today.

DYNETTE. Oh . . . you'll be all right!

JACKIE. Supposing . . .

DYNETTE (*interrupting*). Stop it, you'll be OK.

JACKIE. It's easy for you to say.

DYNETTE. No it isn't.

JACKIE. It's funny but when we were at school I always thought I'd be the family one.

DYNETTE. There's nowt stopping yer.

JACKIE. We're Thirty Dynette! Thirty!

DYNETTE. So!

JACKIE. Dynette, I rang 'cos I needed to talk but if yer gonna be like that –

DYNETTE. I just don't understand what your problem is?

JACKIE. I want a baby! There, is that clear enough for yer. Jesus you always have to analyse.

DYNETTE. I didn't say a word.

JACKIE. I know what yer thinking . . .

DYNETTE. But it's just the way . . .

JACKIE. I haven't got time to go courting . . . I'm not a kid any more –

DYNETTE. You're behaving like one . . . Me and Ricky find it hard and there's two of us. I've got to say it, I've been meaning to say it . . .

JACKIE. Oh don't start Dynette, I know what I'm doing.

DYNETTE. Do yer? Do yer?

JACKIE. I want a kid now . . . I might not be settled for another ten years . . .

DYNETTE. But the way yer going about it . . . It's not . . .

JACKIE. Not what?

DYNETTE. . . . you. You could catch 'anything' . . . You can't be too careful.

JACKIE. I've had it with being too careful. I know the risks Dee. I can't wait any more.

DYNETTE. But on yer own Jackie.

Silence.

JACKIE. But you're on yer own most of the time aren't yer? Ricky doesn't get home 'til late.

DYNETTE. You know that's different.

JACKIE. Why?

DYNETTE. 'Cos we planned for Lyvonne together. What you're doing's like . . . like . . . stealing.

JACKIE. What!

DYNETTE. It is . . .

JACKIE. I haven't seen any of them protest.

DYNETTE. You know what I mean . . . It's a baby, a human being and . . . well . . . you should at least let the men that you sleep with know what you're doing.

JACKIE. I'm not even gonna follow that argument through 'cos you're talking out of yer . . .

DYNETTE. Ah come off it Jackie. I'm just a saying what I think.

JACKIE. I'm sure you don't listen to yourself half of the time. Since you moved to London you only see things one way.

DYNETTE. Just because I don't agree with yer . . . ?

JACKIE. I'm not asking yer to agree with me. Just show some compassion. Bloody hell! It's all right for you, you've got Lyvonne, you've got Ricky, you've got everything. Yer job, everything!

DYNETTE. I don't know what I'm supposed to say . . . What am I supposed to say? Sorry?

Pause.

JACKIE. I don't know . . . I don't know . . .

Silence.

I'll see yer. Kiss Lyvonne for me.

JACKIE *hangs up.*

DYNETTE *puts the receiver down and stares at the phone for a moment. She then goes to the typewriter and sits down.*

DYNETTE. Voila, c'est l'heure pour commençer travaille.

The phone rings.

Oh go away Jackie.

She stares at the typewriter. The phone continues to ring. When it stops she rests back and sighs. Her eyes rest on the calendar above her desk. She stares at the typewriter then back at the calendar. She gets up quickly and rushes to the kitchen drawer and takes out a candle which she lights. She lights a cigarette from it and looks at the candle for some time.

DYNETTE *(to candle)*. Happy birthday my little God.

Lights dim.

Enter CHORUS 1, 2 *and* 3.

CHORUS *(All)*. Summer day.

CHORUS 1. Kids laughing.

CHORUS 2. Skipping.

CHORUS 3. Eating ice-cream.

CHORUS 2. The sound of radios, soft murmurs . . . slow cricket matches.

CHORUS 3. Speeding wasps.

CHORUS 1. Buttercups.

CHORUS 3. Lift up your chin and I'll tell you whether you like butter or not.

CHORUS 1. Daisy chains for jewellery.

DYNETTE. He loves me, he loves me not.

CHORUS 3. Blowing dandelions to tell the time.

CHORUS *(All)*. One o'clock, two o'clock . . . three o'clock.

DYNETTE *looks at her watch.* CHORUS 1 *starts to skip.*

CHORUS 1. Bluebells cockle shells.

CHORUS *(All)*. Evory Ivory over.

DYNETTE *jumps into imaginary rope with* CHORUS 1.

CHORUS *(All)*. Oh Dynette I'm telling your mother
For kissing Eddie Thomas in the parlour
How many kisses did you give him?
One two three four.

CHORUS *turn away.*

Lights back up. DYNETTE *goes to the cupboard and pulls out a suitcase. She opens the suitcase and takes out a school tie; a pair of stiletto heel shoes; and a pink elasticated pointed bra. She puts each of them on then takes out a diary. She flicks through the pages and reads to herself.*

CHORUS 1. She was fourteen. Catching up on last year's fashion. Borrowing her sister's stiletto heels and pencil skirts. Wore her first bra, elasticated, pink and pointed. Didn't feel shame to take off her vest in the swimming bath changing room any more. She received her first Valentine card from the boy in 3A4 she had a crush on. She felt like a grown up for the first time with heels and bra and card. She prayed for three things to confirm her adulthood: A teenage spot; a boyfriend and her periods to start. She did exercises to increase her 30 inch chest size. She pulled at her nipples, pinched her nose, straightened her back and her hair. Her body was changing. She was changing. Her life was changing. Nothing made sense . . .

DYNETTE *does the actions as if in a trance to the following 'Heads and Shoulders'.*

CHORUS (*All*). Heads and shoulders
Knees and toes, knees and toes
Heads and shoulders
Knees and toes, knees and toes
And arms and legs
And . . . (DYNETTE *puts hands on breasts.*)
And . . . (DYNETTE *puts hands between legs.*)

CHORUS (*ordering*). Heads and shoulders
Knees and toes, knees and toes

DYNETTE *does the actions but she is embarrassed when she touches her private parts. Her hands remain there for the next piece.*

DYNETTE. My Mama said I never should
Play with the gipsies in the wood
If I did she would say

CHORUS. Naughty girl to disobey
Naughty girl to . . .

DYNETTE (*innocently*). A sailor went to sea sea sea

CHORUS (*accusingly*). To SEE what he could SEE SEE SEE

DYNETTE. And all that he could see see see

CHORUS. Was the BOTTOM
Was the BOTTOM
Was the BOTTOM

DYNETTE (*pleading innocence*). My Mama told me if I was goody
That she would buy me

CHORUS. A rubber dolly.

DYNETTE. My Auntie told her I kissed a soldier
  Now she won't buy me

CHORUS. A rubber . . .

  All eyes on DYNETTE. *She feels ashamed.*

CHORUS. Naughty girl . . . Naughty girl

DYNETTE (*rocking a baby*). See see my baby.

CHORUS (*taunting* DYNETTE). Come home and play with me
  And bring your kisses free
  Under the apple tree
  In through the cellar
  Into my wheelbarrow
  And we'll be jolly friends
  Forever more more more more.

  DYNETTE *goes back to the diary. She flicks through the pages.*

CHORUS 1. At fifteen her body was developing. She *looked* like a
  young woman and her body demanded the attention of one.
  She wanted to touch and she wanted to be touched. She wanted
  to be like the women in the magazine serials. Those who were
  loved. She wanted to give love. To be in love. She wanted to
  grow up fast.

School toilets.

JACKIE (*lighting a cigarette*). Our Bev did it last night.

DYNETTE. Did what?

JACKIE. Christ . . . *you* know. (*Pause.*) You should have been there
  Dynette. You was the only one who wasn't, your dad's a right . . .

DYNETTE. I'm going out with our Jan on Saturday. Dad says
  week days are for studying . . . that's all right with me.

JACKIE. Caught them at it upstairs.

DYNETTE. Who?

JACKIE. Bev-er-ley and Adrian Banks.

DYNETTE. Adrian Banks!

JACKIE. He's not that bad.

DYNETTE. You reckon they went all the way?

JACKIE. Probably. 'Ere you know who were there? That lad who works at the garage.

DYNETTE. Still fancy him?

JACKIE. He asked me out.

DYNETTE (*sarcastically*). Yeh . . .

JACKIE. He did.

DYNETTE (*seriously*). And what did you say?

JACKIE (*shrugs her shoulders*). Said I'd think about it.

DYNETTE *looks to try and see what* JACKIE's *thoughts are.*

JACKIE. . . . might as well.

JACKIE *starts to put some make up on.*

DYNETTE (*cutting in quickly*). He's not your type.

JACKIE. What d'you mean?

DYNETTE. Too old.

JACKIE. Mature.

DYNETTE. OLD.

JACKIE. Ah yer just jealous . . .

DYNETTE. Jackie if I wanted to go out with somebody with a receding hair line I'd go out with me dad!

JACKIE. What's up with yer? I can't talk to yer these days, not about owt important.

DYNETTE. And that's important then? A bald-headed car mechanic asks you out and that's important!

JACKIE. Well I'd like to see you do better!

DYNETTE. Wouldn't be hard . . .

JACKIE. Oh yeh I'd like to see you try.

DYNETTE. Oh stop being childish.

JACKIE. No, I mean it! You like to criticise but I've never seen you with anybody bald-headed or otherwise. The closest you ever got to it was that precious Valentine card from Malcolm Green when we were in t' third form and then you didn't even have the guts to follow it up.

DYNETTE. I wasn't interested.

JACKIE. You were scared.

DYNETTE. Give me some credit. I didn't fancy him.

JACKIE. You didn't have the guts.

JACKIE *lights a cigarette. She takes a puff and hands it to* DYNETTE *who refuses it.*

. . . and you still haven't.

DYNETTE *goes to the mirror and starts squeezing her spots.*

Well . . . Terry asked if I'd like to go for a meal on Saturday. Best thing about 'mature' car mechanics is they can afford to take you out. Where is it you said you were going Saturday?

DYNETTE. Club with our Jan. There's a band on.

JACKIE. There'll be plenty of OLD men there then?

DYNETTE. Oh stop it.

JACKIE. Still not interested or just scared?

DYNETTE. Jackie leave me alone. Look I've got to get to French . . . See yer later.

JACKIE. Dynette!

DYNETTE *goes back to the diary.*

CHORUS 1. She wanted to know what she was missing. She wanted to know what IT was like. She imagined. She touched . . .

CHORUS (*All*). Touching, touching.

DYNETTE. Can they see?

CHORUS. All the eyes.

DYNETTE. Are watching me.

CHORUS. Locking doors.

DYNETTE. To keep them out.

CHORUS. In case we find –

DYNETTE. What I'm about –

CHORUS. Dream –

DYNETTE. Of loving –

CHORUS. Dream –

DYNETTE. Of kissing.

CHORUS. Of all the things –

DYNETTE. That I've been missing. Dare I –

CHORUS (*coaxing*). Try it.

DYNETTE. Dare I –

CHORUS. Go.

DYNETTE. Where my heart's –

CHORUS. Never been before.

DYNETTE. Legs are –

CHORUS. Open.

DYNETTE. On my bed and –

CHORUS. In between –

DYNETTE. Is someone's head. Oh . . . my –

CHORUS. Cheeks –

DYNETTE. Are burning red, for this –

CHORUS. Feeling –

DYNETTE. Is –

DYNETTE/CHORUS. Dread.

DYNETTE. Sorry God Sorry
Sorry God Sorry
Please forgive me I'll never . . .
I'll never. (*She genuflects.*)
Forgive me Father for I have sinned.
It is three weeks since my last confession.
These are my sins.

CHORUS. She lay on her bed and she played with herself.
Touching. Touching herself. Knowing herself.

CHORUS 3. She thinks she can shut herself out from God.

CHORUS (*All*). And please herself?

CHORUS 2. She closed her bedroom door.

CHORUS 1. She closed her eyes.

CHORUS 3. She opened her legs.

CHORUS (*All*). And we saw. We saw her lying naked on her bed. And Touching. (*They laugh.*) Touching. Touching herself.

Club toilet

DYNETTE *is touching her face and looking in the mirror.* JAN *comes in.*

JAN. God, it's hot out there.

DYNETTE. Good though aren't they?

DYNETTE *sings and dances.*

'Oh . . . oh . . . you make me feel . . .'

They laugh.

JAN. Boy, that lead singer.

DYNETTE. Yeh . . . sweet!

JAN. Don't look too close, he's too old for you. (*She wipes the sweat from her face and freshens up.*)

DYNETTE. I'd say mature.

JAN. Eh eh, pardon me. Anyway Eddie Thomas keeps on asking me about you.

DYNETTE. Who?

JAN. When we go out look to your left. He was standing by the pool table just as I came in. Used to go to school with him. (*Teasing.*) Fancies yer!

DYNETTE. Yer lying.

JAN. Mwoi? Next stop blues, fancy it?

DYNETTE (*full of energy*). Yeh I'm raring to go! (*She turns to leave.*)

JAN. Wait . . . (*She takes fluff from* DYNETTE's *hair.*) That's better . . .

They leave. As they leave they sing together.

JAN/DYNETTE (*singing*). Oh . . . oh . . . you make me feel . . .

DYNETTE *turns her head to the left. They giggle.*

CHORUS 1. Then it happened to her. Whirlwind romance? Well . . . not exactly like the magazines or the films or the books. No flowers. No chocolates. No champagne. Just the not knowing. That was the exciting part. That was IT.

CHORUS (*All*). The blues still a bubble.

CHORUS 2. And the bodies still a grind.

CHORUS 3. Slower than a wind.

CHORUS (*All*). Slow-er . . .

CHORUS 3. than a wind.

DYNETTE. And his . . .

CHORUS (*All*). Eyes . . .

DYNETTE. pierce the night.

CHORUS (*All*). Searching. Eyes . . .

DYNETTE. land on me

CHORUS (*All*). Finding

DYNETTE. I

DYNETTE/CHORUS. dance.

DYNETTE. He pass me once
  He pass me twice
  He stare again
  He stare

CHORUS (*All*). Again.

DYNETTE. And

DYNETTE/CHORUS. Stop.

EDDIE. A dance Sis?

DYNETTE. And me leg buckle over
  In one.

CHORUS (1 *and* 3). In a two time.

DYNETTE. In one

CHORUS (1 *and* 3). In a two time.

DYNETTE. In time

CHORUS (1 *and* 3). In time.

DYNETTE/EDDIE. We arrive

CHORUS (1 *and* 3). To the beat.

DYNETTE/EDDIE. In and out.

CHORUS (1 *and* 3). To the beat. In and out. To the *heavy* beat.

DYNETTE/EDDIE. We dance

CHORUS (1 *and* 3). In the night.

DYNETTE/EDDIE. We love

CHORUS (1 *and* 3). The sound. The bass sound

DYNETTE. Caresses my chest

EDDIE. With its

EDDIE/CHORUS (1 *and* 3). Solid vibrations. The sweat smell is good

DYNETTE. is good.

CHORUS (1 *and* 3). Soft bodies grinding

DYNETTE. Moving

EDDIE/CHORUS (1 *and* 3). So hard.

EDDIE. So hard.

DYNETTE. Forcing.

EDDIE. Pushing.

DYNETTE. Hurting.

CHORUS (1 *and* 3). Forgetting pain.

DYNETTE. Hurting.

DYNETTE/CHORUS (1 *and* 3). Escaping.

DYNETTE/EDDIE/CHORUS. Yes.

CHORUS (1 *and* 3). The blues still a bubble
And the bodies still a grind
Slower than a wind
Slower than a wind

DYNETTE. Stop.

CHORUS (1 *and* 3). Fresh air.

Outside the Blues

EDDIE. Hi. You don't remember me do you?

DYNETTE. Sorry, where do I know you from?

EDDIE. I just danced with you.

DYNETTE (*embarrassed*). Oh it was you. It's so dark in there, I couldn't see.

EDDIE. You're Jan's sister right? I'm Eddie, a friend of Jan's. We go way back, school days. (*Pause.*) You not cold out here?

DYNETTE. I needed some fresh air. It's hot in there. The music's loud. I can feel the bass line in my chest.

EDDIE. Want to sit in my car?

DYNETTE (*quickly*). No.

EDDIE. Just thought it would be better than standing in the cold. (*Pause.*) You look like Jan you know. Yes . . . same mouth. Smile.

DYNETTE *can't help it. She smiles.*

EDDIE. Yeh man, you smile same way . . . But you . . . you prettier.

DYNETTE *turns to go back inside.*

EDDIE. You don't go out much do you. I've never seen you out before.

DYNETTE. I've got exams coming up.

EDDIE. Still at school? (*He steps back.*)

DYNETTE. Er, college.

EDDIE. Oh you're an intellectual. What are you studying?

DYNETTE. Languages . . . mainly.

EDDIE. Is there room for me after your exams?

DYNETTE. Maybe. (*Pause.*) Which car is yours?

EDDIE. Guess.

DYNETTE. Well you don't look like a Mini man. That leaves the other five hundred on this road. But I'd say you look like a person who would like to make a quick getaway so it's either that Escort parked nearest or the one behind.

EDDIE. What about that smart BMW over there?

DYNETTE. You don't look like a BMW man.

EDDIE *(taking out keys)*. What do you mean I don't look like a BMW . . .

DYNETTE. Oh I didn't mean . . .

EDDIE. That's OK, that's my Escort. *(Pause.)* Fancy going for a patty?

DYNETTE. OK. I'm starving. *(She looks back into the Blues.)*

EDDIE. Jan won't miss you. She doesn't stop dancing 'til daylight, and we'll be back before then. OK?

DYNETTE/CHORUS (1 *and* 3). Yes.

The night cafe

JACKO *(singing and drinking from a bottle)*.
Come in Abraham
Where you been so long?
Every time I turn on me bed
I take me pillow for you.
Nobody know
How dry we are.
I sold my shoes
For a bottle of booze . . .

(Muttering.) I don't know . . . Life . . . life. Eh eh Eddie? How's things man? Where you going? Look like King himself . . .
Is Maria dat ne? Maria? But wait you is Skol chil' enn it?

JACKO *looks closely at* DYNETTE.

But look a girl dat favour her modder. Boi Maria. So how you ol' man these days? Skolar and me is good good friend you know . . . but long time me don't see him. He and Maria still togedder?

DYNETTE. Mum?

JACKO. I beg you puddin' darling. Your 'mum' and 'dad' still fighting?

DYNETTE. Don't think they'll stop 'til one of them is dead.

JACKO. I don't know. Those two. Huh, and if you did see them back home heh . . . a better looking woman you never did see and Skolar wid his press suit and thing . . . Girl they was de envy of everybody, man and woman alike. And love, girl, you two stan' up there don't know the meaning of what your mammy and daddy had in those days . . . no seh. Skolar would a walk to Timbuktu to please your mammy and she self would a die in de road if it was what would make him happy.

DYNETTE. So what happened then?

JACKO (*to himself*). Look like she die in de road but it wasn't enough . . .

(*To* DYNETTE.) Love happens – dats what.

Pause.

Your daddy girl, he used to start walking in de night so's he could reach where you mammy living by morning. Now dats love eh? And Skolar and me. We was boys togedder. And you mammy now, now she was de Queen. Lovely woman. Was a time when she was staying by her auntie in de town and she come look for Skol but was me she fin' and we spen' all night chat . . . me and Maria, talk about life and love and . . . I did think that maybe me and she . . . (*Pause.*) but she say is Skolar she want.

DYNETTE (*dryly*). And is Skolar she get. (*Pause.*) Eddie have you got the time?

EDDIE/CHORUS (1 *and* 3). Still early.

DYNETTE (*getting up rudely*). Well it's been nice talking to you Mr . . .

JACKO. What you kids don't understand is, was all you we did make decision for. For all you we did come to dis country. (*Waving his arms about obviously drunk.*) You work you arse off for dem, clocking into work every damn morning, when you bones want to rest . . . Every kiss me arse morning. And you work and you work and you see your own dream fadin' but you still have you kid so you work harder put de little overtime in. Go to work in dark come back in night, but you kid dem you know they'll be all right. Next time round they'll be de one wid de factory and to see Carl like dat I'd be proud . . . but Carl . . . you know Carl enn it Eddie? Him turn Rasta Man. Say is wha' 'im call it again . . . Say 'is red or dread or what I don't know. After me sweat to make him study to be accountant. The people dem say his face don't look 'trustworthy' and is de same face . . . de same face. We come here in '58, '59, we come here for all you to live better and you get up one morning eh and you bloody son don't want to comb his hair again. Was a time when style was press suit and clean cut . . .

DYNETTE. I'm sorry but I've got to go. (*She looks at* EDDIE *for support*.) It's getting late.

JACKO. Don't want to listen to an ol' man talk eh? Don't blame you. Can't say I blame you. (*As* DYNETTE *and* EDDIE *leave he calls after them*.) Say Howdi to de ol' Skol for me . . . and Maria . . . sweet Maria . . .

Car journey

EDDIE. I'll take you back to the blues.

DYNETTE. I'll have to leave without Jan if she isn't ready. (*She explains*.) Jan's got her own flat. I live at home. (*She looks out of the car window and wants to cry*.)

EDDIE. Want to talk? (*Slight pause*.) Jacko's not bad . . . likes his drink but he's OK. (*He hands* DYNETTE *a handkerchief*.)

DYNETTE. I've heard his name come up in many . . . conversations. (*She takes the handkerchief*.) Thank you.

EDDIE. There you go again with that Janet smile. I think I'd have known you two were sisters even if I'd have seen you out on your own.

DYNETTE. Chance would be a fine thing.

EDDIE. Your exams right? Too much study not good for nobody you know.

DYNETTE. I didn't know what I was missing. (*She looks at him*.) Now I do. Can I drive?

EDDIE (*hesitating*). Have you . . . passed your test?

DYNETTE/CHORUS (1 *and* 3). No

DYNETTE. . . . but I'm learning.

They swap seats. EDDIE *is apprehensive.*

CHORUS (1 *and* 3). She found love on a one-way street.

CHORUS 3. Mad Saturday night.

CHORUS 1. Early Sunday morning.

CHORUS 3. Driving up one-way streets.

CHORUS 1. Without a driving licence.

CHORUS 3. Or a tax disc.

CHORUS (1 *and* 3). Without a care in the world.

DYNETTE. Well this is it . . . home.

EDDIE. OK. Car keys please.

DYNETTE. Want to come in?

EDDIE *looks at his car keys.*

EDDIE. OK . . . For five minutes.

EDDIE *kisses her on the cheek.* DYNETTE *tenses up.*

EDDIE. Relax girl. I don't need to come inside if you don't want.

DYNETTE. I want you to. Come.

They go inside.

EDDIE (*looking around*). Jesus Christ.

DYNETTE. Yes he's a close relative. (*Pointing to pictures on the wall.*) This one's when he came to dinner, those are my cousins at the table with him, and this is him doing his sponsored walk . . . some superman . . . carried that piece of wood for miles . . . like I say he's a member of the family.

EDDIE (*laughing*). You're telling me. I thought my old lady was bad. You a regular little church-goer then?

DYNETTE. No. I don't go any more. Leave that to Mum.

EDDIE. Come here. (EDDIE *begins to unfasten her bra. There is the sound of banging.* EDDIE *and* DYNETTE *look up.*)

EDDIE. Your ol' man, what's he like?

DYNETTE. OK. A bit mad. He'll be down in a bit.

EDDIE. What . . .

DYNETTE. Likes to make his presence known.

EDDIE. Well I'll be going then.

DYNETTE. He's all right really . . . just a bit . . . possessive when it comes to his daughters.

EDDIE *gets ready to leave.*

DYNETTE. I was joking. He won't come down. He would at one time but not now. I think he's mellowed with old age.

EDDIE *relaxes.*

DYNETTE. You going out with anyone?

EDDIE. Not really.

DYNETTE. What's that mean?

EDDIE. I've just split up with someone. I don't really want to get involved with anyone just yet.

DYNETTE. Oh. What's she like?

EDDIE. A bit like you. Pretty. Likes to talk. (*He gets closer to her.*) You're a nice girl.

DYNETTE. Is *she* a nice girl too?

EDDIE. She can be 'cept when she's in a mood.

DYNETTE. Is she often in moods?

EDDIE (*putting conversation to an end*). Yep. (*He kisses her. She backs away.*)

DYNETTE. Why did you split up?

EDDIE. She's seeing someone else.

DYNETTE (*relaxing*). Oh. So it's over?

EDDIE. Looks that way . . . yes.

She relaxes more. He moves in on her.

CHORUS (1 *and* 3). Four walls.

CHORUS 1. Floral walls.
Flowers and frills closing in.

CHORUS (1 *and* 3). Jesus Christ watching her
Spying on her while she sins.

CHORUS 3. Instinct calls.

CHORUS 1. Moral falls.
And his body's moving in.

DYNETTE. I don't care who's

DYNETTE/CHORUS (1 *and* 3). Watching

DYNETTE. me

DYNETTE/CHORUS (1 *and* 3). Spying

DYNETTE. on me while I sin. I don't

DYNETTE/CHORUS (1 *and* 3). care

DYNETTE. I won't

DYNETTE/CHORUS (1 *and* 3). care

DYNETTE. I . . .

CHORUS (1 *and* 3 *teasing* DYNETTE). . . . didn't take any
precaution.

DYNETTE *backs away suddenly.*

DYNETTE. IT

DYNETTE/CHORUS (1 *and* 3). hurt.

CHORUS 1. Like fire in her belly.

CHORUS 3. Like a knife in her gut.

CHORUS 1. Like a punch in her insides.

DYNETTE/EDDIE/CHORUS. Reach in her throat. Wrenching
her throat. Wrenching her throat. It made her sick.

DYNETTE. But it freed me
From the rut I was in.

CHORUS (1 *and* 3). For a moment for a second she was free.

DYNETTE. Mammy

CHORUS (1 *and* 3). Could never hol' her again.

DYNETTE. Daddy

CHORUS (1 *and* 3). Could never scold her again.

DYNETTE. And my friends

CHORUS (1 *and* 3). Could never have told her about the freedom, about the knowledge,

CHORUS 1. How the moment could a jus' come

CHORUS (1 *and* 3). And how it could a go.

DYNETTE. I found love on a one-way street,
Mad Saturday night.
Early Sunday morning,
Driving up one-way streets without a driving licence,
Or a tax disc,
Without a care in the world.

DYNETTE/CHORUS (1 *and* 3). And lost IT

DYNETTE. on a lonely by-way.

CHORUS 1. What happened?

CHORUS 3. Did you get caught?

CHORUS 1. Did you get ketch?

CHORUS 3. Did you crash?

DYNETTE. He wanted his old banger back.

She hands EDDIE *back the keys, then takes off the school tie and puts on the rosary. She begins to sing.*

Avé Avé Avé Maria
Avé Avé Avé Maria

MOTHER *joins in song. She reaches out to touch* DYNETTE.
DYNETTE *backs away and watches.*

The Kitchen

MARIA (*singing*). Avé Avé Avé Maria
mm mm mm mm mm mm mm mm (*Humming tune.*)
Emaculet Mayray
Arr Hats arr on fiarr
mm mm mm mm mm mm mm mmm mm mm mm

SKOLAR. Woman stop dat blasted noise in me head.

MARIA (*louder*). Avé Avé Arrrvay Ma ree aaah
Avé Avé . . .

SKOLAR. Shot your mout!

MARIA *stops mid song, shuts her eyes, then begins the tune again.*

SKOLAR. I tell you to stop wid dat dam noise in me head dis
morning you know . . .

MARIA. Wait wait a minute. Since morning you get up your face
humph humph, like is something you want to say but you
don't want to say it. Is what on your min' Skolar?

SKOLAR. Jus' don't sing no church song, I don't want to hear no
church song.

Pause.

You don't hear de time your daughter come in my house las'
night.

MARIA. Oh, is dat you want to say.

SKOLAR. Think I was sleeping? Think is only you alone care
what time she in street.

MARIA. Is street you worry for? (*She laughs.*)

(*She sings more militant.*) Em-ac-u-let May-ray
Ar-hats arr on fi-a –

SKOLAR. Woman I say Shot op!

MARIA. Is street you worry for Skol? Is really street you does put
your min' on when you turn turn in you bed at night eh? Is
really street?

He hits her. She hits him back. He hits her again.

MARIA. You think I never see you when you hear de car stop
outside? Stan' up like a fool fool holdin' on to you pyjama.
Why you hol' it so tight? You 'fraid it gonna drop. You forget is
me you wife and I see it all before. Why you was spying on de
children Skol? You jealous of de man? Eh Skol? You useless . . .
You ol' man . . .

SKOLAR. No man going touch my daughter . . . No kiss me arse
dirty . . . Not my girl no . . .

MARIA. Hear yourself. You is a sick ol' man Skol.

SKOLAR. Because I love my kids I sick?

MARIA. There's love and love. And de way you shame your daughters is a sick ol' man love.

SKOLAR. Is you de one dat jealous. Whappen Jacko don't visit you no more.

MARIA. Same ol' story eh Skol? Jus' can't let it res'. When is time for us to enjoy life togedder, look how we does jus' hurt one anodder. And it hurt you to think of me and Jacko enn it? Good. I glad it hurt you, you hear. I glad. Because you does hurt me too. Everyday I wake up you hurt me. Every day I see where I still is you hurt me. Every day you hear? I did have a life too, you know. I did use to want things too. I was a person too. I did use to want more but now I don't want any more. I can't stan' any more. I tired. So, is you is de man me true? And is you Skol, *you* I follow Inglan wid me big belly so you tell me where we go now. Two ol' people fightin', calling an ol' story to make de time go. Well go on Mr Skolar I right behind you, Maria gonna follow. You is de man and I is you dog . . . I is you dog . . .

SKOLAR. I going . . . I going for a drink.

SKOLAR *turns away.* DYNETTE *turns to face her mother.*

DYNETTE. I heard the noise.

MARIA. You fardhar do some johnny cake and there's saltfish in de pot.

DYNETTE. Don't you get tired.

MARIA. Save some for you fardhar, he don't eat his yet.

DYNETTE. Mum . . . I saw Jacko last night.

MARIA. Jacko, which Jacko? Who tell you about Jacko?

DYNETTE. Nobody's told me anything about anybody. I saw a man. He said his name was Jacko and he said for me to say 'Howdi' to you and Dad. That's all.

MARIA. Oh. Where you see him?

DYNETTE. In the Night Cafe.

MARIA. Dynette what you was doing dem place? ' Is there Jan does take you? If ' is there all you does go ' is no wonder you fardhar does make noise.

DYNETTE. Jan didn't take me there. I went with a friend.

MARIA. Which friend?

DYNETTE. Oh no one special.

MARIA. Oh and no one special take you to ol' break-down cafe
in red light district? Well tell no one special dat you is a
respectable well brought up girl and you have school exam and
dis no one special not going to have a chance to take you to
such a place again and . . . You jus' turn sixteen. You is a chil'!
You' fardhar say you mus' not disrespec' his house so, know
what time you coming back in his house and de no one special
mus' drop you off and go home. So . . . you see ol' Jacko eh?
What he was doing wid himself?

DYNETTE. Drinking mostly.

MARIA. Drinking? Jacko? Back home he never touch a drop.
Always call it liqueur, fire water, de devil drink he use to say.
'Im and you fardhar was like brodder. Jacko was a fine man. A
fine man.

DYNETTE (teasing).He said you and him had a 'likkle ting'.

MARIA. Jacko like to talk out, is talk dat does put people in
trouble. Is talk dat make him and you fardhar break up. And is
talk talk talk dat make us kill one anodder every day and every
night. Yes . . . your fardhar did think dat we was . . . Oh
Dynette life is funny. Let me clean up me kitchen so I can go
church, you hear . . .

DYNETTE. Did you?

MARIA. Did I what?

DYNETTE. You know . . . with Jacko?

MARIA. Chil' move from me way, you don't see how de place in
a mess. And is talk you want me to talk! Why you cannot gi' me
some help in de house? Every day de same. Every day I sit
down at dem people sewing machine making teddy bear. Ten
pence they does gi' me for one, yes, two shillin' and they does
sell de same teddy bear wid my number on it for five pound.
You see how life is? And if I did study maybe it would be me
wid de five pound not de small change. You know how many
teddy bear I have to make to come home wid a decent wage?
Plenty. And I tired work now Dyn, you don't think is time one
of me chil' come home wid some good good news. I sick of
hearing de same 'Mom I expectin'.' I sick of being

grandmother. I sick and I tired Dynette. Come home and tell me dat you pass your exam and 'Mom I want to be a doctor or a lawyer or something special.' I did think dat all a my babies is something special but nearly all a dem do like me. So you want to talk. Don't talk, listen. Dats de bes' advice I can gi' you. And don't jus' listen, listen good. (*Pause.*) Back home I did always say I would make a seamstress but is me own dress shop I did want, yes girl, you ol' modder had big dream. I did think of going America to study . . . open a fancy clothes shop . . . Maria Fashion. Those were de days . . . I use to make all me own clothes you know, now I so tired when I finish work all I have time to do is cook and clean. What I am saying is I could a had all of those things if I had kept myself to myself . . . if I had take care. (*She looks at* DYNETTE *hard*.) But I meet a man and I start to make children for him. Don't follow me Dynette. Is not a life for you. You is me, las' chil', do me proud ne?

DYNETTE. Mum sit down . . .

MARIA. I got to go Church. I don't want to hear no news.

DYNETTE. Was Jacko the first man you . . . made love with?

MARIA (*shocked*). Jesus, listen to de chil', stop me from going church to talk nonsense.

DYNETTE, *serious, waits for a reply.*

MARIA. Skolar, your Daddy, is de firs' and de *only* one I breed wid, but let me tell you something, you don't have to have sex wid a man to love him.

DYNETTE. But if you do have . . . if you do 'make love' it's love . . . isn't it?

MARIA. Is whatever you want it to be when it happening but after, dat is when de real test begin. You can meet a man and love him but when he go, he go for good. Now when you 'breed' wid him dats a different story. When you breed wid him is like he have a hold on you. You can't make a move widout him putting his mouf in it and you can't say noffin because is his chil' too . . . I going now. You make me late enough already. I hope I reach in time.

MARIA *leaves.*

DYNETTE (*to herself*). But Mum . . . did it feel like this for you the first time . . .

CHORUS (2 *and* 3). When the pain is physical
   The doctor will prescribe a twice-a-day remedy
   But when you can't define the ache
   Who do you go to then?

Jan's flat

DYNETTE *knocks on the door.*

DYNETTE. Anybody home? Jan, Jan, Jan. Come on!

JAN (*holding her head*). Easy easy . . . (*She opens the door.*) I'll have to
   give you a key.

DYNETTE (*still buzzing from the night before*). Oh, last night . . . last
   night! Wasn't it good? It were great!

   JAN *puts her head down to sleep.*

JAN. Mmm mmm. Make us a coffee Dee . . . ?

   DYNETTE *goes to make coffee.*

DYNETTE. What time did you get home?

JAN (*wakes up*). Yer what . . . Don't ask me what time . . . What
   the frig happened to you? Where was yer?

DYNETTE. Are yer still on yer diet?

JAN. Eh . . . ?

DYNETTE. Sugar?

JAN. Don't bloody change t' subject.

DYNETTE. I saw yer chatting to that singer. At the blues . . . saw
   yer chatting to . . .

JAN. Dynette!

DYNETTE. I went home – Gotta lift.

JAN. Who with?

DYNETTE. Your mate.

JAN. Mine?

DYNETTE. That lad, whats-his-name. Eddie somebody . . .

JAN. Eddie! Drop you home? Bloody hell. What's up with him? You could have said 'Tarah' I were worried sick. Good job I didn't ring Mum.

DYNETTE. I never thought . . . Anyhow I were in good hands.

JAN. I bet you was. Charmed yer off yer feet I'll bet.

DYNETTE *hands* JAN *the coffee with a grin.*

He took you straight home I hope!

DYNETTE. So, you two good mates then?

JAN. I wouldn't say that exactly. We used to go to school together but since (*She prods* DYNETTE.) he 'started going out with Sonia' I don't see that much of him.

DYNETTE. They've finished.

JAN. They've got a kid. They'll never finish. Why what did he tell yer? What nonsense he fill your head with?

DYNETTE. Nowt. I wasn't interested anyway.

JAN. Good. Don't want you messing your head up on that man! Time is it?

DYNETTE. Quarter past ten.

JAN. Dee . . . ?

DYNETTE. What?

JAN. Do us a favour . . . Pick Tania up for us . . . ? Dee?

DYNETTE. I heard yer!

JAN. Owt the matter? He didn't ask you out did he?

DYNETTE *shakes her head. She takes an apple from the table and bites into it.*

Don't tell me yer fancied him?

DYNETTE. Did I heck! *You* pointed him out . . . I didn't even notice.

JAN. You did! Yer fancied him!

DYNETTE. Don't be daft I've got more to do than waste me time on stupid men. Got me exams in June. I don't want no man to come and do his business and then just piss off out of it.

JAN. Like what happened to me yer mean?

DYNETTE. Yer know that's not what I meant. You and Tania are happy the way things are.

JAN. Happy with Donnovan knocking on me door anytime he sees fit. Like he only remembers he got a child when it's convenient for him to feel guilty . . . Huh, if I could go back in time Dynette I'd gladly swap places with yer . . . 'Young free and single . . .' and contraceptives are so much easier to get hold of these days. If I were your age now you think I'd have Tania . . . ? as much as I love her and everything I'd still . . .

DYNETTE (*interrupting*). I'll go get her . . . I'll see yer later.

DYNETTE *leaves.*

JAN (*shocked at the quick exit, shouts after her*). Forget him Dee it's only a crush!

DYNETTE *takes off the stiletto heels, and puts the bra with them. She holds the rosary in her hand.*

CHORUS 1. She went to church and begged. Begged God for forgiveness. Promised she would never do IT again if only this time, her one and only time, she could get away with it. She promised she would never do IT again. She would never never never . . .

DYNETTE *kneels at the candle holding the rosary in her hand.*

CHORUS (*All*). Nomini Patri
Et de filius
Et de Sanctus Animus

They do the sign of the cross as they speak.

DYNETTE. Hail Mary, full of grace, the Lord is with thee.
Blessed art thou amongst women,
And blessed is the fruit of thy womb, Jesus.
Holy Mary, mother of God, pray for us sinners,
Now and at the hour of our death.
Amen.

She throws the rosary on the floor.

School toilets

DYNETTE. How was Saturday?

JACKIE (*starry-eyed*). Great!

DYNETTE. Where d'you go?

JACKIE. La Grandes. The meal was nice. Candlelit, the works. I could hardly eat though, my throat was dry. I couldn't even talk. He did though. He told me all about himself. He's lovely. We had champagne . . .

DYNETTE. And . . . ?

JACKIE. What d'you mean 'and . . . ?'

DYNETTE (*interrupting*). I meant 'and . . . WHAT HAPPENED NEXT?'

JACKIE. Oh. He took me home.

DYNETTE. That all?

JACKIE. Yeh.

DYNETTE. Didn't yer . . . ? You know . . .

JACKIE. I'm not that . . . not on the first date Dynette. What d'you take me for? He kissed me goodnight, nothing more.

JACKIE. Anyway how about you? Any 'mature' men *interest* you?

DYNETTE. No . . . it was boring.

JACKIE. I heard 'Cool Medallion' are good!

DYNETTE. Oh yeh, the band was good.

JACKIE. So *who* was boring?

DYNETTE. Nobody. Look leave me alone.

JACKIE. Touchy.

DYNETTE. I think I'm catching the 'flu . . . feel a bit on edge that's all.

JACKIE. Taking summat for it?

DYNETTE. No . . . It should clear. Look come round tonight we'll listen to some records and chat . . . ?

JACKIE. I can't, he's taking me to meet his sister tonight. I said I'd go.

DYNETTE. OK, tomorrow then?

JACKIE. He's been working on this car for weeks. He's put a new engine in, brakes, resprayed it.

Pause.

Summat bothering yer?

DYNETTE. No . . . Just this cold.

Pause.

So . . . you'd never do IT the first time . . . on the first meeting . . . I mean, the first date?

JACKIE. Nah . . .

DYNETTE. Me neither.

JACKIE. I mean it would make it too easy for 'em wouldn't it? No mystery, no romance. I could have said yes to Terry but I thought if he really likes me he'll ask again. I might say yes in a month . . . I'm thinking of going on the pill.

DYNETTE. Why the wait? You've done it before without using anything and nothing happened.

JACKIE *shakes her head.*

But I thought . . .

JACKIE. Then you thought wrong didn't yer. I want the first time to be just right. It might be with Terry, it might not, but I want to go on the pill anyway, just in case. We could go to the doctors together if you want. I could do with the support.

DYNETTE (*hesitantly*). Jackie . . .

JACKIE. Yeh.

DYNETTE. When you going?

JACKIE. Wednesday night. Terry's playing pool.

DYNETTE. Oh I see. You sure you can fit me in?

JACKIE. Don't be like that.

DYNETTE. Like what? I'm not being like anything.

JACKIE. Yes you are, you're snapping at me!

DYNETTE. Well it's *you*. Everything's Terry this, Terry that. Don't I exist anymore?

JACKIE. How could you understand? You've never been through it. You don't know what it's like. I like him a lot Dee. I can see you any time . . .

DYNETTE (*leaving*). Don't count on it.

CHORUS 1. When her body started changing and her stomach felt unsettled she put it down to nerves. Every time she was sick she had another excuse ready . . . 'something she had eaten', 'indigestion', 'wind'. Anything so as not to acknowledge the fact that she might be . . . the word stuck in her throat.

CHORUS (2 *and* 3). One two three four five

DYNETTE. Once I caught a dish alive

CHORUS (2 *and* 3). And his hands were meek and mild

DYNETTE. 'Til he gave to me his child
'til he gave to me . . .

School toilets

Six weeks later.

DYNETTE *is being sick in the toilet.*

JACKIE. You'll have to go to the doctor's Dynette. Morning sickness? Very risky.

DYNETTE. It's not funny. It's not . . .

JACKIE. Calm down, there's got to be a bug going round or something, I mean *you* can't be pregnant. Can yer?

Pause.

Can yer? Dynette?

DYNETTE *does not answer.*

You sneaky cow! You bloody sneaky cow. And you never told me. All that time you *had* and you never . . . Who was it?

DYNETTE (*sick again*). Jesus Christ.

JACKIE. 'Ere do you think you really might be? God Dynette, tell me who!

DYNETTE. This isn't happening, please God tell me it's not.

Pause.

JACKIE. You've gone and dunnit now.

DYNETTE. Leave me alone please Jackie . . . just go!

JACKIE *hesitates, then starts to go.*

DYNETTE. And not a word Jack . . . to anyone.

CHORUS (2 *and* 3). Panic Pains?

DYNETTE. How do I cope?

CHORUS (2 *and* 3). She needs someone to talk to.

DYNETTE. Where do I go?

CHORUS (2 *and* 3). She needs a shoulder to cry on.

Jan's flat

JAN. What are you doing here? Why aren't yer at school?

DYNETTE. Took t' afternoon off . . . Came to see me niece, where is she?

JAN. She's at school, eh eh why t' sudden interest?

DYNETTE. Just came to say hello but if she's not here . . .

DYNETTE *turns to leave.*

JAN. Summats wrong!

DYNETTE. Nah it's nowt. Just fed up.

JAN. Fed up! You don't know t' meaning of t' word.

DYNETTE *steps inside.*

DYNETTE (*looking at* JAN's *magazine*). What yer reading? (*She picks it up.*) That's a nice skirt.

JAN. The slit's too high.

DYNETTE. Yer can't take big strides if you haven't got a high slit.

JAN. Yer what?

DYNETTE. *I* like it.

JAN. Brazen.

DYNETTE. Is it heck. Anyhow sometimes yer want to be . . . a bit . . . you know.

JAN (*clips her around the head playfully*). You wouldn't come behind me dressed like that.

DYNETTE. You wear 'em.

JAN. You've got to have t' legs for it.

DYNETTE. Give up. Owt to eat?

DYNETTE *goes to the kitchen.*

JAN. Leave the sausage, it's Tania's tea. There's eggs though if yer want to make us a sandwich.

DYNETTE (*coming back in*). Can't be bothered.

JAN (*flicks through the magazine*). Please yerself.

Pause.

DYNETTE (*hesitantly*). You know when . . .

JAN. You've put t' taste in me mouth now.

DYNETTE. . . . yer first found out you were pregnant . . .

JAN. Oh go on make us a sarni.

DYNETTE. I've got some crisps in me bag d'yer want 'em?

JAN. What flavour?

DYNETTE. Cheese and onion.

JAN. Right what were yer saying?

DYNETTE. I were asking what it felt like when yer first found out you were having Tania.

JAN *continues flicking through the pages of the magazine and eating the crisps.*

JAN. Oh. That colour'd suit you. You ought to wear more green.

DYNETTE. I bet you were scared . . . ?

JAN. When?

DYNETTE. When yer told Mum. God, I wonder what she'd say if I told her I was . . .

JAN. Heaven forbid! She went mad.

DYNETTE. I thought they were gonna make yer get married.

JAN. They tried.

DYNETTE. I didn't know what were going on, me.

JAN (*pinching* DYNETTE). Ah, you were just a kid.

DYNETTE. So did yer just do it then?

JAN. Do what?

DYNETTE. Tell Mum? Did yer just tell her?

JAN. *She* told me. She could tell.

DYNETTE. What, when yer started getting big?

JAN. Nah she knew before that. She just knew. Summat in me face. She just knew . . .

DYNETTE (*looking away*). How?

JAN. I don't know. Bloody hell what's with t' questions? It's not one of them bloody essays, is it?

DYNETTE. No I'm . . .

JAN. How is school anyhow?

DYNETTE. OK.

JAN. Ready for yer exams then?

DYNETTE. I'll take 'em as they come.

JAN. No yer bloody won't you'll work hard for 'em.

DYNETTE. Exams aren't everything.

JAN. No but that bit of paper at t' end of 'em is. How many you doing again?

DYNETTE. Eight. If I didn't pass 'em you'd be dead disappointed wouldn't yer?

JAN. You're gonna pass 'em.

DYNETTE. But what if . . . Jan?

JAN. What?

DYNETTE. I missed a period.

JAN *looks at the magazine.*

JAN. God! You'd get bloody backache with them shoes!

DYNETTE. Did yer hear me?

JAN. I heard. I wouldn't worry about it. It happens . . . Have yer seen heel on them!

DYNETTE. I bought one of them home test-kits from t' chemist.

JAN *looks at* DYNETTE.

I'm pregnant Jan.

JAN. Yer what?

DYNETTE. I'm . . .

JAN. What the fuck . . .

DYNETTE. I didn't do it on purpose.

JAN. Yes you did, yes you bloody did.

DYNETTE. It were a mistake.

JAN. Are you stupid or summat?

DYNETTE. I just wanted to –

JAN. *You* wanted . . . Who was it? It were that Eddie Thomas wasn't it? (*Putting her coat on.*) I'll fucking kill him!

DYNETTE. Jan it were me. I did it. He didn't force me.

JAN. Fucking bastard.

DYNETTE. I should have used summat.

JAN. Yer didn't use owt?

DYNETTE. I didn't think –

JAN. Jesus Christ . . . Hang on, hang on . . .

DYNETTE (*in tears*). How am I gonna tell Mum?

JAN. Where's me fags?

JAN *searches around the room frantically. When she finds the cigarettes she lights one and calms down.*

Right let's start again.

DYNETTE. I'm going to have a baby.

JAN (*angrily*). Haven't yer got any eyes? Can't yer see? Aren't me, Mum and Ingrid enough for yer?

JAN *smokes.*

How many weeks?

DYNETTE. Six.

JAN. Right. OK. Yer not gonna tell Mum.

DYNETTE. She's gonna find out . . . She probably knows already.

JAN. I said yer not gonna tell her. I've got some money . . . some money I was putting away for Tania.

DYNETTE. What you on about?

JAN. I'll take yer to a private clinic.

DYNETTE. Hold on . . . I don't want . . .

JAN. Yer a smart lass Dynette.

DYNETTE. What's that got to do with it?

JAN. It's the best thing.

DYNETTE. For who?

JAN. Think of Mum . . . D' yer know what this will . . .

DYNETTE. Don't! I can't be everyone's puppet Jan. I can't be what everybody else wants me to be all t' time! Everyone keeps putting their dreams on my shoulders. I can't correct everybody else's mistakes. What about me!

JAN. They got back together yer know, Eddie and Sonia. She's pregnant again. Rumour has it could be his or Clifton's, the guy she was seeing.

DYNETTE. And Eddie's gone back to her?

JAN/CHORUS (2 *and* 3). Love.

JAN. Do yer want a baby Dynette?

DYNETTE. I'll have to cope won't I?

JAN. That's not what I asked.

DYNETTE. Course I don't but I can't . . .

JAN. Think about it. If you need to get out of the house for some space you can always come here. We'll sort summat out.

DYNETTE. What's there to think about? I'm gonna have a baby.

JAN *holds* DYNETTE *close.*

JAN You stupid, stupid cow.

At Home

DYNETTE *takes a comb from her suitcase and begins to comb her hair.*
MARIA *takes the comb and combs* DYNETTE's *hair for her.*

DYNETTE. Ow Mam!

MARIA. When I finish wid your hair, you make a start on de
plate.

DYNETTE *is not listening.*

You hear what I saying Dynette?

DYNETTE. What . . . ?

MARIA. Who you saying 'what'?

DYNETTE. I didn't hear what yer said.

MARIA. No. Your mind jus' drifting like you have all de world
problem on your head. Where your mind is? When is study
you should study to pass at school is man you study.

DYNETTE. Mam!

MARIA. Wha' 'appen you don't like to hear de truth?

Pause.

DYNETTE. You and Jacko, Mum did . . .

MARIA. Back to dat again. You and you fardhar is de same.
Pickin', pickin' me brain. For what eh? What you think you
going find?

DYNETTE. I'm just trying to make sense of things.

MARIA. Make sense of what concern you. This is me and you
fardhar fight. Nothing to do wid you.

DYNETTE. It has plenty to do with me. I'm the one who has to
hear it every day.

Pause.

Mum are you going to tell me or not?

MARIA. You wouldn't understand chil'. All you talking is *sex*.
And is not sex I talking. I have sex wid a man and look where
it leave me.

DYNETTE (*looks away embarrassed, then makes a joke*). Mum, you had three beautiful daughters.

DYNETTE *flicks her head back posing.*

MARIA (*laughing*). Oh Dynette, Dynette you is a joker.

DYNETTE. Mum I . . . I'm being serious. Children are important aren't they? I mean at the right time . . .

MARIA (*looks at* DYNETTE *curiously*). At the right time yes, but too early . . . (*She shakes her head.*) When I fall pregnant wid Ingrid, I was 'fraid to go to de modder. 'Fraid. So I go by a friend and we talk. We talk about life. We talk about me and Skolar. Skolar was planning to go Inglan at that time and I was 'fraid to lose him, but I didn't want to tell him about de baby and tie him down, but I didn't know what to do. We did talk all night me and . . . daylight catch us sleeping in de ol' bunk bed de two of dem did share sometime. And you daddy see what he want to see. He didn't see me sleeping wid me friend. He see his woman sleeping wid his brodder man. Dats all he see . . . What eyes does see is not always what is.

When Ingrid was born he never say nothing, but I could see him working something out in his mind . . . could see de man brain working over.

I don't know what was in me mind de odder day when he was fighting. I don't know why. I jus' wanted to hurt him bad. So I tell him after all these years what he did want to hear. Tell him Ingrid not his chil' and I mash him up. Yes dat one hurt.

Pause.

You is me las' daughter. Make me proud. You study. Finish school. Be a seamstress, a fashion designer or . . .

DYNETTE. I want to be a language interpreter. I can't sew.

MARIA. You can learn. Anyway you have brain you can do anything you want.

DYNETTE. Can I? What if I don't know what I want?

MARIA. What you mean? (*Pause.*) What on your mind Dynette? No better you don't talk . . . Listen. Don't let noffin pass you by. Don't do like me . . .

DYNETTE. Mum I . . .

MARIA (*not letting* DYNETTE *interrupt*). But you smart, *you* wouldn't be foolish like your modder.

DYNETTE. Mum . . .

MARIA. Yes.

DYNETTE. Have you nearly finished?

MARIA. Why, you in a hurry to go somewhere? I tell you wash de plate before you go anywhere you know. You have no time these days to spend a little time wid your modder.

DYNETTE. Oh Mam.

Enter SKOLAR. DYNETTE *steps aside. She puts her hands over her ears and watches her mother and father.*

CHORUS (*All*). Duck.

CHORUS 1. The heater, and the TV and the pictures of Our Lord.

CHORUS 2. It isn't raining sun clouds with pretty rainbows in the sky.

CHORUS (*All*). But dangerous missiles

DYNETTE. Keep grazing my head.

CHORUS (*All*). And words used in love

DYNETTE. Keep burning my ears.

CHORUS (*All*). Duck this. Duck that. Duck this. Duck that. Duck . . .

CHORUS 1. The shoves and the pushes and the flying bottles,

CHORUS 2. And the slaps and the cuts and the telephone calls.

CHORUS (*All*). Duck it all. Duck it all.

CHORUS 3. And it may just skim your skin

DYNETTE. But it is remembered . . .

Mid Argument

MARIA. And Jacko was a better man than you. Think he would a plan go Inglan widout me. Think he would a run leave me.

SKOLAR. If is Jacko you did a want so bad why you never stay wid Jacko. Why?

MARIA. Because I was expectin' your chil' you hear me I was breedin' for *you*.

SKOLAR. For me you was breedin? You take me for fool. When you sleep wid two man how you can so sure?

MARIA. When you already expectin' and you lie wid anodder man how dis man can change de one you already have in you belly?

SKOLAR. No woman, don't make story in me head. I tired.

Silence.

I jus' can't understand why . . .

MARIA. Maybe I did love de both of you for true. And then it all mess up. I sleep wid a man.

SKOLAR. One man or two?

MARIA. Is when you have to ax those question I want to know is who I wid.

SKOLAR. You never answer de question.

MARIA. I sleep wid two man Skolar. Two. But I *make love* wid only one.

SKOLAR. Oh. You didn't make love wid him den?

MARIA. I say I didn't make love to one a dem.

SKOLAR. So why you cannot talk straight. You and me do a ting so is me is de one you make love wid.

MARIA. I 'make love' wid only one man.

SKOLAR *puts his arms around her. She shrugs him off.*

MARIA. And after thirty-one years you still can't understand what I am saying.

SKOLAR. I understand one thing. You and Jacko never . . .

MARIA. No Skolar we never . . . And is dat what is all about enn it?

DYNETTE (*calmly to her mother and father*). I'm staying by Jan.

Silence.

DYNETTE. Tania's sick so Jan wants me to stay with her for the week. Jan has to work.

MARIA. Tania sick? Why Jan never phone me?

DYNETTE. It's nothing, just a cold.

MARIA. What about you school work?

DYNETTE. It's just revision. I've just got books to read.

MARIA. I don't see why Tania cannot stay here wid you while you read you books. Why you have to go over there?

DYNETTE. Mum, I 'need' to stay at Jan's. Give me a break. I need a break from you two at each other's throats all the time.

SKOLAR. Let her go. Is go she want to go. I don' having no vemin woman in me house. If is tramp she want to tramp herself better she do it in de street than inside my house.

MARIA. Skolar . . .

DYNETTE. I'm not a tramp dad. I'm *your* daughter.

SKOLAR. Yeh is true. *You* is mine. (*He looks dejectedly at* MARIA, *then hands the suitcase to* DYNETTE.) But the place not big enough for two woman one time. If you want to stay have respec'. If you can't have respec' get out.

DYNETTE *takes the suitcase and watches* SKOLAR *walk away from her.*

The Street

SKOLAR *and* JACKO *pass each other. They turn back and look at one another.* SKOLAR *recognises* JACKO *but turns his back on him and carries on walking.*

JACKO. Skolar . . . Whooi Skol. Skol, is me, is me man.

JACKO *holds* SKOLAR.

Sacca fet?

SKOLAR. Moi la. I still here. (SKOLAR *softens. He is genuinely glad to see his old friend.*) I living man. Cha' is in street we have to chat? Annu boire. I will buy you a 'Coke' man, for ol' time.

JACKO. Which coke? Me turn drinker now you know. I like me gwag same like you.

SKOLAR. It not too early?

JACKO. Which early? It nearly too late.

They laugh and go into the pub.

JACKO. So how is . . .

SKOLAR. Maria eh? (*He laughs.*) Hi Jacko, life is dread.

JACKO. But what I hearing? You turn Rasta too? (*He lifts up* SKOLAR*'s hat.*) No you hair not locked up.

SKOLAR. You raise up me hat you don't see how me head white already. (*Stuups.*) Jacko man . . . life eh.
    I see . . . (*Pause.*) I see me las' chil' turn woman on me. Think she can treat my house how she want. Bring man at all hours. All night I hear dem humph humph on me hire purchase sofa . . . makin' noise in me head all night. And is me las' girl Jacko. She have brains dat one. She me las' girl, me las' hope to make me know I didn't come to dis damn place for nothing . . . All night Jacko I hearing de spring in me sofa and me baby going away from me man. And it was de firs' time, de firs' time in the line of girl chil' I have there, the firs' time I stay in me bed, hol' onto de sheet and try and block out de noise. De firs' time I never hol' a knife to his throat and run de likkle skunt outta me house, outta me daughter . . . de firs' time Jacko . . . And you know why man . . . you know why? Cos I was scared. I was scared, and wouldn't I be a sick man if it *was* true what Maria say mm? Dat I was jealous of de man lying on me sofa wid me daughter. Jealous of de man who taste firs'.

He looks at JACKO *hard.*

Now wouldn't I be a sick man?

JACKO (*trying to avoid the conclusion of the conversation*). Man is long time since I see you. I see you daughter; she real pretty. You should be proud . . .

SKOLAR. Yes . . . I would be a sick man. You know what I saying enn it Jacko. It like a burning right in you stomach, right in de pit of you stomach . . . Like when you have a cake dat don't cut yet and somebody come in de night and take piece . . . when somebody cut de cake before you birthday den de birthday spoil ne true. Well is that what I talking.

JACKO. Ah man stop wid that.

SKOLAR. Jacko you know what it is when a man take anodder man woman? You know what it is?

JACKO. Man you let it play on you brain too much . . . too long.

SKOLAR. And after thirty-one years, she spring on you dat you chil' not you chil'.

JACKO. What?

SKOLAR. And you spend thirty-one years wid a woman eh, and you learn in a second dat de las' thirty-one years was for nothing.

JACKO. Not for nothing man.

SKOLAR. Thirty-one years eh and look how things does jus' fly back in you face . . . jus' cut you gut like a knife . . . things in front of you nose all you life and you never see it.

JACKO. Maria lie man . . . How a man chil' cannot be *his* chil' after thirty-one years.

SKOLAR. Jacko wasn't me and you dat use to stan' up on street corner . . . pose. Was de same Jacko and Skolar use to teef chicken from yard and sell in market. Was me and you dat could have any woman and we dat respec' de brodder woman . . . Was me and you dat?

JACKO. We always respec' man, always.

SKOLAR. So is whappen Jacko?

Pause.

You did know dat Ingrid was your chil' from time. But you never tell you brodder man . . . you never . . .

JACKO. Hol' it. Wha you say? No man. Is Maria and you Skol. You is joke man. (*He looks at* SKOLAR *who is deadly serious.*) I is Jacko man. Is me. You brodder. Maria was you woman. And de night you fin' us togedder I tried tell you is *you* she come look for and is talk we talk man. Talk. Now drink you drink and tired waste you breath.

They drink.

I is you brodder, Maria is you wife, and Ingrid is you chil' know dat.

Pause.

Skol I making tracks man. Take care and say 'Howdi' to Mar . . .

SKOLAR. . . . ria.

JACKO. Is life Skol. Life is de bastard not the two of we. We jus' man.

JACKO *extends his hand to* SKOLAR. *Pause.* SKOLAR *grasps his friend's hand.*

SKOLAR. Jus' *man* man. Man.

CHORUS (*All*). Life!

DYNETTE. If I take your life

CHORUS 3. Will she go to hell?

CHORUS 2. Will she have to suffer for her sin?

DYNETTE. If I give you life.

CHORUS 3. Will she go to heaven?

CHORUS 2. And suffer on this earth instead?

CHORUS (1 *and* 2). We taught her to love.

DYNETTE. I loved. I loved a man. Body and soul loved a man.

CHORUS 1. And you conceived.

DYNETTE (*bitterly*). Romantic dreams.

CHORUS (*All*). We taught her to think.

DYNETTE. I thought. I thought of pretty things. Plastic dolls with cotton dresses.

CHORUS 1. And you conceived.

DYNETTE. Cold reality.

CHORUS (*All*). You can't give up on life so early.

DYNETTE. One life must stop here.

CHORUS (*All*). And *your* mouth is already formed.

DYNETTE. Yes.

School Toilets

DYNETTE *is washing her face.*

JACKIE. Hey Dynette.

DYNETTE. Hi Jack was I missed yesterday?

JACKIE. I signed your name in the late book. As long as no one checks up you're clear. Where did you go?

DYNETTE. To see our Jan.

JACKIE. She all right? How's the little one? Sorry. I mean your niece . . . Tania . . . sorry.

DYNETTE. Why you sorry?

JACKIE. Didn't mean to remind you . . .

DYNETTE. Don't be daft.

JACKIE. What's the latest anyway?

DYNETTE. Latest?

JACKIE. Any sign of the Dreaded Curse?

   JACKIE *puts her fingers up as a Dracula shield.*

DYNETTE. No.

JACKIE. What about the exams?

   DYNETTE *looks at her.* JACKIE *shuts up.*

   Pause.

DYNETTE. I might have an abortion.

JACKIE. You wouldn't . . .

DYNETTE. Wouldn't I? I'm scared Jack.

JACKIE. Does your Mum know?

DYNETTE. No. I swear you say anything and I'll kill you.

JACKIE. I wouldn't.

DYNETTE. I've never thought about abortion before. Never thought about what it means.

JACKIE. It means to terminate the . . .

DYNETTE. I know that, stupid cow, I know what it means in the dictionary but to me it means I'm going to lose my God.

JACKIE *looks puzzled.*

Everything I've been taught to respect. The unquestionable. God's laws. I'm challenging God's laws Jackie. What does that make me . . . ? 'Thou shalt not kill'. I just want another chance. And for the first time in my life it feels like what I say, what I decide counts. And the funny thing is I know God's not going to punish me. Nobody's going to strike me down . . .

JACKIE. You need to talk to somebody.

DYNETTE. But I do. *She* doesn't answer me back or tell me what to do. She listens. She just lies comfortably inside me. (*She laughs.*) She is me Jackie. I found a new God. My own.

JACKIE. Stop it Dynette you're messing about. (*She makes the sign of the cross.*) She doesn't mean it God. For Christ's sake, you've only just missed a period. There's nothing there. You're not pregnant!

DYNETTE. I'm changing.

JACKIE. You're telling me!

DYNETTE. You can't understand. Nobody can, not even our Jan because Tania is Tania but this is something that's me, that thinks me and breathes me.

JACKIE. Breathes you?

DYNETTE. I'm discovering things about myself that I didn't know before. I'm finding out what I want and when I go to bed we talk.

JACKIE. Who?

DYNETTE. Me and my God. I ask her if she'd mind if I postponed her birth . . .

JACKIE (*curiously*). And what does she say?

DYNETTE. She listens . . . she just wraps herself around me and makes me know that whatever I decide is right. I'd like to hold her. I dream of her knees locked round my waist and her arms tight around my shoulders . . . and her head on my chest. She's not a baby. She's my friend and it feels warm when we're like that . . . safe . . . love. I've never been so close to anyone before in my life.

JACKIE. So . . . what you going to do . . . *if* you are . . . ?

DYNETTE. What d'you think about abortion Jack?

JACKIE. It's murder.

DYNETTE. I can't have a baby. Look at me. What would I do with a baby! There's so much I've got to do first. I don't want to end up like Mum.

JACKIE. You're not pregnant, you're not. You can't be . . . it's the pill it sometimes messes up your system.

DYNETTE. I never went on the pill.

JACKIE. But we talked . . . I know you never went with me but I thought . . .

DYNETTE. It was too late.

Pause.

JACKIE. Me and Terry finished last night.

DYNETTE. Oh.

JACKIE. He said I'm a teaser. I told him I wasn't ready.

JACKIE *leaves.*

DYNETTE. I'm not ready.

CHORUS (2 *and* 3). So you think you have the right?

DYNETTE. To determine my own life, yes.

CHORUS (*All*). You are forgetting the life of the baby.

DYNETTE. There is no baby.

CHORUS 3. Don't fool yourself. The 'baby' will always be there. You will always be a back street Mammy. A mother without a child. An orphan mother . . . Think about that . . .

DYNETTE. I thought I had a choice.

CHORUS 3 (*All*). You have a choice. What is your decision?

Silence.

DYNETTE. Terminate the pregnancy.

CHORUS (*All*). Taking off

DYNETTE. my holy socks,

CHORUS (*All*). Taking off

DYNETTE. responsibility

CHORUS (*All*). Putting on

DYNETTE. the gown.

CHORUS (*All*). The white stainless gown.

DYNETTE. And sitting on a plastic chair, my bottom poking through and

CHORUS (*All*). sticking. There are plenty more

DYNETTE. of me.

CHORUS (*All*). Sitting next

DYNETTE. to me

CHORUS (*All*). all with eyes

DYNETTE. as vacant as an empty tank,

CHORUS (*All*). washed out.

DYNETTE. My name is called and you shake,

CHORUS (*All*). or is it because

DYNETTE. I haven't eaten? I walk

CHORUS (*All*). or fly

DYNETTE. to the room.

CHORUS (*All*). Walk or fly

DYNETTE. to the leather bed.

CHORUS (*All*). And they inject,

DYNETTE. me

CHORUS. eject

DYNETTE. you

CHORUS (*All*). and before

DYNETTE. I can change my mind you are

CHORUS (*All*). out

DYNETTE. of my life

CHORUS (*All*). forever.

After

DYNETTE *steps into her parent's home with the suitcase.*

MARIA (*hears the door slam*). Dynette, dat you?

DYNETTE. Yeh Mum.

MARIA (*going to* DYNETTE). So why you stand up there like a . . . (*She notices a 'change' in her daughter.*) You had a nice 'break' by Jan's . . . ? How . . . how is Tania?

DYNETTE. She's better.

MARIA. And you now?

Silence.

Your fardhar didn't mean what he say you know. His mouf does run away wid him sometimes.

DYNETTE. I'm moving out . . . in with Jan.

MARIA. What you talking about? What you saying?

DYNETTE. I just came back to get some things.

MARIA. What Jan been filling your head with?

DYNETTE (*walking away from her mother*). Jan had nothing to do with it. It was my decision. I just think the time is right for me to . . .

MARIA. You think! You don't think! How you can think? You is a chil'. You don't know noffin about life yet.

DYNETTE. I think a lot Mum and I know a lot more than you're allowing me to.

MARIA. So you want to follow Jan. You want to do like me? Is hard times you looking for? Why you cannot use your head?

DYNETTE (*packing*). I've got headache.

MARIA. You think you smart . . . (*Pause.*)
Why you cannot take time . . . (*Pause.*)
So, you going leave me . . . my las' chil' . . .

DYNETTE. I'll be at Jan's. You just have to catch the forty-six bus! I'm not leaving the country.

MARIA. You not waiting to talk to your fardhar?

DYNETTE. He already said his piece.

MARIA. Your fardhar! What your fardhar know? Your fardhar don't know a patat!

SKOLAR (enters). Is dat so?

DYNETTE. Look Dad, I don't want to show disrespect for your house, so I'm moving out.

SKOLAR. Is dat man you bring in my house enn it? What he do?

DYNETTE. Nowt. He didn't do owt you never did!

SKOLAR (raising his hand). So you come woman!

MARIA holds him off.

Woman don't touch me!

DYNETTE. You don't even know what a woman is. How long you been married to Mum? Over thirty years and you haven't got a clue how she feels about anything. You fight, you argue but you never talk. So don't tell me anything about 'Woman'. You don't know!

SKOLAR grabs DYNETTE by the throat.

SKOLAR. I don't know?

MARIA. Skolar you going to murder your chil'!

SKOLAR keeps hold of DYNETTE. MARIA tries to pull him back. DYNETTE and SKOLAR's eyes stay fixed on each other. DYNETTE is crying but staring him out obstinately.

SKOLAR (slackening his grip). I don't know woman eh? (He lets her go.) . . . but now you know man.

DYNETTE takes the suitcase. MARIA goes to her but DYNETTE pulls away and leaves.

DYNETTE kneels at the candle.

DYNETTE. I saw your face for a while 'My Little God'. Kissed your soft brow. Watched you in your sleep, but I did not wake you. You looked so peaceful there and I wanted to prolong the moment. So I gave you death before life; knowledge before ignorance; And love, I gave you love.

She kisses her hand and blows the kiss to the candle until it goes out.

DYNETTE. I do this in memory of you.

> DYNETTE *begins to tidy up the mess by putting the things back in the suitcase. She comes across a red dress. She holds on to the dress.*

JAN. I got a new dress. Do you want to borrow that?

DYNETTE. Stop it Jan, I can't do with all this niceness. I'll borrow this one instead.

JAN. No you bloody won't. I've only worn it once. (*Pause.*) OK. OK. But don't stand near anyone who's smoking. I don't want any burns on it. It cost me a lot of money that dress.

DYNETTE. Thanks Jan.

JAN. Are you sure you want to go out tonight?

DYNETTE. I need to go out. I need to hear some music. I need to dance.

JAN. You sure? The anaesthetic . . . ?

DYNETTE. I *need* to dance.

JAN. OK. I'll ring Ingrid, see if she minds keeping Tania overnight. As long as you're OK.

> DYNETTE *uses the red dress as a stole. She flicks it over her shoulders, looks confident and then hesitates.*

CHORUS (*All*). Why so hesitant?

The Club

CHORUS (1 *and* 3). Eyes. Flickering in the night.

> EDDIE *notices* DYNETTE *and makes his way towards her.*

DYNETTE. We near but do not reach.

CHORUS 3. Have to run back. She is being watched
By eyes flickering in the night.

DYNETTE. I try not to see him in the corner of my eye,
But he fills my view as he performs in my show
And likewise I perform in his.

CHORUS 1. Miss Confident Red Dress sails to the bar
Laughing loudly at no joke

But making it into the best she's ever heard.

CHORUS 3. She concentrates on buying six drinks
While the person she's 'not interested in' nears to say HELLO.

CHORUS 1. She laughs again, hysterically, because the joke is
killing her,
And before HE reaches she makes a deliberate attempt to alter
her pose.

CHORUS (1 *and* 3). Now Miss Elegant.
Now Miss Beautiful.
Return Miss Confident.

CHORUS 3. HE smiles Hello to an actress.

DYNETTE. Boy you turn me into a stranger and a liar and . . .
Standing there as if I'm the only girl you could ever love.
You shitty hypocrite.
You bastard you . . .
Bastard. Bastard.

CHORUS 1. He smiles and the warmth makes her glow in the
dark.

CHORUS 3. But behind his smile he still says sorry

DYNETTE. And I can't cope with wet apologies, too late.

CHORUS (1 *and* 3). He hesitates to speak.
To bring up all avoided conversation.

CHORUS 3. Avoid eye contact for too long in case of telepathy.
Avoid each other like bumper cars at the fair.
If they collide . . .

DYNETTE/CHORUS 3. Will anyone get seriously hurt?

DYNETTE/EDDIE/CHORUS (1 *and* 3). Swerve.

EDDIE. Hi . . . Little Jan. How are you? Haven't seen you
since . . . Exams over yet?

DYNETTE. No. Begin next week.

He looks over his shoulder nervously.

EDDIE. Well . . . How's it going? Want a drink?

DYNETTE. No I'm OK.

EDDIE. Of course, you've just been to the bar. Who you with?

DYNETTE. Jan and some friends over there.

He waves over.

EDDIE. So . . . you've been well then?

DYNETTE. Mmm and you?

EDDIE. Yes . . . fine, fine.

Pause.

Sorry I haven't been in touch. I've been busy.

DYNETTE. Oh?

EDDIE. Had your driving test yet?

DYNETTE. Soon.

CHORUS (1 *and* 3). The test is soon.

EDDIE (*noticing a friend*). I'll catch up with you later. I'm just going over . . .

DYNETTE. Eddie . . .

EDDIE. Yes . . .

DYNETTE. I won't be here when you come back.

EDDIE. Right, well take care of yourself.

DYNETTE. I will.

CHORUS 1. She thinks, after the event has passed, of all the cues he gave her to say cute one-liners, that could have crippled him. But she could not tell him. Not then. Not ever. What was the point? Instead she shouts:

DYNETTE. I will pass my driving test.

CHORUS 1. He stands alone, a reject from her old old world.

EDDIE. I'm sorry.

CHORUS 1. His eyes say but she only sees what she wants to see. She takes her drinks and says to herself

DYNETTE. He still 'loves' me of course.

CHORUS 1. And part of her still wants, but the 'woman' in her says

DYNETTE. No.

(She puts the dress in the suitcase and slams it shut.)

CHORUS *(All)*. And de blues still a bubble

DYNETTE *puts her hands over her ears.*

DYNETTE. No it's finished. Done.

She brings the suitcase back to the cupboard.

My body. My life. There was never a child involved. I had an abortion.

The telephone rings. DYNETTE *sits at the typewriter. When she is ready she goes to answer the phone.*

DYNETTE. Hello?

JACKIE. Hi Dynette . . . I'm sorry for going on like I did.

DYNETTE. What did the doctor say?

JACKIE. I didn't go . . .

DYNETTE. Oh . . .

JACKIE. I'm thirty not dead!

DYNETTE *(laughs)*. Yer mad!

JACKIE. I rang earlier, where d'yer go?

DYNETTE. Here . . . I was here . . . working.

JACKIE. I'll let yer get back to it then . . . You all right?

DYNETTE. Yeh . . . I'll ring yer later on in the week.

DYNETTE *hangs up.*

CHORUS *(All)*. And de blues still a bubble.

Pause.

DYNETTE *puts a clean sheet of paper in the typewriter.*

CHORUS *(All)*. Bubble on . . . bubble on . . .

She begins to type.

Lights fade to blackout as DYNETTE *works.*

SLEEPING NIGHTIE ■ VICTORIA HARDIE

Victoria Hardie left school at sixteen and became a telephonist and shop assistant. She then worked for a documentary film company in New York. She married and produced one child and a play for the Soho Poly, London, called *Us Good Girls*. Another play, *Toy Boy*, was produced at the Riverside Studios, Hammersmith. *Vital Statistics*, an opera written with Michael Nyman, was performed at the Warehouse. She had another child and another play, *Dangerwoman*. Her essay on motherism, entitled 'The World Became a More Dangerous Place', was included in the book *Balancing Acts* published by Virago in 1989. She has lived in the Mato Grosso, Brazil, North Herefordshire and now lives in London with her husband and two sons.

Sleeping Nightie was commissioned by the Royal Court Theatre, London, and was first staged in a co-production at the Warehouse Theatre, Croydon, and then at the Royal Court Theatre Upstairs.

Characters

MOLLY, Sculptress. Lover of ADRIAN. Mother of BOY. Age, mid-thirties.

LAURA, MOLLY's sister. PR woman. Age, thirty.

ADRIAN, Tenor (or light baritone). MOLLY's lover. Father of BOY. Age, early thirties.

DAVID, American tourist. Electrical engineer with Lockheed. Age, late forties.

The Set

The set is the art gallery in which the locations of the scenes outside the gallery take place as well. At the back is MOLLY's icon. The icon should be in proportion to the rest of the set, easily visible without being oppressive. The painting on the icon is of the Virgin Mary. The icon should have two side panels with landscapes on them. There is a TV screen slotted into the crook of the Virgin Mary's arm so she looks as if she is cradling it, like a baby. She gazes down on the screen tenderly. The screen is for MOLLY's videos. The TV screen has two side panels that match the side panels of the main icon. Although the painting on the icon should be clearly a Madonna figure (with nothing abstract about it); the painting can be pretty rough and ready as are the video films. The video screen is slotted back into the icon.

Otherwise a window is needed for ADRIAN and MOLLY's flat, and LAURA's. A bed with a tartan rug on it. An ice bucket, some toys, a drawer of loose socks. Their belongings and the scenes in the flat should evoke the poverty and ordinariness in their domestic lives.

There should also be a slung monitor for use in Scene One and Scene Four.

Sleeping Nightie was written for the Royal Court Theatre and first staged at the Croydon Warehouse on 13 October 1989 and subsequently at the Royal Court Theatre Upstairs on 17 November 1989. The cast was as follows:

MOLLY	Louise Jameson
LAURA	Serena Gordon
ADRIAN	Michael Garner
DAVID	Ray Jewers

Directed by Terry Johnson
Designed by Kathy Strachan
Lighting by Steve Whitson

ACT ONE

Scene One

MOLLY *stands in front of us. Only she and the Madonna are lit. There is a Video 8 camera at her feet.*

MOLLY. The trouble is, I don't like, that I like men.
Since being a mother I have noticed more sharply it is nearly always them . . . men . . . who are doing something crazy on the tele. Officially or unofficially. In or out of uniform. They behave as if it's another species. But it's them. Men who mow the lawn, cry at funerals, loll about.

(Reflects.)

My son might become one of them. Be mugged of himself. Want a Rottweiler. God knows.
I like strangers. Bumping into people. It is hard to trust people you know. Art school was difficult for me. After the first year, I ditched painting for sculpture. But it wasn't enough. Too old. Too slow. I need to say something relevant. I shared an exhibition at the Bristol Warehouse. And three years ago I contributed to a video arts show at the Serpentine Gallery. Twenty artists. Half of them German. I finally settled on this. The image hardly exists at all. It has a ghostliness. Mine's the sort of art you can see through. No. Don't quote me on that. Sorry. Crass. But I am an artist. Video is immediate. Raw. Cheap.

Immediately the rest of the set lights up with lighting appropriate for street lighting.

A street somewhere in London. Enter LAURA. MOLLY *carries a hand-held camera on her shoulder. She wears a red tee-shirt. Pretty skirt with elasticated waist. Red socks and white trainers. Heavy ornate earrings. No make-up.*

LAURA *wears pressed jeans. Expensive blouse. New leather jacket, lipstick and a velvet Alice-band in her hair.*

MOLLY *adjusts the camera on her shoulder.*
The video films play on the icon video screen as MOLLY *films.*

MOLLY (*filming*). Beat me. Rape me. Strangle me.

As she says that we see a DAPPER CHINAMAN *respond to her and what she says, on the slung video screen.*

DAPPER CHINAMAN (*on screen*). Who would care?

The video film continues with a response from another man she has accosted. Meanwhile LAURA *looks round, anxiously tries to separate herself from* MOLLY *in some way.* LAURA *is embarrassed. The man on the screen is now a labourer. Bare chest. Close up of expression on his face.*

MOLLY. Beat me. Rape me. Strangle me.

LABOURER. I have more important things to do.

The video film continues with a response from another man she accosts. LAURA *has walked as far away from* MOLLY *as she can.*

MOLLY. Rape me. Beat me. Strangle me.

VERY RESPECTABLE BANK MANAGER MAN (*on screen*). Are you worth going to jail for? That is the question. Or is it better that I wend my way?

The video film continues with a response from another man she accosts. A man with a hippy appearance, responds.

MOLLY. Beat me. Rape me. Strangle me.

MIDDLE-AGED HIPPY (*on screen*). Don't you put your trip on to my ego man.

The video film continues with another response from a new man. An Asian man carrying a large box full of crisp packets, as if to take them into a corner shop. MOLLY *confronts him.*

MOLLY. Beat me. Rape me. Strangle me.

ASIAN MAN. Good day.

Films stop.

LAURA. I don't understand.

MOLLY. You promised you'd help me out. So what did you think I was doing?

LAURA. Lying to me.

MOLLY. No.

LAURA. Yes.

MOLLY. How?

LAURA. You said. Just come along and see. You said. I'd soon get the hang of it. What you were doing for your exhibition. That you were filming street life.

MOLLY. You said you'd do my PR for my exhibition.

LAURA. Might . . .

MOLLY. You said, I need you to make it proper. I need a real professional like you. Not some . . . broke art student who's passionate about my work but hasn't the faintest idea how to organise publicity.
You've got to help. My life can't go on like this.

LAURA. No. It can't.

MOLLY. I film the expression on each man's face. His response to my accosting him right here in the street. Then I mount the video in the icon in the gallery.

LAURA. I always thought the use of tape or celluloid or whatever was called film.

MOLLY. Sculptures aren't all broken arms and chipped marble willies.

LAURA. You know perfectly well why you're doing this. And I know.

MOLLY. It's my work.

LAURA. OK. Face up to where the inspiration came from. You wouldn't have the guts. (*Lights a cigarette.*)

MOLLY. You're a fine one to talk about guts. Here I am risking life and limb.

LAURA. I'll have you know my firm is in the middle of an extremely lucrative support-smoking campaign. Not easy in these green times.

MOLLY. Does Adrian look cross with me these days. Kind of scowling?

LAURA. Do you tell him you love him?

MOLLY. Not when he criticises my shoes. Anyway declarations of love, gauged wrong, can be the last straw.

A moment.

See that man over there?

LAURA. Black or white?

MOLLY. Coming out of the Nat. West. waving a white hanky.

LAURA. He must be all right. He's wearing a tweed jacket.

MOLLY. I feel sick.

LAURA. Oh Christ.

MOLLY. Just before I accost. I'd give anything to be at home . . . tidying up the toys even. Right, move it.

MOLLY *films. We see* DAVID *on the video screen. An expensive motorised camera round his neck. Close-up of* DAVID's *face on TV screen.*

DAVID (*on screen*). Taxi!

MOLLY *stops filming. Screen goes blank.* MOLLY *approaches him, camera at the ready again. Enter* DAVID *on stage for real.*

MOLLY (*to* DAVID). Beat me!

LAURA. I don't think he heard.

MOLLY. Oh Christ.

LAURA *gives* MOLLY *a shove at* DAVID.

DAVID. Taxi.

MOLLY (*to* DAVID). Beat me. Rape me. Strangle me.

DAVID. What? Hell! London's become just like Sao Paulo, Johannesburg.

DAVID *snaps* MOLLY *with his camera.*

Or L.A. Taxis won't stop for no man.

LAURA. Any . . . man.

MOLLY. Beat me. Rape me. Strangle me.

DAVID. One at a time or all together because I have an appointment . . .

MOLLY. All right. Smother me to death with a shot-silk cushion from Hong Kong.

MOLLY *films.*

DAVID. Hong Kong? I have a cricket bat from Pakistan I bought in Lillywhites.

MOLLY. Lillywhites?

DAVID. On Piccadilly. Around the block from here.

MOLLY. Why don't Americans ever understand anything?

DAVID. That is because the rest of the world is always doing something without our permission.

MOLLY. Sock me on the jaw.

He snaps her with his camera.

DAVID. Take it easy Ma'am. I'm just like a big friendly dog. Just let me sniff your hand and when I know your scent, when I know what and who you are, I'll let you go. So take it easy. OK.

MOLLY *(stops filming).* OK.

DAVID. OK. It's a beautiful day and we have time on our side. The world is our oyster.

MOLLY. This is my sister . . . and I'm . . . her sister.

LAURA. Oh Christ.

DAVID. Tell you what. I'd really appreciate it if you'd both come along with me and we can all explain ourselves toward greater understanding. We haven't exchanged enough to merit a farewell.

MOLLY. You Americans are always so quick.

DAVID *(charm and smiles).* But you're obviously interested in people. I'm fascinated by people. I love people. My chin ain't so photogenic, by the way.

MOLLY. Thank you for being a film star.

DAVID. I'm originally from Texas, matter of fact.

MOLLY. That doesn't matter.

LAURA *(jotting in her notebook).* Where in Texas?

MOLLY. It doesn't matter. You all came from your mothers' wombs and there's no getting away from that.

DAVID. You don't know my mother. Sure as hell I never came from her womb!

MOLLY (*to* DAVID). Is your mother aware of this?

DAVID. You should see the way she looks at me. Kinda as if we were never connected. I just appeared one day. A day so hot the ice caps trickled down the mountainside like fresh cream down the side of a chocolate sundae. Leastways that's what I tell myself when the going gets rough. It was the heat that made me!

LAURA (*looking round*). I hope I don't meet someone I know.

MOLLY. I have to go. Childminder's waiting.

DAVID. What? Already?

MOLLY. Laura will take your name and address and send you an invitation to an exhibition of mine where the cassette of you will be included as a work of art.

DAVID. Me and the Mona Lisa, huh.

MOLLY. There will be other male subjects present. With any luck.

DAVID. OK, OK, OK. Look. I hate giving business cards to someone I like for heaven's sake. But seeing how this is the latter half of the twentieth century.

MOLLY. Fine. Fine.

DAVID (*hands them each a card*). Call me David.

MOLLY. OK David.

DAVID. Name's on the card . . . The designer quality. It was patterned by an acquaintance who wanted to change her life after her kids left home to explore. Do you have a card please?

MOLLY. Well. I am my card really.

DAVID. Should I use extra-sensory perception that I might connect with you?

MOLLY. Hang on.

She delves into her bag and brings out a piece of paper and a pen. She writes her name down and hands the paper to DAVID.

DAVID (*reading it*). Baby oil. Plastic pants. Two holed teats . . . sterilising pills.

MOLLY. I'm on the end of the list.

(*Bending down and picking something up off the pavement*.) It's my lucky day.

DAVID. And mine that's for sure.

MOLLY. Somebody's dropped their Pizza Hut vouchers.

DAVID. Do you collect Pizza Hut vouchers?

MOLLY. We could eat out with these.

LAURA (*embarrassed*). Molly. This gentlemen isn't interested in your housekeeping plans.

DAVID (*peers over* MOLLY's *shoulder at the vouchers*). Yeah but you have to take the pizza out. You can't eat it at the table in the restaurant.

MOLLY. Even if there's a blizzard?

DAVID. It's just for . . . to go. Yeah. To go.

MOLLY. Right.

DAVID. Yeah.

MOLLY. Oh well. Thanks. Bye.

DAVID. Oh. (*Holds his hand out again and clasps her arm with both hands*.) Look forward to talking with you . . .

MOLLY. How does that camera treat you?

DAVID. Oh it's my friend. Once people are in there they are mine.

MOLLY. Really?

DAVID. And thank you.

Exit MOLLY.

Scene Two

LAURA *and* DAVID *in the street. Seconds later.* DAVID *looks out after* MOLLY. LAURA *taps him on the shoulder.*

LAURA. I'll need you to sign a consent form for the artist.

DAVID. Where will that get her?

LAURA. It gives Molly immunity for you.

DAVID. Is that what she wants?

LAURA. It's what is required.

DAVID. From me? Me a plain, ordinary tourist. Thought he'd catch the Trooping of the Colour or whatever.

LAURA. Oh lovely, the Trooping.

DAVID. Now . . .

LAURA. Yes?

DAVID. About the artist.

LAURA. I can send you her details . . .

DAVID. Yeah?

LAURA. Perhaps?

DAVID. Sisters huh?

LAURA. She lives with a singer and they have a baby son. The coast isn't exactly clear. Anyway . . .

  LAURA *makes as if to leave.*

DAVID. Does her boyfriend go out to work?

LAURA. How does opera grab you?

DAVID. Sticks in my throat matter of fact. If you don't mind. No one kinda farts or swears. There's no humanity. Just yelling and I dunno. Gimme humanity, the hard truths.

LAURA (*writing in her notebook*). What do you do?

DAVID. I'm an electrical engineer with Lockheed. We're working with your Ministry of Defence. Helicopters are my speciality matter of fact.

LAURA. Terrifying, helicopters. The motorbikes of the sky.

DAVID. Oh no. Not my Big Mother.

LAURA. Your mother is a helicopter?

DAVID. Big Mother is my pride and joy. Used in combat. It kills with its guns and can swoop real low and kinda scoop up the injured. Kinda killer and Angel of Mercy all in one.

LAURA. Big Mother?

DAVID. I find the connection . . . with the name . . . somewhat tenuous . . . But that's what the men in 'Nam called it.

LAURA. Pity.

DAVID. Why for pity's sake? I take my crossed wires very seriously.

LAURA. I'm not sure that she'd want you to be an exhibit if she knew you made weapons.

DAVID. Oh? It's never bothered anyone before. In fact the world is full of satisfied customers.

LAURA. The exhibition is to do with how she doesn't like violence.

DAVID. Who does Ma'am? . . .

LAURA. Me actually . . . Couldn't you say 'gliders' or something?

DAVID. Perhaps. But I do have this compulsive habit of telling the truth when I'm nervous. It's always been my downfall.

LAURA. Make sure you reach a high nervous point *after* you've bought her cassette. Right?

DAVID. So you want me to sacrifice the truth for art. Be a new experience.

LAURA. Exactly.

DAVID. Send whatever . . . to the Connaught Hotel. David Jackson.

LAURA *shakes his hand.*

LAURA. I'll have it biked over especially and thank you so much.

DAVID. Tell yer what?

LAURA. Yes?

DAVID. I gotta couple o'tickets for the Trooping of the Colour . . .

LAURA. And?

DAVID. Be a nice way to keep in touch . . . all of us? Maybe?

LAURA. Maybe.

Exit LAURA *and* DAVID.

Scene Three

Midday. A few days later.

ADRIAN *and* MOLLY's *flat. The bed with the tartan rug over it.*
ADRIAN *is emptying ice boxes into a green plastic bucket. He is tall with long shiny hair, a thin frame, a loose cotton jacket, a white tee-shirt with a drawing on it. Loose fitting cotton trousers. Polished leather shoes. He is kempt and beautiful.*

Enter LAURA *in a smart suit with the skirt above the knee. Alice-band in hair. Pearl earrings and necklace. She smokes a cigarette and holds a matchbox.*

LAURA. Ashtray?

ADRIAN. My larynx.

LAURA. Sorry. Sorry. Sorry. I forget.

LAURA *stubs the cigarette butt in the matchbox and puts the box in her jacket pocket. She straightens up the tartan rug on the bed, although it's already straight.*

ADRIAN. Killjoy, I know I am sometimes.

LAURA. You know if you two got married one day, in a proper church, invited proper people, if you had proper wedding lists in proper shops then someone would give you an ice bucket. I know you both think it would be meaningless to tie the knot, but you should think materialistically in your precarious cash flow situation.
    Where's the champagne?

ADRIAN. I shoved it in the ice box for ten minutes. We only decided on this naming party at the last minute. You know how she can't stand plans.

LAURA. She plans the videos for hours and hours though. Staring at the icon in the gallery. Must be strange when she's working and you're not. It's usually the other way round.

ADRIAN. There have been gaps before. But this time all the gaps have joined together. There must be a decline in the market for freelance tenors. You either have to be a star, or like me. Scrounging around for a tour if you're lucky, or the odd covering job. Or maybe a modern opera by a brilliant composer no one's heard of and no one gets paid properly.

LAURA. One good thing about my business . . .

ADRIAN. The money . . .

LAURA. A baby son is better than a kick in the teeth. They can't take that away from you.

ADRIAN. Ah, but I was never prepared for the shock of it! To think that there is a shit machine in there asleep in his cot, who is one day going to refer to me as a 'my Dad'. Numbing, really numbing.

LAURA. Molly understands, I know.

ADRIAN. Maybe.

LAURA. She doesn't tell you when there's only 75 pence for weekend food.

ADRIAN. I didn't come into this world to support a family I've only just discovered. Persuade her to take up something that can produce the readies so we can live just a tiny bit. Sisters are always in league.

LAURA. She is going to have to make it clear to me what the cassettes do say. I'm not so hot at interpreting art that isn't . . . a bowl of fruit or a Virgin in a frame. Cassettes . . . I dunno.

ADRIAN. *You* dunno?

LAURA. Video art could come a cropper against market forces.

Enter MOLLY. *She wears a cream suit with a fitted jacket and swirling skirt. Flat black suede shoes. Heavy ornate earrings. No eye make-up but lipstick.*

MOLLY. It's been stolen.

ADRIAN. We have no insurance. What?

LAURA. Baby?

MOLLY. My waist.

LAURA. Having a baby at your age is bound to take its toll.

MOLLY. I'm a tree trunk.

ADRIAN. You look ravishing but rather red shoes with that outfit.

MOLLY. Oh.

ADRIAN. Never mind.

MOLLY. You mean I look terrible. Lost my former glory. Fat. A maturing oak.

ADRIAN. Silver birch.

A moment.

Don't worry. For the time being. You aren't supposed to be thin at the moment.

MOLLY. My body has had a terrible mind lately. I mean *shock*.

LAURA. But you do go in and out. Honestly.

MOLLY. Not like a natural beauty.

LAURA. But you don't want members of the opposite sex to eye you with their minds. Isn't that what you're on about with the sculpture videos?

MOLLY. Just because I don't want my son to grow up to think he can fall back on hitting instead of thinking. Just because I don't want my son to feel he has to be a *real man* with muscles. Getting to the heart and soul of masculinity with my . . . work . . . has nothing to do with the fact that it's elasticated waists from now on. Can you see my hair falling out?

ADRIAN. Fistfuls.

LAURA. What's his name?

MOLLY. We'll announce it when the guests arrive.

LAURA. I must say I would have liked a proper christening. Font, carpet of daffs, train of lace floating from the robe. God.

ADRIAN. I'm the culprit. This non-denominational non-political – do.

MOLLY. It's because of what the monks did to him at school.

ADRIAN. Irrelevant. It's really naff when people winge about their childhoods.

MOLLY. They beat him and . . .

ADRIAN. Doesn't matter . . .

MOLLY. And they made him have a bath with his vest and pants on . . .

LAURA. To save laundry bills?

ADRIAN. Molly I haven't heard the sound of the hoover recently.

MOLLY. He had committed a mortal sin.

LAURA. I hear they're the best kind. What?

ADRIAN. This rug is crying out for a clean. I can hear it.

MOLLY. One that wakes you up in the middle of the night in a cold sweat ever after amen.

LAURA. What was it?

ADRIAN. I had given up sweets for Lent and got caught eating peppermint lumps. Forced me they did. Beat me. Forced me into the bath. And left the cold tap dripping on my head. My vest and pants wet, ringing through.

LAURA. Oh dear.

ADRIAN. They don't make them anymore.

LAURA. What?

ADRIAN. Peppermint lumps.

LAURA. Anyway . . . great fun what they're doing to the council block opposite.

MOLLY. There's a ghost mother in there. The block's empty.

ADRIAN. So they can tart it up for some developer.

MOLLY. It was full of single mothers till the council decided to rehouse them.

LAURA. Well that's all right then, isn't it?

MOLLY. One of the mothers didn't want to move.

LAURA. People can be rather ungrateful.

MOLLY. She threw herself out of the window in protest when the police tried to evict her and her baby. She died. 'Great fun'.

ADRIAN. Every time the builders put a new window in . . . her ghost pushes it out. We saw her do it once.

LAURA. You two are over-imaginative. The putty is probably too weak and they've cut the pane wrong.

(*Flourishing a notebook.*) I need to go over the catalogue and the press release for the exhibition.

ADRIAN. Grown-up stuff.

LAURA. Got to be done.

ADRIAN. Give business a break. This is our son's big day.

MOLLY. That's right. The idea of the videos grew in my head as he grew in my body. The minute I saw his sweet little balls on the hospital scan.

LAURA. Were they to have a name?

MOLLY. No. He is to have a name.

LAURA. I know. How about Rodney after Uncle Rodney?

ADRIAN. Would that be an honour?

LAURA. He was cox for Cambridge.

MOLLY. The year they sunk.

LAURA. But at least he was somebody.

ADRIAN. To forget.

LAURA. Ooh nasty.

MOLLY. You'll find out the name when the guests arrive.

ADRIAN. I thought you went out earlier for a takeaway pizza. I haven't had any lunch.

MOLLY. Food, fucking and song. That's the life of a singer for you.

ADRIAN. You understand me so well.

MOLLY. I did go out for a takeaway pizza, yes. But it wasn't as simple as that.

ADRIAN. Pizzas are very simple. They know who they are and what is going to happen to them.

MOLLY. Do sit down.

ADRIAN *gets the hoover out. He hoovers.* MOLLY *goes off and gets a camera. Films* ADRIAN.

MOLLY. Like to record rare moments in history from time to time.

MOLLY *stops filming.*

MOLLY. The *noise!*

ADRIAN. It has a certain musical tone; it seems that only I have the ear to appreciate in this house.

LAURA. And what tone is that?

MOLLY. Don't rise to it Laura. Let's just get on.

ADRIAN. Castrato.

MOLLY. Please. We're all . . .

LAURA. Here to help each other.

ADRIAN *switches the hoover off.*

MOLLY. There. Now.

LAURA. The American. I've organised his consent.

MOLLY. I really liked him. He obviously didn't think I was at all weird.

ADRIAN. Why on earth should he?

LAURA. He seems such a nice man. An electrical engineer.

ADRIAN. Very useful in a power-cut.

LAURA. The bumph has to be at the printers two months ahead of the exhibition. And that was four weeks ago.

MOLLY. So. His face. His tweed jacket. His features on the screen . . . like a baby being cradled in her arms. The proportions of the installation are as important as the materials . . .

LAURA. No aesthetics . . .

ADRIAN *switches the hoover on.*

MOLLY (*shouting above noise*). When you're a mother you feel as if you've got no one on your side.

ADRIAN *switches the hoover off.*

Like the ghost mother.

ADRIAN. I'm on your side.

MOLLY. Then will you look after him tomorrow while I do the last video sculpture?

ADRIAN. Of course I will. But he's got a sniffle. Might do my throat in.

LAURA. Don't you approve of the video sculptures?

MOLLY. I've lost an ear-ring.

LAURA. Have any of the sculptures retaliated when accosted?

MOLLY. No. If they did what I asked, that would give me control. That is the thing most men most fear about a woman. So I confront them with what they think they want. The kind of madnesses you hear about, fear about, dread.

The response is the sculpture. The video of the man's response is the sculpture.

Each man is supposed to come to the exhibition and buy himself. A view of himself . . . not needing to be violent. So that . . . each time he assumes he has the right to be out of control . . . he has this to remind himself . . . and others who will flock to the show . . . he has the tape to show the absurdity . . . how it looks even to think about those terrible madnesses and that he needn't be a real man.

A moment.

LAURA (*jotting in her notebook*). Male violence is a global problem.

ADRIAN. Our son is no more likely to grow up violent than any other man, as long as you're a good mother to him.

MOLLY. I don't know what a good mother is.

LAURA (*to* MOLLY). A good mother rings the gallery every time we have a meeting on the installation and winges about the babysitter being late, or the pushchair getting a puncture or whatever. It's so unprofessional.

MOLLY. The world is divided between sculptresses who do have children and those who don't.

ADRIAN. And singers who are hungry and those who are starving.

LAURA. Be realistic. No one wants to know about that side of your life when struggling with art forms.

MOLLY. Even when I'm engrossed in my work, his face burns at the back of my mind. Anything could happen to him. God knows.

LAURA. Everything will be all right. Who do you admire? Other artists?

MOLLY. Leni Riefenstahl, Mr Kodak.

LAURA. Leni Riefenstahl?

MOLLY. She was a woman. She was an artist and she worked for the Nazis. Three greater disadvantages would be hard to find.

ADRIAN *makes a show of coiling up the hoover lead.*

LAURA. Reifenwhat?
Right. This is you Moll.

MOLLY. Thank you very much.

LAURA (*reads from her notebook*). 'This is Molly's first major exhibition. Her other shows include paintings in a mixed show before working in Germany . . .'

MOLLY. We only went to Hamburg for a weekend.

ADRIAN. Those were the days.

MOLLY. Oh. We'll have them back. Promise.

LAURA. Having become disillusioned with her college training she worked alongside video artists then individually. She now combines technology with the traditional Virgin image. She has filmed innocent male passers-by . . .

MOLLY. You don't know they are innocent.

LAURA. Innocent male passers-by, attacking them with obscene aggressive suggestions . . .

MOLLY. It's their . . . thoughts I attack them with . . . oh help.

LAURA. Trust me.

MOLLY. What about what I mean?

ADRIAN. What about me? Don't I mean anything any more?

LAURA. This is new territory to me. I don't have to be doing this you know. I'm doing this because I want to help you. And my firm is hot at the moment.

ADRIAN. It won't be for much longer.

LAURA. Oh shut up.

ADRIAN. I intend to swallow that pizza whole . . . wherever it is.

Pause.

MOLLY. There isn't one.

ADRIAN. What d'you mean?

MOLLY. I didn't have the right sort of money.

ADRIAN. But you had six vouchers . . . from Pizza Hut!

MOLLY. Yes, but they're not right.

ADRIAN. You've been deceiving me! You could have got a country vegetarian deep-pan for free with a portion of garlic bread. I've been dreaming of that bread all morning.

MOLLY. I got over-excited and didn't focus on the small print.

ADRIAN. Are you suggesting I call a lawyer?

LAURA. You have to use one voucher at a time perhaps.

MOLLY. For each pizza. Yes.

ADRIAN. What if you sit down and eat there? In the actual . . . hut?

MOLLY. You have to leave.

ADRIAN. You mean you have to eat six pizzas to use up six vouchers?

MOLLY. Yes but each medium pizza costs £5.95, but you get a pound off each 'cos of the pound vouchers.

ADRIAN. So in order to save £6 we have to spend . . .

LAURA. £35.70 pence.

ADRIAN. So where is the pizza?

MOLLY. Where the £4.95 is, which is a mystery.

ADRIAN. Molly!

MOLLY. And we have to eat six vouchers within six weeks.

LAURA. You can have three and she can have three.

ADRIAN. What if I get a tour?

MOLLY. Only accept the job when you've checked the stops are in towns with Pizza Huts.

ADRIAN *advances towards her threateningly.*

ADRIAN. Fine. Meanwhile I'll stay hungry.

MOLLY (*arms raised*). All right. Beat me. Rape me. Strangle me. Pour boiling oil over me. On second thoughts lay off the boiling oil. Just go and boil an egg.

Tense moments.

ADRIAN. I suppose we'd have to take out a bank loan for a coleslaw.

MOLLY (*looking out of window*). The ghost mother . . . she's pushing her hands against the window-pane.

LAURA. Nonsense. I bet it's someone measuring for curtains.

MOLLY. She's going to push the window out.

ADRIAN. Is there anyone walking underneath?

MOLLY. Yes. God yes there is. A woman with a pushchair and a baby. She's wearing trainers like mine. Looks like me.
  Sing. Soothe her. You might stop her pushing the window out.

LAURA. Hit that top C and you might have the window out. I mean . . . really you two.

ADRIAN *sings the opening lines of 'Che Faro Euridice' beautifully.* MOLLY *looks agonisingly out of the window.*

ADRIAN. She's stepping back. She's left the window in.

MOLLY. She loved your voice. Heart stopper.

Pause. They embrace.

LAURA. Tell us his name before the others arrive. Damnit I am family.

MOLLY. He's called 'Boy'.

LAURA. What's that?

ADRIAN. Take the champagne out of the ice-box for us Laura. Before it explodes?

LAURA. Right. I can understand that.

Exit LAURA.

MOLLY *and* ADRIAN *embrace.*

MOLLY. When people are just about to arrive I'm never in the mood for them.

Is my bottom thinner? I know my breasts have had an identity crisis . . . my tummy too . . .

Lights.

Scene Four

Next day. Horseguards Parade. The Trooping of the Colour. Military Band plays.

LAURA *looks out at the audience as if she's watching the Trooping. We see video of the Trooping on the slung TV screen. She wears an expensive dress and hat and gloves.*

DAVID *in a light summer suit approaches her as if clambering over people and benches, clasping his camera.*

LAURA *then notices him.*

The Trooping music softens as they talk. The screen filled with Guardsmen in red tunics and busbies.

LAURA. Stirring stuff. The Trooping.

DAVID. One hundred rifles as one. Capable of thirty or forty well-aimed shots a minute . . . for automatic fire, or street fighting.

LAURA. Not in Fulham I hope . . .

DAVID. My, what a beautiful sight. Brings defence, arms, to the level of art . . . yeah art . . . You know each of those soldiers has a thirty-six inch pace and is allotted a twenty-four inch frontage.

LAURA. You really do know an awful lot.

DAVID. Whole bang show fitted into four hundred square yards of parade ground. Five hundred more men lining the route.

LAURA. The sun glinting on the bayonets. So pretty.

DAVID. Oh they just stick those on for tradition's sake. These new automatic rifles are positively stunted, matter of fact.

LAURA. Oh.

DAVID. Weapons are friendly. Like that extra bolt on the front door that you don't really need . . .

LAURA. I've got a Siamese . . .

DAVID. That's neat. I mean you know there's an enemy out there somewhere. Even if you don't know what or who it is.

LAURA. Exactly . . .

DAVID. The precision of the march with the music . . .

LAURA. Lovely tune . . .

DAVID. Not a connection missing not a foot wrong . . .

LAURA. Why does the Queen dress like a blue pineapple in a skirt? Still, her birthday.

DAVID. One missing connection on an automatic missile and all the wrong people could get killed . . .

LAURA. Every foot in step . . .

DAVID. A mathematical extravaganza . . .

LAURA. So seductive . . .

DAVID. I trust you didn't tell your sister about the real me?

LAURA *turns and looks at him sharply as if he's spoilt the moment.*

The Trooping video plays. The military band volume increases. Video stops. Video screen doors should be closed over screen; perhaps by LAURA.

Exit DAVID.

Scene Five

ADRIAN *and* MOLLY's *flat. A few days later.*

MOLLY *rummages through a black plastic bag full of rubbish.*

LAURA *lights up a Marlborough cigarette with a matchbox from her pocket.*

MOLLY. I've got to find my other ear-ring.

LAURA. He's sleeping a long time.

MOLLY. Goes like that. Other times he never sleeps. Exhausting. Drives his father mad.

LAURA. How mad is he at the moment?

MOLLY. Can't you tell?

LAURA. Having never lived with a man I've got no yardstick. They all seem roughly the same. Always needing so much attention. Girlfriends often say. 'Let's meet when he's away, then we can really talk'. As if they are censored when their men are at home.

MOLLY. It's the waiting for work . . . the not knowing. The lack of control. It permeates everything till I feel like a bundle of ashes. It's so hard to deal with. Never knowing what sort of mood he'll be in. Charm? Rage? Charm?

LAURA. Beneath all that trendiness he is a traditional public schoolboy. He'll always be one-up on you. He's better educated.

MOLLY. Educated a lot. I wouldn't use the word 'better'. Christ.

LAURA. Deep down he wants a proper wife.

MOLLY (rummaging). My favourite ear-rings damnit.

LAURA. And it was a nasty business with the monks at bathtime.

MOLLY. Don't.

LAURA. Well. He's obviously got over it. All quite jokey now.

MOLLY. He's only the third man I've ever wanted to stay for breakfast with on the first night. The first time I saw him I was furious. He was laughing with a friend . . . doubled up . . . then he caught my eye as if I'd caught him out. I knew I had to look no further. Something in him was me. Something.

LAURA. All very significant.

MOLLY. Love.

Enter ADRIAN.

ADRIAN. Where's my gargle?

MOLLY. In the medicine cupboard next to the baby oil.

Exit ADRIAN.

LAURA. Anyway. You've done it all for me. With the romance side of life.

MOLLY. Well it was all so womb-like at art school. Passions rising over transparent coffee. Arguing about art but thinking about romance. Just fell into bed with whoever it was. Thinking . . . I . . . well . . . persuading myself I was in love. Always needed to be in love. But the real test was whether I could stay for breakfast . . .

LAURA. Cold light of day kind of thing?

MOLLY. When I couldn't. I'd wake in the dark hours, a sense of asphyxiation rising in my throat. It wasn't till I hit the empty streets that I could breathe freely.

LAURA. You are like me. You don't trust. Deep down.

MOLLY. Not true. We made love under the tartan rug . . .

LAURA. On the Welsh borders. I know.

MOLLY. Yes, but at an open-air jazz concert. I didn't care if anyone saw us really. Swop away.

LAURA. You didn't tell me that before.

MOLLY. Very precious to me. The first time with him.

LAURA. So you don't get asphyxiated with him then?

MOLLY. It passes. It's OK.
Let's talk about you.

LAURA. Talking about you means talking about me and talking about me means talking about you.

We hear ADRIAN *sing a few lines of 'It's all right Mama' by Elvis Presley; then he enters.*

ADRIAN. How much longer exactly are you going to talk?

MOLLY. Couple of inches.

LAURA. Nothing less than three-feet-worth as far as I'm concerned.

ADRIAN. Well I've done my gargling and now I don't know what to do and I can't go into Boy's room, and the only other place is to sit on the lavatory with the lid down. Can I join in?

LAURA. Yes.

MOLLY. No. There's a chocolate mousse in the fridge.

ADRIAN. Mine.

ADRIAN *exits.*

LAURA. If you told him what happened you wouldn't have to do the videos.

MOLLY. Thanks.

LAURA. I wish you would tell. I want the world to know.

MOLLY. Always me who had to take the risks. Tread on thin ice. Like the row about refusing to wear a vest when we were little. I had to go through it so you could benefit too.
  The Admiral has won. He won by being dead.

LAURA. Always the Admiral, never his name.

MOLLY (*rummaging*). Boy was conceived in these ear-rings. They're irreplaceable. Adrian gave them to me.

LAURA. Listen.

MOLLY. I am, I am.

LAURA. I want what I daren't have.

  MOLLY *rummages more in hoover bag.*

  I'm fed up with being . . . I want a complete . . . I'm a fucking virgin . . . I mean I've never . . . you know what I mean.

MOLLY. What do you mean?

LAURA. What did I just say?

MOLLY. But you're much nicer than me. Men with proper jobs used to fall all over you. What did you do? Or do you do?

LAURA. I never went back for coffee. And they moved on.

MOLLY. I don't want to tell Adrian. He only has to lose his comb and he goes up the wall and round the bend. He feels a failure when there's nothing he can do about something. Besides I'm a different person . . . I shed layers off my life like throwing off heavy blankets when the Spring comes.

LAURA. Bullshit.

MOLLY. We've got enough worries . . . of . . . hitting top C's and facing brown envelopes. Please. These are real problems to us at the moment.

LAURA. And what about your nightie?

MOLLY. What nightie?

LAURA. The one I saw you bury in the woods.

MOLLY. I need sleep, lots of sleep.

LAURA. I want a baby. You've got everything.

MOLLY. Sorry.

LAURA *takes the hoover bag from* MOLLY *and rummages around. She takes out a torn letter.*

LAURA. It kills me when I see lovers in the dark kissing like the world is about to end. When all I can manage is a peck on the cheek on the doorstep.

MOLLY. You make me feel as if everything is my fault. Everybody makes me feel as if everything they do is my fault.

LAURA *reads the letter.*

LAURA. 'My kids asked me how fast the train went. Where it was going. But I couldn't tell them everything'. Who's it from?

MOLLY. It's not mine. Gimme it.

LAURA. Couldn't tell them what? Who?

MOLLY. I don't know. It's someone else's letter.

MOLLY *takes the letter from* LAURA.

Earring's vanished anyway.

Scene Six

Moments later in MOLLY *and* ADRIAN's *flat.*

ADRIAN. I stroked some Bonjela on his gums. No sign of our ghost friend?

MOLLY. It's all right. You don't have to try.

ADRIAN. Fatherhood doesn't come naturally except for the initial contribution.

MOLLY. That's what you're best at!

ADRIAN. But he does look adorable with his bottom in the air.

MOLLY. Don't we all.

ADRIAN. It's the constant pressure.

MOLLY. Something will turn up. It always does. Just when you can't stand the hanging around waiting another minute.

ADRIAN. It's the tone when he cries. It's programmed to drive me mad. Brings out my Wagnerian streak.

MOLLY. It's programmed for survival.

ADRIAN. It makes me want to throttle him.

MOLLY *lifts her skirt up and pulls an elastic 'roll on' off down her legs.*

MOLLY. Oooohaa. I can breathe again.

MOLLY *undoes the button of her skirt.*

Phew.

ADRIAN. I'll run you a bath and put some nice smelly things in.

MOLLY. Rather salt.

ADRIAN. Right.

MOLLY. Don't you want to know why?

ADRIAN. You know what you want.

MOLLY. It's to keep the soreness, left over from the stitches and the forceps, at bay. It's taken six months to learn how to walk normally instead of like a bow-legged jockey.

ADRIAN. Right, Right, right.

MOLLY. Let's go to bed. Make everything right.

ADRIAN. You have your bath and then we'll just close our eyes and settle for the night.

MOLLY. Oh. That sort of bed. I am awake now. Second wind. Sometimes when I have a bath . . . it's like a ritual . . . before . . . but if we're not going to . . . after . . . that's OK, I won't bother with the bath . . . I'll just flick through a magazine and drop off . . .

ADRIAN. But I put the heating dial on 'hot water' earlier. You'll have to turn it off now if you don't have a bath.

MOLLY. But I never asked for a bath!

ADRIAN. I just thought you ought to have one.

MOLLY (*smelling an armpit surreptitiously*). Why?

ADRIAN. You'll still have to turn the dial off. It's a waste.

MOLLY. You're filling my mind up with the wrong things when I'm being pulled in so many different directions.

ADRIAN. We have to keep everything under control.

MOLLY. Right. Water dial.

ADRIAN. I'll deal with it just this once tonight.

MOLLY. Fantastic!

ADRIAN. Is the towel on the bathroom rail?

MOLLY. It was when I last saw it. Settled for the night in fact!

MOLLY undresses and gets into a thigh length tee-shirt. ADRIAN watches her. He takes a pyjama top from under the pillow. He undresses and puts the pyjama top on. He takes his clothes out and comes back.

MOLLY. And don't ask me where all the bottoms have gone.

ADRIAN. Nothing was further from my mind.

He touches MOLLY's breasts.

MOLLY. I've wound myself down now.

ADRIAN. You are difficult these days. Never mind.

They get into bed. Lights down.

Scene Seven

Enter DAVID.

Same evening. Connaught Hotel Bar. Lonely lighting. He holds a glass of whisky on the rocks.

DAVID (*as if he's talking to someone at the bar*). Need plenty of ice on a day like today huh? You don't mind if I talk to a fellow American? It felt like a sharing a kind of a day. So sunny. (*Holds up a cricket bat.*) Bought this for my son back home. He wanted something real British.

You should stay and talk to me. I'm an interesting phenomena. Hell. No one ever exchanges enough to merit a farewell these days.

I wonder what Molly is wearing now?

Shit. The sunniest days can be the cruellest.

Exit DAVID.

Scene Eight

That night MOLLY *and* ADRIAN's *flat.* MOLLY, *still asleep beats*
ADRIAN *up.* ADRIAN *pins her down as she remains asleep. Still asleep*
she stops and curls up. Darkness.

Morning next day. About 6 a.m.

MOLLY *gets out of bed as if nothing has happened.*

ADRIAN *lies in bed and doesn't move.*

MOLLY. Time to get up. There's a lot to do today and I can't
think straight till the bed's made.

ADRIAN *pulls covers over his head.*

Even if you've got nowhere to go and nothing to do, act as if
you've got somewhere to go, then something will happen when
you least expect because of something you haven't realised
you've done.

ADRIAN (*tense*). Keep going.

MOLLY. I'll make you some lemon and honey for your throat.

ADRIAN. You did it again last night.

MOLLY. What?

ADRIAN. What you haven't done for ages. An impersonation of a
middleweight on his last legs.

MOLLY. You should have woken me up.

ADRIAN. I'm scared. It's as if you're possessed. I can't believe
you can't remember.

MOLLY. Do you want to hear? Laura knows. But it's bygones be
bygones honestly.

ADRIAN. OK. Gimme the bygones.

MOLLY. What?

ADRIAN. Or will I have to ask Laura?

MOLLY. No. It's for me to say if anyone. The best way to help . . .
is to help me . . . make Boy . . . all right. Protect him from . . .
what we talked about . . . so he doesn't get mugged of himself . . .
protect him . . . somehow.

ADRIAN. Fine, fine, but . . . I've got my audition on the horizon.

MOLLY. 11 o'clock today.

ADRIAN. They need someone with experience. Someone with a ready wit and a stable personality on top of everything else.

MOLLY. How will you manage that?

ADRIAN. After last night, God knows. I do love you but where are my socks?

MOLLY. Where they usually are.

ADRIAN. There's no such place.

MOLLY. Look, I'm very sorry. What can I say? Let's get on.

ADRIAN. You pack a right left hook.

MOLLY. And when fast asleep . . .

ADRIAN. Come here and get warm.

She snuggles down beside him. The sheet is pulled back. She kisses the palms of his hands.

MOLLY. How are your ears?

ADRIAN. Need attention.

MOLLY (*kisses his ears*). You know Wales?

ADRIAN. A thistle up my bum. And I'm certain we had an audience.

MOLLY (*stroking his bottom*). Yes. Aaaah fuck.

Her head travels down his chest and she pulls the sheet over her. ADRIAN *lies back and enjoys it.*

ADRIAN. Aah . . .

MOLLY *props herself up on one elbow. Her head moves under the sheet.*

ADRIAN. Oh 's nice.

MOLLY (*pops her head out from under the sheet*). Did you do the hot water dial in the end.

ADRIAN. I may have.

MOLLY. I love the feel of your surrender when I wrap you in my mouth.

MOLLY *dives back under the sheet again. Her head moves under the sheet.*

ADRIAN. Mmmmm there. Oh beautiful girl. Yes. Aah . . .

The baby cries.

BOY (*voice over*). Waaaaaawa.

MOLLY's *head stops still under the sheet. Exit* MOLLY. ADRIAN *hurls the pillow across the stage.*

ADRIAN. I can't stand it. He'll have to go.

Exit ADRIAN.

Scene Nine

The day before the exhibition. Four weeks later.

MOLLY *is alone in the art gallery. She takes the Trooping video out. She completes some finishing touches to the icon with a paint brush and generally tidies up. She moves a wastepaper basket offstage. She takes a cassette out of a large hold-all type bag. She puts the paint brush back in a wooden case for paint brushes and oils. She puts the cassette in the video.*

We watch the cassette with her and see a close-up of the word 'GENTS' outside a Gents' toilet.

A man, big in stature, emerges. He wears sturdy shoes and a riding mac that looks a size too small. He holds a handkerchief to his face.

MOLLY (*voice over*). Rape me. Beat me. Strangle me.

MAN (*to camera*). My wife has taken everything. My house, my records, my sons. You women have the best of all worlds these days. I can't even afford to go to the toilet.

The MAN *runs off sobbing.*

MOLLY (*voice over*). Don't cry. Please stop. Wait. Damnit.

MOLLY *polishes the screen, then takes out the cassette from the video and replaces it with another video cassette which she takes from her hold-all bag.*

MOLLY *turns the new cassette on. It is of* ADRIAN *and* BOY. BOY *is a tiny baby in* ADRIAN's *arms.* ADRIAN *smiles. We see close-up of* BOY *fill the screen.*

MOLLY *dusts his image and kisses his image on the screen.*

She then turns the cassette off, takes it out of the video and closes the icon doors over the screen.

MOLLY *exits.*

Scene Ten

Same day. Evening before exhibition.

Enter ADRIAN *with drawer full of socks. He drops the drawer on the floor. He sits down on chair with tartan rug.*

Enter LAURA.

LAURA. Heard about the tour yet?

ADRIAN. Would I be sitting here like a squashed canary if I had?

LAURA. Here's the bumph and the press release.

ADRIAN. She went to the chemist after the gallery . . .

LAURA *drops the pages of bumph on the floor near the drawer.*

LAURA. My God. The dreaded sock drawer!
Let's go out for a drink.

ADRIAN. No. Take the pain out of waiting for the phone. That's what you're thinking.

LAURA. Yes. Matter of fact.

ADRIAN. S'right.

Enter MOLLY. *Black tee-shirt. Black skirt. Shopping bag.*

MOLLY. They had the wrong teats.

ADRIAN. I dunno what to say to that.

MOLLY. You never shave these days. I should have bought you some razors.

ADRIAN. What with?

MOLLY. All right.

LAURA. I rang the nice American . . . from the gallery. He'll definitely come to the exhibition.

MOLLY *takes a good look at the sock drawer and its socks.*

MOLLY. Stay for an iceberg lettuce Laura. That's an order not an invite.

LAURA. Regrets but got to go.

MOLLY. Right.

LAURA. The press release is in the drawer. Didn't you see?

MOLLY. I was so shocked by the socks.

LAURA. Sure you'll be all right?

MOLLY. As long as you don't ask me if I'm all right.

LAURA. Sorry.

MOLLY. Go.

   Exit LAURA.

Scene Eleven

Same evening. Minutes later.

MOLLY. Before he wakes up. How about a salad?

ADRIAN. My socks.

MOLLY. What?

ADRIAN. They need matching.

MOLLY. They can't do it by themselves!

ADRIAN. No.

MOLLY. Leave them till the morning. Just eat and go to bed, or watch a film.

ADRIAN. You won't get out of it that way.

MOLLY. Out of it?

ADRIAN. Go on. Match them.

MOLLY. You!

ADRIAN. Don't adopt that tone with me.

MOLLY. What tone?

ADRIAN. You know.

MOLLY. I'm racking my brains.

ADRIAN. What brains?

MOLLY. It won't work talking to me like that.

ADRIAN. I'm in the middle of talking.

MOLLY. I thought you'd finished for the moment.

ADRIAN. Don't lie. I do a lot for this family. I do an audition to some director who fancies himself. Thinks I'm some stuffed shirt frilly shirt opera singer . . . he can switch off and on like a tape-recorder . . . after a night of you fucking me about.

MOLLY. That was weeks ago. I'm sure they'll ring soon. I know you need undivided attention but when the exhibition is over . . . we'll go for a drive . . . take the tartan rug . . .

ADRIAN. We have not got a car any more.

MOLLY. Hire one, we could!

ADRIAN. God, I feel like a nice steak and some Burgundy. Lettuce?! Babies! Gone are the days of yesteryear.
 They ground you. That's what they do. Babies. They show up all your weaknesses. I didn't know I could love anything so much or anything could make me so confused.
 Life used to be so simple. Spontaneous. When you could watch me, any night, the way you did. Armed with a comp.

MOLLY. The lights go up. The chocolate boxes stop rustling. The conductor waves his baton. Your voice floats in front of me.

ADRIAN. All being well in the vocal dungeon of my mind.

MOLLY. Just – hang on . . .

ADRIAN. They want a natural rasping sound for the part.

MOLLY. You should cut down on technique and let your passions take over.

ADRIAN. I'm so frightened of losing control.

MOLLY. I know.

ADRIAN. No you don't.

MOLLY. Oh. Well, let's get rid of today.

ADRIAN. The socks.

MOLLY. Stop it.

ADRIAN. I'm warning you. Go on.

MOLLY. God, what language do I have to speak to make you understand English?

MOLLY *bends down and picks up two black socks and hands them to* ADRIAN. ADRIAN *punches her on the face.*

MOLLY (*yelling*). Go away go away go away.

He slaps her hard on her face as if to stop her yelling.

Lights go off them.

Scene Twelve

Lights up on LAURA. *Same night.*

In her flat. Separate from them. She gazes out of the window. She smokes.

A Catherine Cookson novel in the other hand.

With her back to the audience LAURA *undresses down to her bra and pants, in front of the window. She stands for a second squarely in front of the window. She then draws the curtains and puts a dressing gown on.*

LAURA. There's a lovely couple in the flat opposite. They're always embracing in their sitting room. Sometimes she goes out of the room first at night, when they've got back from a concert or whatever it is. Sometimes he just sits and pours himself a brandy and thinks on his own, while she gets ready for bed.

    I undress for him. But he never takes any notice. I fantasise that I can break up their marriage. But the chair he sits in is at an odd angle. I don't think he can even see me.

Scene Thirteen

Back to ADRIAN *and* MOLLY. *Same night a few moments later.*

ADRIAN *takes two dressing-gowns off hangers. His is a worn woolly one with silk braiding round the edges. Hers is a towelling bathrobe. They undress down to their underwear.*

ADRIAN *starts to undo her bra.*

MOLLY *stops him and wanders off.*

ADRIAN. Oi.

MOLLY. What?

ADRIAN. Take off your clothes.

MOLLY. Well. No.

ADRIAN. Come on. Let's go to bed properly . . .

MOLLY. I can't.

ADRIAN. Oh?

MOLLY. I just can't.

ADRIAN. You've got your big moment tomorrow. Let's make things right.

MOLLY. Don't feel good.

ADRIAN. Let me run the tip of my tongue down the line of your hip bone like you love.

MOLLY. This has happened before.

ADRIAN. I have never struck you before in my life.

MOLLY. Not you. I'm trying to tell you something.

ADRIAN. I suppose I'm going to have to enter into a debate with you as to whether to untie your belt or not?

MOLLY. It's happened before.

ADRIAN. You worry about Boy. You worry about him all the time.

MOLLY. That's got nothing to do with it. Please don't be jealous of Boy.

ADRIAN *forces her belt undone. There is a stock still struggle between them and he forces her hand between his legs. They stop struggling.*

ADRIAN *storms off.*

MOLLY. Listen.

Lights down on her.

Scene Fourteen

Same night. Same time. Connaught Hotel.

DAVID *in his hotel room. He shows us a new fashionable baggy grey linen suit. He is in shirt and trousers. The cricket bat against the wall with the price tag still on.*

DAVID *(as he changes into the suit which doesn't look quite right on him).*
The assistant in the store said this would be most suitable for
an *avant garde* private view. I haven't bought a new suit in years.
But I am not certain of what to wear on these occasions. At
arms fairs, I just wear, hell, what do I wear? Something
anonymous. But this ain't tailored and maybe I look several
pounds heavier in it.
I've booked a table at a Thai Restaurant in Chinatown for
after the exhibition. I made instructions for it to be against the
wall . . . so as I can sit next to her . . . and when she's over the
nerves of the evening . . . the wine is softening her up . . . I'll
slip my arm round the back of the banquette whatsit . . .
casual . . . as if I've got cramp in my arm or somethin'. Her
fella and Laura will sit opposite. We won't actually look at each
other, me and Molly . . . but I'll know she's there . . . I can't
make out if she wears a bra or not . . . no tights. I've never
been in close contact with that kind of woman before . . . I see
them in magazines . . . in cafés . . . but never real close to me.
They are not the same as the Laura type . . . I meet them all
the time . . . looking beautiful in men's suits . . . no mystery
there. By the end of the evening . . . we'll know . . . that when
she comes alone to my hotel room . . . Christ, I didn't realise
how lonely I've been till now.

DAVID *flaps his suit about with his hands. He takes the trousers off.
Boxer shorts underneath.*

Who am I kidding?

Holds up baggy trousers.

It's me she wants.
The real me.
She picked the real me.

Exit DAVID.

Scene Fifteen

LAURA's *flat. Same night. Late.*

The moon is out. She stubs her cigarette out in an ashtray. She lies down on the floor. She pulls her dressing gown and nightie up and puts her hand between her legs and moves her hand. Rolls over. She cries.

LAURA. I am not crying.

Scene Sixteen

Same night. MOLLY *and* ADRIAN's *flat. Moon out.* MOLLY *sits on the bed. She takes a hairbrush out of her handbag which is lying around. She brushes her hair falteringly.*

MOLLY. Aaah.

Brushing her hair clearly hurts her beaten up head.

Enter ADRIAN. *He is in his underwear. He is soaked to the skin. He has had a bath in his underwear to punish himself, like he was punished by the monks.*

MOLLY *takes the tartan rug off the bed and wraps it round him.*

MOLLY. To hell with the monks.

Exit ADRIAN *and* MOLLY.

End of Act One

ACT TWO

Scene One

The following evening. The gallery. Everyone has left. Empty bottles. Dirty glasses. DAVID, LAURA *and* ADRIAN *watch* MOLLY's *videos which have been edited together.* DAVID *wears the jacket of his new suit with conventional grey flannel trousers, blue silk shirt and tasteful silk tie.*

MOLLY (*on video screen to* BLACK POLICEMAN). Rape me. Beat me. Strangle me.

Close up of BLACK POLICEMAN's *face on video screen.*

ADRIAN *switches off video and closes the icon doors over the screen.*

ADRIAN. I liked the one of the man who couldn't afford the loo.

LAURA. But only one bloody critic turned up after all my hard work.

DAVID. Yeah. I thought I was going to be world famous.

LAURA. Pity Molly wasn't here to chat him up.

ADRIAN. She's still hiding in the pub opposite.

LAURA. Go on fetch her.

ADRIAN. . . .

ADRIAN *empties ashtrays into the wastepaper basket.*

DAVID. Yeah. She must be scared outa her mind. Hell.

Enter MOLLY *rather drunk. Cream suit. Black shoes.*

MOLLY. Everything going wrong all right then?

ADRIAN. You know what people are like. They come to private views for a drink and a flirt and to get ideas for their own work.

MOLLY. Where's the red dots then?

DAVID (*walks over to his screen and takes out his cassette from video*). Da-da! I bought my cassette.

ADRIAN. No one else did. Nothing sold.

MOLLY. Understand the Virgin Mary is optional, but you can buy her as well if you want.

DAVID. Sure. She's extra baggage but that's OK. Hell I bought myself and I'm mighty proud of it . . . me.

ADRIAN. Something to show the folks back home.

DAVID. And Laura gave me this here leaflet thing.

MOLLY. Nicely put together Laura.

LAURA. It's been a fascinating experience.

MOLLY. Oh Laura you don't have to say. I do know when people are just saying. I do know.

LAURA. No you don't.

DAVID. Let me say, just let me say. Darn well never struck a woman hell! Matter of fact, shows of physical strength, don't impress. Give me strength of mind every time . . .

MOLLY. I wish I'd put on the leaflet what I ought to have, not what I thought I ought to have. That would have sorted out the buyers from the boys.

ADRIAN. I'm hungry.

DAVID. I've booked a table at a restaurant with a great kitchen . . .

MOLLY. Our parents had gone to Paris for the weekend.

LAURA. Not the time not the place Molly.

LAURA *lights up cigarette.* ADRIAN *takes it off her and stubs it out.*

ADRIAN. What weekend?

DAVID. Some people think that no weekend is complete without Paris. Me, I prefer New York.

MOLLY. They hadn't been alone together for years I suppose. Always going off into a daze Mum was. She packed her best dress and favourite brooch. We were sent to stay with my Godfather. He ran a kind of pedigree dog kennels outside Guildford.

LAURA. Before that he was an admiral in the Navy.

MOLLY. I'd packed my Viyella nightie with the yellow flowers on it. I was ten and a bit.

LAURA. Nearly six. Five only five. Me. We asked to sleep in the same room but he said we would stay awake all night giggling.

MOLLY. He could be very sweet to me. He made Instant Whip puddings . . . all sugary and delicious and bad for the teeth. He drew pictures of farm animals and made up rhymes to go with them.

DAVID. Huh uh?

ADRIAN. Look . . .

MOLLY. I trusted him. He was my friend. I think the first night it was all right. He kissed us goodnight. Lined us both up for clean teeth inspection. then the next night, he insisted on giving me a massage and wouldn't let me put my nightie on.

ADRIAN. England must seem very foreign to you . . . Sir.

DAVID. That's right. I'm just some stoopid Texan.

ADRIAN. I didn't mean that.

DAVID. Sure.

MOLLY. He said he'd been to India once and had been taught massage by a Guru and how to relax. He breathed very close to me and I could smell the gin and tonic on his breath. His coarse fingers kneading my thighs too near my bottom.

DAVID. I'll cancel the table. Don't stop.

MOLLY. But I still wanted to trust him.

ADRIAN. We've got the gist. We've got the gist.

MOLLY. Then one of the days, slight blur on the days, Tuesday, Wednesday, I dunno. He sat me on his lap. He pulled my trousers down and patted me with one hand and kept his other hand in his trouser pocket masturbating. But I'd never heard of masturbating then. So I didn't know what he was doing. But I do remember thinking at the time, why is he doing this? Why can't I go and sweep out my favourite Bassett's kennel? Have some fun.

DAVID. I hope he's in jail. Son of a bitch.

ADRIAN. Try not to cry.

MOLLY. I'm not.

DAVID. Cry cry.

MOLLY. No. Certainly not. You all right, Laura?

LAURA. Yes.

MOLLY. Are you feeling better now? Are you?

LAURA. You're very brave. If that's what you want me to say.

MOLLY. No. Then one night I was planning some adventure for
the next day . . . dreaming away . . . and he came into tuck me
up with a hot milk. I held my nightie firmly down. I didn't
want a massage . . . he held my hair very hard so I couldn't
move my head . . . then he pinned one arm down by my side
. . . I could hear his belt buckle unlocking . . . swearing at his
fly buttons . . . that wouldn't undo . . . he put my free hand on
his penis. It felt soft and hard at the same time, and gristly. I
couldn't think what it was to start with. I tried to struggle free
but he kept such a tight grip on my wrist. Laura walked in . . .

LAURA. I'd never seen a man's genitals before . . . they looked
huge at eye level . . . sort of bald and hairy at the same time.
He grabbed hold of me, dragged me into my bedroom and
threw me against the wall.

MOLLY. I screamed and screamed. He came back and slapped
me hard across the face and forced my hand on his cock until
he got what he wanted.

LAURA. He said no one would believe us because he'd once
been a very important man. So we wouldn't tell.

MOLLY. My hand was all sticky and there was sticky stuff all over
my nightie. There were patches of sperm on the sheet but I
didn't know what sperm was then. I didn't know it was a
creative substance. The next day when I was out for a walk with
the Bassett I buried my nightie in the woods. He took us to the
local circus.

LAURA. We made a pact we wouldn't tell.

MOLLY. I knew I'd done something wrong. I thought I'd done
something wrong but I didn't know what. When Mum got back
from Paris, she looked so different and happy and young. I
remember how much younger she looked, and smiley. I
hugged her but I knew in my heart of hearts I would never
forgive her for failing to protect me . . . from being forced . . .
it's the being forced. I'm so angry . . . just so angry . . . I'll
never know what I might have been like if it hadn't happened . . .

I might be . . . confident . . . I dunno whatever people are . . . breezy . . . or no different . . . the point is I'll never know. I've never had a fair start. I was born complete then broken up and put back together with jagged edges . . . no frame . . .

Silence.

When I became a mother I wanted to make it right.

ADRIAN (*trapped feeling*). It's all right.

MOLLY. What I mean is . . . that by having a baby . . . when the baby lands . . . I thought . . . the world would tip a fraction to accommodate a new soul where it's needed. One tiny pink toe in the huge sea of continents, (natural extravagances and moments of largesse), would send ripples that change the universe imperceptibly, but irreversibly for the better. But it doesn't.

ADRIAN. Anyway . . .

MOLLY. Right, dinner.

DAVID. Anyway right dinner? Don't you foreigners ever say anything about anything?

ADRIAN. In our way.

DAVID. Your way my ass. This is mega trauma man. Sweet Jesus if this was my home town we'd all be on our hands and knees praying.

ADRIAN. We can't rewind it. Make it different. And it's strictly family.

LAURA. Thank you so much for coming to the exhibition. The last few minutes are not your concern really.

DAVID. But everybody is everybody. We're all everybody!

ADRIAN. Speak for yourself.

DAVID. Oh.

ADRIAN. What exactly is your line of business?

DAVID. Lockheed Engineer.

ADRIAN. Ah. Right.

Pause.

DAVID. Do you go to an analyst?

MOLLY. Who?

DAVID. Who? You askin' me who? Well how about all of you?

LAURA. I smoke too much.

ADRIAN. I take baths.

MOLLY. I don't. Go to an analyst.

ADRIAN (*highly irritated*). You been to an analyst?

DAVID. I went to a therapy group in California once. Northern California when my marriage broke up, yeah.

ADRIAN. I suppose it was one of those set-ups where you have to sit in a circle and hug strangers.

They exit. Music. Perhaps opera.

Scene Two

The following evening. MOLLY *and* ADRIAN's *flat.* ADRIAN *sits in a chair with the tartan rug on it.*

MOLLY *is dressed in a flower printed dress.*

MOLLY. You don't mind if I spend some time alone?

ADRIAN *is silent.*

MOLLY. Laura will put Boy to bed.

ADRIAN *is silent.*

MOLLY. I don't want to be disturbed and I want to sleep right through. I'll ring to check all is well from the hotel.

ADRIAN *is silent.*

MOLLY. The hot water dial is on if you want a bath.

ADRIAN. Look, I'm likely to be really ratty waiting for the call about the part. They are going to ring this evening. In fact I'd really appreciate it if you go out. It's less pressure on me.

MOLLY. I do need a night apart from you.

ADRIAN. That's right. Get yourself on an even keel after last night. You make sure you have a nice rest and a good breakfast.

MOLLY. Don't worry about me. Just make sure Boy's all right. If he wakes up when Laura's gone, all you have to do is change his nappy and give him a bottle of milk. The nappies are in the airing cupboard.

Exit MOLLY.

ADRIAN. Which is the airing cupboard?

ADRIAN *remains on stage like a shadow in the background.*

Scene Three

DAVID's *hotel suite. One hour later. Same evening.*

DAVID *combs his hair and feels his chin as if looking in a mirror. He walks round with a lamp, puts it down and puts a cloth over it so that the lighting is subtler. There is a satin sheet on the floor and a couple of pillows. Arts magazines on the floor including* MOLLY's *catalogue. The cricket bat against the wall. Price tag on.*

Enter MOLLY.

MOLLY. Phew.

DAVID. What?

MOLLY. I dunno.

DAVID. Let me take your coat.

MOLLY. Where to?

DAVID. A closet.

MOLLY. I haven't got one.

DAVID. Oh.

MOLLY. All right?

DAVID. Great.

MOLLY. Thirsty.

DAVID. A drink?

MOLLY. Champagne anywhere?

DAVID. Sure.

He takes an ice bucket with champagne from beside the lamp.

MOLLY. Oh I didn't see.

DAVID *pops the cork.*

DAVID. Where does Adrian think you are?

MOLLY. In a hotel.

DAVID. Which?

MOLLY. Just a hotel.

DAVID. With me?

MOLLY. No. Just with me.

DAVID. He believes that?

MOLLY. He thinks it was his idea.

DAVID. Ah.

He hands her glass of champagne.

MOLLY. I couldn't drink champagne when I was breastfeeding.

DAVID. My ex-wife was the same with our kids.

MOLLY. Gives the baby diarrhoea.

DAVID. Gee.

MOLLY. It was your ex-wife who designed your card wasn't it?

DAVID. Yeah. She's very clever.

MOLLY. You parted because you were away too much on business?

DAVID. No no no.

MOLLY. The towel wasn't on the bathroom rail?

DAVID. Sometimes it was.

MOLLY. She didn't pair your socks?

DAVID. All my socks were the same colour.

MOLLY. She left the hot water on and didn't have a bath?

DAVID. Shower. Matter of fact we had constant hot water!

MOLLY. She didn't earn enough money?

DAVID. She did a great job with the kids.

MOLLY. You wanted sex when she didn't and vice versa?

DAVID. Only toward the end.

MOLLY (*puzzled*). So?

DAVID. It just wasn't there.

They kiss and sink on to the bed. Passionate stuff.

DAVID. Is this OK?

MOLLY. Yes.

DAVID. Now are you sure?

MOLLY. Very.

DAVID. I want to make you come.

MOLLY. Please don't take offence if I don't. I've had a lot to do lately.

DAVID. OK OK. But I just wanna be there when you *do*.

MOLLY. And *I* want to be the when *you* do. And . . . I want to see the expression on your face.

DAVID. Babe . . .

Hands all over each other.

MOLLY. I'll just undo your trousers if you don't mind.

DAVID. Please don't hesitate.

MOLLY *does so. She pulls the trousers down.* DAVID *has boxer underpants on.* MOLLY *studies them.*

MOLLY. Real silk!

DAVID. Who cares?

MOLLY *takes her pants off. Then she puts his hand back under her skirt.*

MOLLY. Oh.

DAVID (*exploring under skirt with his hand*). There?

MOLLY. More there.

She guides his hand.

Ah.

She puts her hand down the front of his boxer shorts.

DAVID. Oh.

MOLLY. Mmm . . .

DAVID (*moving his hand up her skirt*). Is that right?

MOLLY. Just . . . yes . . . there.

DAVID. I could hold you while you make yourself come if you want. Or if you don't want I could read an arts magazine so we have something in common.

MOLLY. Delicious . . . there . . .

DAVID. Oh hell. Is it safe for me to come inside you.

MOLLY. Hang on. (*Thinks and counts on her fingers briefly.*) Yes. But is it safe for you to be inside me?

DAVID. I swear on my kids' lives.

They kiss.

Lights down on them.

Scene Four

Same evening. Back in ADRIAN *and* MOLLY's *flat.*

Enter LAURA. *More casually dressed than usual.*

LAURA. He's settled now with his bottom in the air.

ADRIAN. I hope Molly is. Settled.

LAURA. Did you ask her which hotel she's going to?

ADRIAN. No . . .

LAURA. Why not?

ADRIAN. . . .

LAURA. She said she'd be back in time to get Boy up.

ADRIAN. It doesn't matter if she isn't, I can manage.

LAURA. Everything all right?

ADRIAN. I start rehearsals in three weeks. Second lead. Expenses. They rang a minute ago. I can do anything now. I wish Molly had been here.

LAURA. If you had responded to her revelation . . .

ADRIAN. Crack up.

LAURA. Revelation. Instead of just pretending she'd talked about the weather or something. She'd be here.

ADRIAN. You think I don't know what she's doing now? You think I don't know she could have easily told me that horror story before the exhibition? You think I don't know she had to humiliate me in front of you all? You think I don't know she's with that American? You think I'm some idiot who thinks about nothing but being an opera star . . . who never notices anything about the woman he loves? Some people notice everything and say nothing. What am I supposed to do? Raid the Connaught with the Vice Squad? That crack up . . . sorry revelation . . . was for his benefit not mine. She may not know it herself.

LAURA. I think it was for her benefit actually. And mine.

ADRIAN. She's paying me back. She could have left it at that. Not gone to *his* hotel . . . to *him*. 'Oh I'll make you a lemon and honey' she says cheerfully. Have you any idea the nightmares I have at the thought of being on stage and my voice being stuck in my belly and a fart coming out instead?

LAURA. And have you any idea that you might have driven her to it?

ADRIAN. How? Apart from the odd tiff?

LAURA. It terrifies you that she got savaged . . . because you did . . . in your way by the monks. I suppose you'd hoped you'd connected up with a woman . . . who was undamaged. As if you could spirit away her . . . completeness, and make yourself whole. She's let you down.

ADRIAN. Christ. Sorry Laura. I never understood why you never had a boyfriend. But I bet you have lots of good friends eh? Who understand. I mean nowadays . . . anything goes . . . even celibacy . . .

LAURA. I've never talked about it to anyone. That's why I'm grateful to her . . . for a kind of release.

ADRIAN. Boy's being such a good boy tonight. As if he knows not to push his luck. Not a squeak. Would you like to be his guardian?

LAURA. Thank you. If Molly wants it.

ADRIAN. She'll do what I bloody well say.

LAURA. That's not the way to set about her . . . or anyone . . .

ADRIAN. As long as she doesn't stay for breakfast eh?

LAURA. Yes.

ADRIAN. Tell me she won't.

LAURA. Look. It's fantastic about the job. Things are moving in
the right direction for you.

Pause.

ADRIAN. If I don't have work I don't care about love. And if I
don't have love, work seems pointless; apart from the money.
   Everybody needs all, all the time, but I can't control . . .
any . . .
   Always something getting in the way of something.

LAURA. Why don't you tell her that sort of thing?

ADRIAN. I can't. It's the sort of thing I confide in to a man.

LAURA. Ah. Well. This '*man*' is sick of being . . . on call for you
two. Your buffer . . . crisis upon crisis. So you listen to me and
what I have to say. Swill it around in your mouth and taste it.
   I go home to the fridge changing gear each time I open the
front door.
   My cat greets me.
   Miaow he says. Miaow I say. I give him his cat meat churned
up in a special way with his biscuits. The biscuits have to be
folded up with the meat; else he won't eat, then he won't purr.
   When he's finished he leaves through the cat-flap and joins
his friends. Friends I don't know about. When he returns he
sits on my chest. He likes my bosom. I do have breasts you
know. He perches himself on my breasts as if I'm his favourite
armchair. Just like a baby. I've unplugged the answering
machine. I don't want to know who hasn't rung either. Thought
of keeping it for the cat. I mean he has such a social life.
   He purrs, digging his claws in.
   Who's doing the PR for the opera company?

ADRIAN *is silent.*

Scene Five

DAVID's *suite. Dawn the following morning.*

DAVID *and* MOLLY *are asleep, arms round each other under the satin sheet.*

ADRIAN *remains separate from them on stage.*

Cricket bat against the wall with the price tag still on.

MOLLY *turns in bed and beats* DAVID *up in her sleep.*

DAVID. What the . . . ?!

MOLLY *pounds him with her fists and feet.*

DAVID. Wake up . . . For Chrissake . . . Jesus.

He gets up and puts his trousers on. He bends down and shakes her shoulders.

DAVID. Wake up!

MOLLY *belts him.* DAVID *takes the bottle of champagne out of the ice bucket and tips the bucket of water over her.*

MOLLY *wakes up.*

MOLLY. Why did you do that?

DAVID. I had to.

MOLLY. You maniac. I gotta go anyway.

DAVID *puts a towel on her and starts to dry her.*

DAVID. You thumped me in your sleep!

MOLLY. I can't help that.

DAVID. Oh no?

MOLLY. No. And I can't stay for breakfast.

DAVID. But you said you could last night. That the kid was organised. You wanted to . . . 'cuddle' after.

MOLLY. Don't force me.

DAVID. OK, OK . . .

MOLLY *stands up and winds the towel round her naked body.*

MOLLY. Just don't come near me, OK?

DAVID. No need to yell. That's OK.

MOLLY *buries her head in her hands.*

MOLLY. Help.

DAVID. Sure. (DAVID *tries to hold her.*)

MOLLY. Leave me alone.

DAVID *reaches for the cricket bat and holds it up. He tries to get* MOLLY *to hold it.*

MOLLY. Leave me alone.

DAVID. I want you to do something. I'm not forcing you. If it doesn't work you leave right away and I'll never bother you again. I swear.

DAVID *piles the pillows on the floor in front of her.*

DAVID *folds* MOLLY's *fingers round the cricket bat handle.*

DAVID. Hit the pillows.

MOLLY. What in cold blood?

DAVID. Slowly first.

MOLLY. I feel silly!

DAVID. Try. We did it at the therapy group. Let me help. I'm begging.

MOLLY. You're mad. There are shoes lined up under doors along this corridor listening to us.

DAVID. They won't tell.

MOLLY. Over arm?

DAVID. Sure . . .

MOLLY *hits the pillows with the bat.*

DAVID. And again!

MOLLY *hits the pillows with the bat.*

DAVID. And again!

MOLLY *hits the pillows harder and harder.*

MOLLY. Agh . . .

DAVID. That's it! Imagine the pillows are . . . the Navy guy, your mother for not protecting you, the hot water dial, the socks, the babysitters who didn't turn up, all the guys you did want but didn't want. All the things you told me before we slept. Think of all the people down the ages from the beginning of time who've shattered and smashed before you. Who splintered people apart and we all carry their burdens of guilt and damage.

DAVID *reaches into his TWA bag and takes out his camera and films* MOLLY *hitting the pillows.*

MOLLY *hits a little longer then stops exhausted.*

MOLLY. Ha. Well. Thank you.

DAVID *(puts camera down).* Coffee, scrambled egg, croissant. *(He takes menu from round the door handle.)* . . . er porridge. Porridge?

MOLLY. You know. One day . . . maybe . . . when he's eighteen Boy will bring me to tea here and tell me about his life. He'll say 'Mum, I'm doing this or that', and with any luck I'll give a huge sigh of relief because it'll be something I haven't thought of that makes him happy, and me knowing that he's chosen something . . . life making . . . or something that makes the world . . . easier, safer . . . Croissant, coffee, and . . . all right, porridge.

DAVID. Sure. And let's all be there on that great day in eighteen year's time if we may.

MOLLY. Sure. But with sugar not salt. The porridge.

DAVID. C'm here.

MOLLY. What?

They lie down on the bed again.

DAVID. I wanna hold you.

MOLLY *lies down on the bed on top of him, her head resting under his chin.*

MOLLY. I have to get back to Boy soon.

DAVID. I know. Stay for breakfast.

MOLLY. Promise.

DAVID. Laura told me not to tell you. But I wanna be honest with you.

MOLLY *sits up and across* DAVID *so she is sitting on his cock having a very nice time, slowly, and wraps sheet round herself.*

DAVID. Oh . . . she . . . said . . . aah . . .

MOLLY. Go on . . .

DAVID. Look . . . you wouldn't get off and leave me now if I told you I made a helicopter that was the greatest defence helicopter and that sometimes I deal in conventional weapons? Would you? There now I've said it.

MOLLY *gets off him. Gets dressed. Takes the film out of his camera.*

DAVID. Please. You don't understand. What about me? The me you know? God, you should see the expression on your face.

MOLLY. . . . Maiden over.

Exit MOLLY.
Lights.
Exit DAVID.

Scene Six

ADRIAN *and* MOLLY's *flat. That morning. The video 8 camera is on the floor.*

Enter MOLLY.

MOLLY. I've just checked him . . .

ADRIAN. . . .

MOLLY. Somebody put a pillow under his head. Everyone knows you can't put a pillow under a baby's head.

ADRIAN. Why?

MOLLY. That's such a stupid question I won't answer it. I can't relax for a second. I thought I'd thought of everything. It didn't occur to me you'd put a pillow under his head.

ADRIAN. It might have been Laura.

MOLLY. Well was it?

ADRIAN. . . .

MOLLY. That's not the point. The point is you don't think. You don't . . . fuck . . . He could have smothered himself.

ADRIAN. Why don't you shut up?

MOLLY. Thanks for changing him. He's nice and dry anyway.

ADRIAN. Oh fuck off.

MOLLY. Oh?

ADRIAN. Coffee's in the kitchen.

MOLLY. Thanks.

ADRIAN. Or was breakfast included in the price of the hotel room?

MOLLY. I'd love some.

ADRIAN. Better watch the waist.

MOLLY. It's all right. I'm thinner now. Been doing some exercises.

ADRIAN. We've run out of Boy's strained apple and we've got no cash.

MOLLY. The camera has to go back to the hire shop, so with the deposit money I'll go to the corner shop.

ADRIAN. There are apples in the kitchen.

MOLLY. That's very observant of you.

ADRIAN. Why don't you do something with them?

MOLLY. Like what?

ADRIAN. Why don't you tread on them like the French do with grapes?

MOLLY. Then one of us'd have to clean the floor.

ADRIAN. . . .

MOLLY. They have to be puréed . . . the lumps . . .

ADRIAN. With your size feet that should be no problem.

MOLLY. Otherwise he chokes . . .

ADRIAN. Keep going . . .

MOLLY. . . .

ADRIAN. Why don't you take the camera and take a couple of snaps of them? It's all right. They won't shout at you. And feed Boy that?

MOLLY. Perhaps they wouldn't hit me either.

ADRIAN. You can take it.

MOLLY. I'll be the judge of that.

ADRIAN. You did it to me in your sleep.

MOLLY. But you were awake. You knew what you were doing.

ADRIAN. I don't actually fucking care.

MOLLY. What?

ADRIAN. 'Gee I thought I was going to be world famous'.

MOLLY. Don't you criticise him and don't tell me you haven't had the odd tumble with an occasional second violinist in some lonely provincial town behind my back.

ADRIAN. I haven't said a word.

MOLLY. You were so distant when I was pregnant . . . and . . . always disappearing . . . leaving me flatly gazing on to the world over my lump.

ADRIAN. I couldn't help it.

MOLLY. I felt so vulnerable.

ADRIAN. Your pregnancy wasn't real to me.

MOLLY. But you felt him kicking!

ADRIAN. Yes but as a man you have no control over . . . the whole thing.

MOLLY. Control control always control! It was when I saw you off on the train. She was on it . . . waiting . . .

ADRIAN. Lay off.

MOLLY. I just want to know one thing.

ADRIAN. And another and another and another.

MOLLY. Did you take the tartan rug?

ADRIAN. . . .

MOLLY. I can't remember. I can't fucking remember. But it was a cold day. My stomach was so big I couldn't bend down to put my tights on, and you were yelling about clean shirts.

ADRIAN. Oh God . . .

MOLLY. I can't remember if you took the rug.

ADRIAN. Nor can I.

MOLLY. You fucking can.

ADRIAN. I fucking can't.

MOLLY. You can, you can.

ADRIAN. Shut up. You'll wake Boy.

MOLLY. Oh, very cossetting all of a sudden. What's her address?

ADRIAN. What?

MOLLY. I'm going to send her your socks.

A moment.

ADRIAN. She was married with a couple of kids. It didn't matter. Hardly knew each other. And now you've had your revenge.

MOLLY. It wasn't revenge. He was there at the right moment. But it was a mistake.

ADRIAN. Why? Did he want to tie you to the bedpost and recite the ten commandments or something?

MOLLY. So what if he had? He wanted to help me.

ADRIAN. Ah. The nightie.

MOLLY. I haven't asked for your sympathy.

ADRIAN. Your secret. Whores keep secrets.

MOLLY. Misogynists have baths with their clothes on.

ADRIAN. Your art stinks.

MOLLY. You're nobody till someone shoves . . . a warble . . . down your gullet. I've got me and what I see all the time and you can't take that away . . . I don't need anyone for that. I've got me all the time.

ADRIAN. Poor you.

A moment.

MOLLY. Well I'm home now. Broke. With nothing to do except

look after you and Boy. You're quite safe. We'll have to do
exactly what you want. Me and Boy. Come on. Come on. What
do you want?

You want a woman who has a lot of money but never moves
an inch. I don't blame you. After all there's nothing secret
about the world out there . . . it's staring us in the face.
Nothing secret. That's what you don't want me to discover . . .
there is nothing to discover . . . it's all just there . . . sitting
there. 'Everybody is everybody', to quote. Boy's going to learn
a lot from you. How to be a real man; if you'd just . . . let go.

A moment.

ADRIAN. I've got the second lead. Bristol.

A moment.

MOLLY. I'm glad for you. I am.

ADRIAN. I believe you.

MOLLY. I didn't stay for croissant and orange juice.

ADRIAN. Drop it.

MOLLY. As long as you haven't got a network rail card season
ticket.

ADRIAN. Not a chance. With the price of British Rail 'real leaf'
tea, as it stands.

MOLLY. Right.

ADRIAN. Right.

MOLLY. It's not us. It's everything out there.

ADRIAN. 'K.
Where exactly did you bury the nightie?

MOLLY. We'll hire a car. Go for a drive.

ADRIAN. After Bristol.

MOLLY. Oh.

Enter LAURA.

LAURA. I can't say you look very refreshed.

MOLLY. Where's the money from David's cassette?

LAURA. Here.

LAURA *gives* MOLLY *the money.*

ADRIAN. At least he did something useful.

MOLLY. Doesn't bother me the likes of him bought it. I'll take Boy with me to the corner shop so you can practise properly.

ADRIAN. We've run out of baby shampoo.

LAURA *looks on in amazement at their talk. She expected big dramas.*

MOLLY. 'K.

ADRIAN. It suits my hair.

MOLLY. It needs one of my special haircuts.

ADRIAN. Certainly does.

MOLLY. Right. Bottle of Burgundy.

ADRIAN. And some Italian bread.

MOLLY. And I'll hire a video.

Exit MOLLY.

LAURA. I'm angling to do the PR for the opera company.

ADRIAN. Tell me Laura.

LAURA. What?

ADRIAN. Why didn't you stop her?

LAURA. What? Going to the hotel?

ADRIAN. No. Telling.

LAURA. She chose to.

ADRIAN. I'll have to think twice every time I touch her, every time I talk to her. In case I get her all wrong. Nothing'll be natural any more. I can't deal with it and that's the truth.

How's it for you now eh? Endless candlelit dinners with understanding men operating their rescue fantasies on you? Until the novelty wears off eh?

LAURA. As a matter of fact, no. Now I have the choice as to whether to explore the male of the species or not, I have no great urgency. But the answer machine is plugged in.

I'm going to make you into a star who can't bear to leave his family behind.

They've built a leisure centre next to the wood.

ADRIAN. Christ.

LAURA *walks over to the window and looks out.*

LAURA. Molly and Boy are walking underneath. Just in case . . . Adrian quick . . . just in case it isn't someone measuring for curtains. Molly and Boy are nearly underneath that window. It could fall and kill them. Quick . . . opposite. Sing.

ADRIAN. . . .

LAURA. Here.

ADRIAN *looks out of the window.*

LAURA. Sing for Chrissake. Stop the ghost pushing the window out. Stop her. Sing . . . anything.

ADRIAN. I can't. It won't . . .

ADRIAN *turns away from the window because he can't bear to look. We hear the crash of the window.* LAURA *exits in panic.*

ADRIAN. Boy?

BOY (*voice over*). Waaaawaaaawaa.

Scene Seven.

Sometime soon after MOLLY's *death. The spot where she buried the nightie.*

Enter ADRIAN. *With his hands he digs up the school satchel which contains the tattered remains of the yellow Viyella nightie. He holds it tenderly.*

Lights.

Exit ADRIAN.

Eighteen years later. London. Trooping the Colour. Military Band plays.

DAVID *in top hat and tails with his camera round his neck approaching front of stage as if clambering over people and benches as in Scene Four.*

He snaps away. Enter LAURA *in her late forties. Glam. dress and hat.*

DAVID. Hi. Thanks for sending me the ticket.

LAURA. And thank you for dressing up for Boy's big day.

DAVID. He sure is a man now.

LAURA. A proper man.

DAVID. Amongst men.

LAURA. He'll fight off the enemy any day.

DAVID. Which one is he?

LAURA. The one in the busby.

DAVID. You bet.

LAURA. I got your letter and kept the stamps for Boy's album, as I always have over the years.

DAVID. My pleasure. His father is away till when?

LAURA. He's locked in a recording studio till after you leave. So don't worry. He couldn't understand why his son isn't in the band. Music. Something of him. Then I reminded him that he'd hardly been around for Boy anyway. So he shouldn't complain.

DAVID. Around enough but not enough huh?

LAURA. Exactly.

DAVID. Well. It's good to know that the peace of the world depends on the likes of him being fighting fit. Fighting.

LAURA. It's a shame the rifles don't really go with the uniform. Your lot should have designed something neo-classical.

DAVID. But they are so lightweight . . . and lethal. Easy to carry in this stifling heat.

LAURA. Look. The King's about to ride past Boy.
Hold your head up high darling.

DAVID. He will he will.

LAURA. He's the opposite of what Molly would have wanted I know. But she gave him to me when she died and he's fulfilled me.

DAVID. That's right.

LAURA. Please. Can I hold your arm?

DAVID *takes her arm.*

Military band plays. Trooping of the Colour plays on the TV screen. One of the soldiers on the TV screen disappears off the screen as he crumples to the ground.

LAURA *withdraws her arm from* DAVID.

LAURA. Oh my God.

DAVID. What?

LAURA. He's fainted. After all I've done. (*Angry.*) He'll always be Molly's.

UNA POOKA ■ MICHAEL HARDING

Michael Harding was born in Cavan, Ireland, in 1953 and has lived and worked on both sides of the Irish border. He has published poetry and was awarded the Hennessy Literary Award for short stories in 1980. He received an Irish Arts Council bursary in 1985. His first novel, *Priest*, was published in 1986 and was shortlisted for the Book of the Year, Ireland. His latest, *The Trouble with Sarah Gullion*, published in 1988, was shortlisted for the Aer Lingus/Irish Times Literature Prize.

Una Pooka is his second play for the Abbey Theatre, Dublin; the first, *Strawboys*, was presented on the Abbey's Peacock stage in 1987 to both critical and box-office success and was nominated for a Harveys Award.

Author's note

Holy week is punctuated by the Eucharist of Thursday evening. It is an event which looks not back to the splendid certainties of Palm Sunday but rather forward to the silence of the morrow.

In 1979 we in Ireland, I believe, rooted ourselves too firmly in the unfurled banners of Palm Sunday. We cheered and swooned, and in the end, were ill-prepared for the absurd and macabre nightmare that has been an aspect of our being in the world since.

Statues moving – serial hunger strikes – death by ritual – Enniskillen and all its works – the venomous political feuding over private morality and the civil law.

When we turned our faces towards the triumphal spectacle in the Phoenix Park that September, we were already turning away from the terrible prospect of accompanying the Victim, on his journey. A journey out beyond the walls of political and religious righteousness, out beyond fancy painted streets, into the dark solitude of death and silence. We would not be led out into the terrible unease where faith is measured by despair. We would not be led to where the victim cries out, and even God himself is silent. We preferred instead to rinse our ears in jubilation certainty and strength.

But those who will not be led will be dragged. We were dragged, and the palms we still clutched in our fists were pitiable compensation.

It is the dream in which Palm Sunday meets Good Friday that finds implicit remembrance in *Una Pooka*.

Just as the church constantly reaffirms its identity in remembering the Truth of its original Event, so Theatre, at certain times can have no higher function than to be faithful, both actors and audience, in remembering the interior truth of specific historical events which bear upon the ground of our being, and touch upon the ground of our anxieties, even in the present.

The play is just a play and that is important. But it attempts to catch in some small way, that interior dream, that moment of human frailty when we look for signs and certainties, only to end up discovering that all the while, we were looking in the wrong direction.

Michael Harding

Characters

UNA, a single woman in her early thirties
AIDAN, Una's elder brother
LIAM, Una's young brother
MRS KEVITT, Una's mother
NUALA, a Dublin woman in her twenties married to AIDAN.
ANGELO, The Pooka Man
FATHER SIMEON
DOCTOR

Setting

The action takes place in a two-storey street house, the play areas being a dining room, bedroom, corridor and outside bathroom. A naturalistic set is not recommended.

The play begins on the eve of the Pope's visit to Ireland in September 1979.

Una Pooka was first performed on 17 April 1989 on the Abbey Theatre's Peacock stage, Dublin, with the following cast:

AIDAN KEVITT	Sean McGinley
NUALA KEVITT	Hilary Fannin
MRS KEVITT	Doreen Keogh
UNA KEVITT	Gabrielle Reidy
LIAM KEVITT	Jonathan Sharpe
FR SIMEON/ THE POOKA MAN	Barry McGovern
PRIEST/DOCTOR	Kevin Flood

Directed by Patrick Mason
Designed by Monica Frawley
Lighting by Tony Wakefield

ACT ONE

Late evening 28 September 1979.

NUALA *is in the kitchen, washing dishes.* AIDAN *is in the sitting room watching TV. We hear snatches of the television commentary under the dialogue:* 'Rome 1978. Smoke wafts into the Italian sky like incense rising to the nostrils of the gods. A new pope is declared . . . Clonmacnoise, today. A refuge of broken stone in a troubled land. Silent stones waiting, almost with anticipation, because it is to here the Pope will come to pray, at the well-spring of Christianity.'

AIDAN *(shouts).* Apparently he's going to stop over at Clonmacnoise, if there's time.

    Pause.

    AIDAN *shouts again.*

    Apparently he's going to stop over at Clonmacnoise, if there's time.

NUALA. What?

AIDAN. He's going to stop at Clonmacnoise. On the way to Galway.

    NUALA *enters the room, wiping a pot with a towel.*

NUALA. Sorry?

AIDAN. The Pope.

NUALA. What about him now?

AIDAN. I'm saying he's going to stop off at Clonmacnoise. On his way to Galway. If there's time. Shhh.

NUALA. Oh good. Good. That's good. (*She returns to the kitchen.*)

    AIDAN *is still watching TV. We hear the television commentary* '. . . and so to Dublin. Rehearsals on the eve of this most glorious event. Into which almost one million Irish people are expected tonight to pray with the Bishop of Rome in the historic Phoenix Park.'

AIDAN. They're expecting at least a million people in the park in the morning.

Pause.

A million people. Nuala. Nuala.

NUALA. What?

AIDAN. They're expecting at least a million people in the Park. In the morning.

NUALA *enters wiping another pot with a towel.*

AIDAN. I say. A million people pet.

NUALA. Aidan, how are we going to put up all these people if we have no extra mattresses?

AIDAN. Sure we're not putting up a million people love.

NUALA. Aidan, your mother.

AIDAN. What?

NUALA. Your mother.

AIDAN. Ah, I forgot.

NUALA. You forgot your mother was coming?

AIDAN. I forgot to go over to Sean, for the mattresses.

NUALA. Your mother, your brother, your sister, and that mysterious cousin of your mothers.

AIDAN. Me fathers.

NUALA. . . . of your fathers, what's his name, Father Semen.

AIDAN. Simeon. Father Simeon.

NUALA. Yeah, well, whatever his name is; they can't all sleep on the floor. (*She goes back to the kitchen.*)

AIDAN. No, they can't. That's true . . . love.

The doorbell rings.

NUALA. Oh no. They're not here already.

AIDAN. I'll get it.

The doorbell rings. The Pope appears on TV.

AIDAN. That's him.

We hear the voice of the Pope. The doorbell rings.

AIDAN. OK, OK. I'm coming.

AIDAN *opens the front door to* MRS KEVITT, UNA *and* LIAM.

MRS KEVITT. You took your time about opening the door.

Sound of a Papal blessing on TV. MRS KEVITT *and* AIDAN *cross themselves. We hear the TV commentator:* 'It is just over a year ago that Karol Wojtya, poet, actor, humble priest, bishop and archbishop of Krakow came out into the sunlight of Michelangelo's great monument to the Church, and gave his first blessing as Vicar of Christ on Earth.'

AIDAN. Sorry. Hello Mum. Una. Liam.

MRS KEVITT. Such a journey. Here Liam, bring those cases in for your mother, Is that Father Magee?

NUALA *enters.*

UNA. Nuala, how are you?

NUALA. Hello Una.

MRS KEVITT. Oh you're wasting away child. Mmmm. Well, sure it's good to see the both of ye . . . once in a while.

LIAM. Where will I put these cases Aidan?

MRS KEVITT. Put them in one of the bedrooms Liam. Wherever we're sleeping.

AIDAN. No. Yes. Here. We'll leave them here for the moment. Yes.

We hear the TV commentator: 'and so the Army bands stand to attention. The flags snap reverently in the wind and a nation waits for a man from a far country. Waiting in hope: waiting in hope and expectation'. *Then we hear:* 'Habemus Papem. The conclave has chosen. Habemus Papem. The church has decided. Habemus Papem. The spirit has spoken. Habemus Papem. And the children of God are no longer fatherless. Habemus Papem'.

NUALA *switches off the TV.*

NUALA. So, how is everyone in the country?

MRS KEVITT. The country is fine dear. The country is fine. I don't know why Aidan ever had to leave it.

NUALA. Well, do you think he'll go to Clonmacnoise?

MRS KEVITT. Who? Our Aidan?

NUALA. No. I mean the Pope. Do you think he'll go to Clonmacnoise?

MRS KEVITT. Oh the Pope.

NUALA. Yes. The Pope.

MRS KEVITT. Well Nuala, the Holy Father knows best, in these matters. The Holy Father knows best.
    The Maguires were asking for you Aidan.

UNA. Oh Mam, don't start that again.

MRS KEVITT. Tommy's in the hospital.

NUALA. I'll make a cup of tea.

MRS KEVITT. Nothing for me dear. I'm fasting.

NUALA. Fasting?

MRS KEVITT. Fasting?

NUALA. You're not . . . unwell?

MRS KEVITT. Didn't all the priests ask the people to fast for these few days? Before the Pope arrived.

NUALA. Really.

MRS KEVITT. It was read out at all the Masses dear.

NUALA. Oh.

UNA. I'd love a cup of tea Nuala, thanks.

LIAM. Yeah me too. If you've nothing stronger.

MRS KEVITT. Liam.

LIAM. Joking.

    NUALA *exits*.

AIDAN. So. I'll leave your bags away.

UNA. I'll help you.

AIDAN. No.

AIDAN *exits with luggage.*

In the silence that follows, MRS KEVITT *casts a hawk's eye round the room. She examines the lace curtains and the table tops.*

MRS KEVITT. Very luxurious, I must say.

UNA. Mam, don't start.

MRS KEVITT. I said nothing.

LIAM. Is Uncle Sam staying here tonight?

MRS KEVITT. Father Simeon. I told you he'd be here later. I'm quite looking forward to meeting him. Although why he didn't stay with the Jesuits, I don't know.

LIAM. But Uncle Sam isn't a Jesuit.

MRS KEVITT. He has friends in the Jesuits. And they've a big house somewhere, and that's where all the priests from home are staying. And I told you before that your uncle is an ordained priest, and if his name in community life is Father Simeon, then you should pay him the respect of calling him that.

LIAM. I didn't call him anything yet, did I? He's not even here.

UNA. Does he have the address?

MRS KEVITT. Oh he'll find us alright. 247. 247. Your father and I spent every penny we had to put Aidan through college; I never thought I'd see the day when he'd be living in a council terrace.

UNA. Mam, it's an estate, not a terrace. And if Nuala was able to get the house, then fair play to her; why should they waste money buying one.

MRS KEVITT. Who ever heard of a teacher marrying one of the pupils anyhow. Ugh. Oh, but she was the cute girl alright. Make no mistake about that. (*To* LIAM.) Where's your beads?

LIAM. What?

MRS KEVITT. Where's your beads? I told you to bring your beads.

LIAM. What am I supposed to bring me beads for? It's Mass we're going to, not the Rosary.

MRS KEVITT. Liam I told you to bring them to get them blessed. The Holy Father is hardly going to leave Ireland without blessing all the holy objects. And of course my son will be the only one without.

LIAM (going out). Spare me.

MRS KEVITT. Where are you going?

LIAM. Gimme a break.

MRS KEVITT. I asked you where you are going Liam? You're not in your own house now.

LIAM. I'm going to the Jacks. OK?

MRS KEVITT. Oh the language of that child.

Enter AIDAN.

AIDAN. Now. Mammy. Una.

Enter NUALA from the kitchen, with tea and sandwiches.

AIDAN. Ah! The tea. Now.

NUALA. The mattresses Aidan.

AIDAN. Yes. Yes pet. (Exits.)

NUALA. Now Una. A cuppa for you, and a cuppa for Liam. Are you sure you won't have a cuppa?

MRS KEVITT. Sure.

NUALA. Sure you're sure?

MRS KEVITT. Well I'll just have the tea. I don't think that breaks the fast anyhow. Oh by the way . . . Liam . . . Liam. I brought . . . Li-am.

LIAM. Ye – es.

MRS KEVITT. Bring in the white plastic bag when you're coming. I brought you a little bit of jam Nuala. We were just saying here, you have a lovely home, thank God.

NUALA. Yeah. It's nice now.

UNA. Where did Aidan go to?

NUALA. To get mattresses.

MRS KEVITT. Oh?

NUALA. He has this friend that he runs the scouts with. So they're taking the loan of a few mattresses. Y'see. For here. For the few days. (*Pause.*) Like we've only the one bed.

MRS KEVITT. Just so. Well of course, that's all you'd need. You're a married couple . . . and you don't have . . . any . . . other troubles.

NUALA (*a touch angered*). I mean like for these few days. I wouldn't want yous sleeping on the floor.

Enter LIAM *with a white plastic bag, from which* MRS KEVITT *delivers: two pots of jam, a cake, buns, meat sandwiches, eggs, rashers, chops, black pudding, and the local paper.*

MRS KEVITT. Now say nothing. It's just a few things. I didn't want to be putting either of yous to any trouble. And you're so good to put us up for the night. And I know Aidan is very fond of the bit of black pudding. Oh and I brought him the Western Gazette; there's a report of the match in it.

MRS KEVITT *pauses before extracting the final item.*

MRS KEVITT. Did you buy him any winter things yet?

NUALA. What?

MRS KEVITT. Winter things.

NUALA. No.

MRS KEVITT. He was down home the week before last, and he was saying by the looks of the weather he'd soon be needing to buy some thermal vests. Apparently the pre-fabs in that 'technical school' are a disgrace. But sure you must know, you were a student there. Anyhow; I thought since I was coming up, and they were only 1.99 in Super Sons, you wouldn't get the quality of them in Dublin, I'd get a couple and bring them up for him. Just in case.

NUALA *takes the vests.* MRS KEVITT, *quite pleased, moves to the next task.*

MRS KEVITT. Well, I'll just leave these things in the kitchen, out of your way. You two girls sit there and finish your tea. Liam come out and give me a hand to put these things away. Liam. Liam.

MRS KEVITT *exits to kitchen followed by* LIAM, *both carry groceries.*

NUALA *sits, head down, with the vests on her lap.*

UNA (*sipping tea*). Nuala, don't be upset. She doesn't mean it.

NUALA. You got your hair done.

UNA. Yeah.

NUALA. It's nice.

UNA (*going over to hold her*). Look Nuala, it'll be OK. You and Aidan are doing fine. You've a lovely home. Aidan has his job back . . . Now don't mind Mother. She's excited. That's all. Relax. Things are going to be OK.

NUALA. Things won't be OK Una. They'll never be OK. I didn't even get me hair done.

UNA. Nuala, what's eating you?

NUALA. There's something wrong Una. There's something very wrong . . .

NUALA *flicks on the TV. Someone is talking about the Pope's attitude to the IRA.* UNA *is silent.*

NUALA. The Pope, the Pope, the Pope; the whole bleedin' country is gone daft about the Pope. It's a pity the IRA or someone wouldn't give him a good kick up the arse.

UNA. Nuala, that's a terrible thing to say.

NUALA. I'm only joking.

The doorbell rings furiously. NUALA *moves to answer it but so does* MRS KEVITT *who gets to the door first.*

MRS KEVITT. OK, OK, OK.

AIDAN (*grappling with four mattresses*). Clear the way. Clear the way. Mind now. Watch it, they're heavy. OK.

MRS KEVITT. Liam. Liam. Help your brother with these things.

NUALA *returns to* UNA *in the sitting room.*

MRS KEVITT *enters with a parcel she has picked up from outside the door.*

NUALA. What's that?

MRS KEVITT. Something Aidan brought.

AIDAN *enters.*

AIDAN. There. We'll make them up later on. Mam, you and Una can have the bed. (NUALA *stares at him*.) Being the visitors. And eh . . . well, we can divide out the four mattresses between the rest of us. Isn't that right Nuala?

NUALA. Oh yeah. That's just what we were saying earlier.

MRS KEVITT. What's this Aidan?

AIDAN. Oh yeah, that. (*Taking parcel from her*.) I'll leave that away.

MRS KEVITT. Well what is it?

AIDAN. It's me uniform. Me scout uniform.

MRS KEVITT. Your scout uniform.

NUALA. Aidan's squadron commander now, Mrs Kevitt. And they'll all be on parade tomorrow, for the Pope and they'll all be wearing their uniforms. Including the leaders. Isn't that right Aidan? Did you not tell your mammy?

MRS KEVITT. And will you not be able to come with us?

AIDAN. Well like, I'll be with the scouts.

MRS KEVITT. You never told me that. Sure I thought you'd be with us. That we'd all go together. To see the Pope.

NUALA. Here gimme it. (*Takes the parcel briskly from* AIDAN.) I'll leave it up with your shirts. (*Goes out*.)

MRS KEVITT. Did you have your tea?

AIDAN. No.

MRS KEVITT. Will I make you some . . . ? I brought you up a wee bit of boxty. Mmmm?

AIDAN. Alright.

MRS KEVITT. Good.

AIDAN. Yeah. Sure that'd be great. Great Mam, great.

MRS KEVITT *much delighted, goes to the kitchen.*

AIDAN *remains with* UNA.

AIDAN. So how is little sister?

UNA. Little sister is fine Aidan. How are you and Nuala?

AIDAN. I'm fine. Just fine. I'm back at the school, and everyone is just totally apologetic.

UNA. Do they mention it?

AIDAN. Not a word. But you know . . . when they're . . . apologetic. I should have never been suspended. Y'know. Implication there was that they believed the allegation.

UNA. And is the young girl still at the school?

AIDAN. Gone. Gone . . . little rat. (*Looks about him and keeps his voice down.*) I'll tell you, I had it . . . we had it damn hard here over the summer. Damn hard. Here, tell us, Mammy didn't get wind of it did she?

UNA *rises and lights a cigarette.*

UNA. By God you may be damn sure she didn't hear of it. Do ye think life would be worth living. I'm bad enough listening to her on and on about Christmas. And why Stephen and I aren't married.

AIDAN. What about Christmas?

MRS KEVITT. Aidan. Aidan. Your tea is ready.

AIDAN. Coming. (*Goes into the kitchen to take tea.*)

A ring at the door.

UNA. Oh never mind. It's not important. That's probably Father Simeon now.

Another ring. AIDAN *and* MRS KEVITT *are now out of sight.*

LIAM *is in the corridor with the mattresses and* NUALA *is in the bedroom. They are also out of sight.*

As the door bell rings, UNA *makes her way towards the door then stops; turns for a moment towards the audience and surveys the house. We are aware that she is the only person in the house.*

There has been a time shift.

UNA *then opens the door, and standing there, is an agile fifty-year-old man, in a black polo neck, slacks and black leather coat. He has dark glasses in his hand.*

UNA *stands back, uneasy with him.*

Enter the POOKA MAN, *to be called* ANGELO. *He saunters coolly down-stage to the sitting room before speaking.*

ANGELO. You shouldn't have brought me back, y'know? That was a mistake.

UNA. Well I'm glad you had the decency to come.

ANGELO. Is there any one else here?

UNA. No.

ANGELO. So you want to find out what happened. Yeah? You think I might have had something to do with it.

UNA. I think you might know something. That's all. You seemed to get on well with Aidan. I have a right to know.

ANGELO. What about Nuala, his wife? Couldn't she help you?

UNA. She left. About a month later, she upped and went to America.

ANGELO. Really.

UNA. Really.

ANGELO. Dear oh dear. Just like the Pope.

UNA. Sorry?

ANGELO. Just like the Pope. Isn't that where he went. After Ireland. To America.

UNA. Yes, well I don't see what that has got to do with anything, quite frankly.

ANGELO. Sorry. It's just that the occasion of our meeting, was that papal visit.

UNA. Y'know something?

ANGELO. What?

UNA. I don't like you.

ANGELO. Oh.

UNA. And I don't trust you.

ANGELO. I see.

UNA. And I don't think you were good for Aidan.

ANGELO. Now don't push it too far, my dear girl.

UNA. And don't dear girl me.

ANGELO. And you don't make too many easy implications about whether I was or wasn't good for your brother. He was a sick man.

UNA. It's my family you're talking about.

ANGELO. And your family suffered a terrible blow. A violent
death is difficult to live with. There's no use in blaming me.
And if you want my honest and professional opinion on your
brother, then I have to say he was sick. You're foolish to go
raking up the muck y' know.

UNA. My family are normal, happy, content ordinary people. We
live normal lives in a normal country town.

ANGELO. Village.

UNA. Village. We're not the kind of people who suddenly decide
to go into the toilet and commit suicide. We might suffer a bit
of stress now and then, but we handle it. We don't go and
drown ourselves.

ANGELO. Nobody was drowned Una. It was electrocution by
means of the hair-dryer contacting with the water.

UNA. What do you mean, 'your professional opinion?' You're
only a priest.

ANGELO. They know a lot about suicide.

UNA. They know a lot about everything.

ANGELO. Yeah.

UNA. Yeah.

ANGELO. I am professionally trained. Human psychology. I
knew. I knew from the moment I walked in the door, that
something was terribly wrong. And I had the objectivity of an
outsider. You see, though Mrs Kevitt's husband, your father,
was my cousin, I had never met her. I have been a
contemplative for many years. I've never really belonged in the
world. It was only because of the Pope's visit that we were
dispensed to travel out to see him. That's why I say that it was
a mistake for you to send a message asking me to come again.

UNA. Well you got here. Someone must have let you out.

ANGELO. The message said it was desperately urgent.

UNA. And did you have to ask permission?

ANGELO. We do take a vow of obedience.

UNA. And what if your superior said no?

ANGELO. Oh that's not likely. Not when the request was so urgent.

UNA *chuckles.*

ANGELO. As I was saying, from the moment I stepped into this house – I knew something was wrong.

We return to the earlier time.

First the TV comes on: Papal images, then NUALA *enters wearing scout shorts.*

NUALA. Una. Una. These won't fit him. Oh sorry.

UNA. Oh Nuala, this is my cousin – Father Simeon.

NUALA. Hullo. Sorry. It's my husband's. Sorry. You're welcome.

ANGELO (*puts on glasses and becomes more the elderly cleric*). God bless you child, you are very kind to offer the hospitality of your home . . .

Enter MRS KEVITT.

MRS KEVITT (*arms out*). Ohhhh, Father . . . Simeon . . . After . . . all these years.

ANGELO. Dear cousin. (*They embrace.*)

AIDAN *enters, still chewing the last of his supper. He extends his hand to* ANGELO.

AIDAN. How do you do. I'm Aidan Kevitt. You must be the Father's cousin.

MRS KEVITT. Oh Aidan, Father is not just Father's cousin. He's our cousin.

NUALA. Eh, let me take your coat Father. Yeah. (*She places it on the bottom of the bannister.*)

MRS KEVITT. And sit down won't you Father. Will you have a cup of tea?

AIDAN. We get all your letters. (*Stares at* ANGELO.) Yeah. Every Christmas. Gosh it's great to meet you.

ANGELO. I have, eh, got all your letters too.

AIDAN. Is that a fact? Well well. Ah now, it's just hilarious; meeting you in the flesh. After all these years.

MRS KEVITT. Would you mind telling me what she's doing in them trousers. Where did Liam go. (*She rises to search.*) Liam. Liam. Come in and meet your cousin, Father Simeon.

AIDAN. And are you allowed to read letters in there.

MRS KEVITT. Oh Aidan, where's your manners.

ANGELO. On Sundays and feast day. Just those from close relatives.

NUALA. Well you'd hardly be gettin' any others, would you. I mean like, after being out of the world all your life.

ANGELO (*sad*). True. Eh, true. True.

NUALA. I mean like you don't have a girl friend waiting for you, like they do in 'the Joy.'

AIDAN. You're upsetting me.

NUALA *and* UNA *enjoy a restrained giggle.*

MRS KEVITT. Well what do you think of the Holy Father visiting our little country Father?

ANGELO. Oh it is wonderful. Wonderful.

MRS KEVITT. Yes.

AIDAN. Yes.

UNA. Yes.

NUALA. Yes.

LIAM *enters and stands at the door.*

LIAM. Yes what? (*Sees* NUALA *who is still wearing the scout shorts and laughs.*) You're not going out in them are you?

AIDAN. That's enough, now.

MRS KEVITT. Yes it's wonderful, Father. Isn't it. Thank God.

All bow their heads for a solemn moment.

ANGELO. Oh the Holy Father . . . is . . . mmmm . . . very close to Ireland.

NUALA. Really? Is he coming tonight?

ANGELO. Eh spiritually, the Holy Father is eh . . . eh . . . eh . . .

MRS KEVITT. All the same father, God must be very cross with the people. What with some of the things that go on . . .

ANGELO. I had the privilege of meeting him once.

NUALA. Who; God?

ANGELO. The present Pope.

MRS KEVITT. You had the privilege of meeting him. My goodness.

ANGELO. Our Congregation were in Rome, two years ago; for the canonization of Saint Prudentiano, a brother of the order who was hanged, drawn and quartered in the twelfth century, for refusing to relinquish his virginity.

AIDAN. Gosh. That must have been very beautiful.

ANGELO. There must have been a certain beatific beauty about the occasion, though according to the historical record, it was quite a gory incident.

Pause.

NUALA. I think that what Aidan meant was that meeting the Pope must have been a beautiful occasion.

AIDAN (*eyeing* NUALA). Yeah. That is what I meant.

ANGELO. Oh it was. Of course. It was most beautiful.

Pause.

ANGELO. We had a very small, intimate meeting with him afterwards. Just himself and the one and a half thousand Irish people that were there. And he shook hands with a great number of them.

A titter of laughter from UNA *and* NUALA.

He spoke about his deep affection for Ireland, and how he would long very deeply to visit our country.

Pause.

NUALA. Are you in the Boy Scouts Liam?

LIAM. Lay off me will ye? (*Exits to kitchen.*)

AIDAN *and* MRS KEVITT *are aware of the giggling.*

MRS KEVITT. Well it seems to me a very fine thing to be 'away from the world,' as you are Father, in the days that are in it. What with all the temptations there are in the world.

UNA. Well Father if you'll excuse us for a moment maybe we'll get Aidan's things ready for tomorrow.

NUALA *and* UNA *go out.*

ANGELO. But I have no doubt that the Holy Father's visit is doing something very extraordinary for our country. It's eh, bringing, eh, so many people . . . together . . . and . . . eh . . . back to the sacraments.

MRS KEVITT. That reminds me Aidan. You're sure you and Nuala were at confessions.

AIDAN. Oh yeah. Yeah. Sure.

ANGELO. At the church down the road, they are still hearing confessions. And a vigil, until midnight.

MRS KEVITT. A vigil 'til midnight. Isn't that beautiful. I think Una and I might pop down there and get confessions as well. (*To* ANGELO.) I don't like going at home, you know. It's not the same. You're sure you've been . . .

AIDAN. Yeah. Oh yeah. So Father, do you think he'll speak out on anything in particular while he's here?

ANGELO. I've no doubt that he will. What, eh, what special word he might have to enlighten us, no one can say.

MRS KEVITT. No one can say.

AIDAN. I suppose.

ANGELO. There is so much, eh, in relation to, eh, you know, eh . . . modern life . . . the . . . eh . . . per-miss-ive society, the kind of problems young people are facing nowadays . . .

Cut to UNA *and* NUALA *in the bedroom.*

UNA. What did you put them on for?

NUALA. They're trousers.

UNA. I know they're trousers. What did you put them on for?

Both continue to examine the trousers and giggle.

NUALA. They're pants. (*Laughs.*) They're short pants. Aidan's. He's (*Laughs.*) going, (*Laughs.*) to wear them . . . tomorrow.

Another eruption of laughter.

UNA. To see the Pope?

NUALA. Apparently all the Boy Scouts are doing a guard of honour tomorrow, and Aidan is one of the generals, and they all have to be in the full regalia.

UNA. Will he fit into them?

NUALA. No. Or if he does it'll be a tight fit.

Pause.

NUALA *looks at* UNA *then starts undressing.*

UNA *produces cigarettes.*

NUALA. Oh Una. Is this monk fella for real?
– No no, it's my flash.

UNA (*flicks through dresses on a clothes-horse, and cosmetics on the table*). Well none of us really knows him. Not even Mam. In fact he was Daddy's cousin. She's not related to him at all.

NUALA. I don't like the smell of him.

Pause.

UNA. I didn't think Aidan would take that fella so seriously. (*Picks up the pants again.*) He's really wound up about all this. Isn't he.

NUALA. Don't talk to me about it. You don't know the half of what goes on. I've had the Pope for breakfast, dinner and tea for the past month. What will he say about the IRA? Should he tell the priests to get back into their collars? And what will he say about abortion, divorce, and . . . contraceptives? Eh? You'd swear the Pope was going to take a bus out here, and ask Aidan for all the answers.

UNA. He's excited.

NUALA. And then he has this big idea that the country is going to be different. Afterwards. When the Pope is gone. Everybody is suddenly going to be good, and perfect, and holy, just like the Boy Scouts. I had a row about that with him this morning. I told him he was raving.

UNA. And what did he say to that?

NUALA. What did he say?

UNA. What did he say?

NUALA. He said I was being disrespectful. He says I'm stupid.

UNA. Ah, he's probably excited because he has a job tomorrow looking after the guard of honour. Who knows, maybe he'll even meet the Pope personally.

NUALA. Looka. When the Pope goes, this place will be exactly the same – exactly.

UNA. OK. But that's no reason not to have one or two days where everybody feels good; where everybody feels together and honoured, because of the Pope.

Back in the sitting room.

MRS KEVITT. U-na. UUU-na.

UNA. Coming.

AIDAN (*offers a cigarette*). Do you smoke Father?

MRS KEVITT. Aidan.

ANGELO. Oh no.

MRS KEVITT. Of course Father doesn't smoke.

AIDAN. I was only offering.

LIAM (*at the door*). Are yis not allowed to smoke inside?

MRS KEVITT. Liam did you wash those dishes I told you to?

UNA (*enters with* NUALA). Right, I suppose you want to go up and say your prayers.

NUALA. Are you going to confessions too Aidan?

AIDAN. I was. We were. Last week.

NUALA. We were?

AIDAN. And we didn't do anything since.

NUALA. Hah?

MRS KEVITT. Oh the world is a changed place Father, since I was a young woman.

ANGELO. Ohhhh yes, Oh yes indeed.

MRS KEVITT. Father. (*Taking his hand.*) It's been lovely to meet you and very interesting chatting. You're such an interesting person. You know . . . when my husband was alive . . .

UNA. Mother. Come on.

MRS KEVITT. . . . we used to have a lot of Jesuits staying. Such interesting people I always thought. So professional.

ANGELO. The Jesuits have their merits.

MRS KEVITT. Yes, well, I hope we'll meet you later Father.

NUALA. Sure you'll be here when she gets back. You're not going out to a night club or anything to have your fling?

ANGELO *affects a hearty laugh.*

MRS KEVITT (*with a knife-like smile*). Oh now. It takes the Dublin ones for the quick remark. Liam. Come on. We'll go Father. God bless. Thank you Nuala.

In the hallway MRS KEVITT's *hand searches for the holy water font before blessing herself a dry blessing.*

MRS KEVITT. Liam. You'll let us in when we get back Aidan?

MRS KEVITT *and* LIAM *go out.*

AIDAN, NUALA *and* FATHER SIMEON (ANGELO) *remain.* AIDAN *is vexed with* NUALA.

AIDAN. Can I get you anything Father?

ANGELO *silently indicates negative.*

NUALA. Well sit down Father. Relax.

AIDAN. Yeah. Here. Have a fag.

ANGELO *sits and takes a cigarette.*

NUALA. Are yis allowed smoke?

ANGELO. I'm just dying for one.

NUALA Yeah?

ANGELO. I just didn't like to . . . eh . . . smoke . . . in front of . . . I mean . . . when I came in at first.

NUALA. Yeah?

AIDAN. He's hardly going to smoke in front of Big Mama. The way her mind works. (*The two boys giggle.*)

NUALA. Oh for fuck sake. (*She exits in disgust and goes to the bedroom.*)

We hear a lot of banging about of furniture upstairs – NUALA *completing the beds.* AIDAN *gives an embarrassed look at* ANGELO. ANGELO *stares back.* AIDAN *tries to defend himself.*

AIDAN (*nervous laugh*). Don't mind her, Father. Just . . . just gets a bit uptight . . . that's all.

ANGELO. Of course.

AIDAN. That's all.

ANGELO. I understand completely.

Banging of bed being moved.

AIDAN. She's just a bit annoyed about something.

ANGELO. Yes.

AIDAN. Well, to come back to the Pope for a moment. (*Bang.*) He's . . . he's . . . he's . . . a great man. Isn't he. Really. I mean . . . he's just like . . . so like . . . like . . . eh . . . good . . . y'know. I suppose good. He's good. And and and you can see it. (*Bang.*) Good God. Excuse me Father. (*He goes to the door and roars.*) Nuala! Nuala!

NUALA. Yeah?

AIDAN. Are you alright?

NUALA (*bang*). Fine.

AIDAN. What are you doing?

NUALA. I'm getting the bed ready – for you mother.

AIDAN (*smouldering, returns to* ANGELO). Ah yes. Well, I think it's going to be the best thing ever happened to this country. I think it's going to make an awful difference in people's lives.

ANGELO. It's certainly bringin' a lot of people back to the church.

AIDAN. Yes. It is.

ANGELO. Wonderful.

AIDAN. Yes. Wonderful. (*Bang.*) Bloody wonderful. Excuse me for a moment Father. (*He marches up to* NUALA *in the bedroom.*)

AIDAN. What the fuck are you at?

NUALA (*just finished the bed, and smiling*). What?

AIDAN. I said what the fuck are you playing at? You've been insulting that man since he came into the house.

NUALA. I'm insulting nobody. And it's my house and I can do what I want with it. What did you give your Mother this room for anyhow?

AIDAN. Because she's sixty-five and I don't expect her to sleep in the bath.

NUALA. You never mentioned it. You never told me.

AIDAN. Nuala, it's only a fucking bed.

NUALA. It's our bed.

AIDAN. It's only two nights.

NUALA. And it's a bed. A bed. Bed. Bed.

AIDAN. That's what I said.

NUALA. You said it was a fucking bed.

AIDAN. So I said it was a fucking bed. What's wrong now.

NUALA. A fucking bed.

AIDAN. You don't like cursing.

NUALA. We don't do much fucking in it do we.

AIDAN. You said you didn't like that word.

NUALA. Oh Christ.

Pause.

AIDAN. Nuala, what is wrong? My mother is going to be here for two nights. Now you may not like that, but you've no choice. It's the biggest moment of her life. She's coming up to see the Pope. Everyone in Dublin is putting someone up.

NUALA. I never said a word about your mother.

AIDAN. Then what is wrong?

NUALA. Nothing. I'm making the beds, OK? I'm taking a few personal things out of the drawers and putting them somewhere she won't be snooping. I'm doing my best. And you come barging up the stairs with a temper on you, and then you want to know what's wrong with me. It's you is too bloody wound up with this Pope thing.

AIDAN. OK, do what you want. I never said a word. Have it your own way. You always do anyway. As you say, it's your house.

NUALA. I'm not leaving this (*Holds up a night-dress.*) around for your mother to be commenting on.

AIDAN. Nuala, will you for one second stop rooting round in that drawer like a skunk and tell me what's the matter.

NUALA. Like a what?

AIDAN. Oh Jesus, do you have to pick up everything. Skunk. Skunk. Skunk.

NUALA. That's sick.

AIDAN. What are you talking about?

NUALA. A skunk. Skunks smell. I don't smell. I may not be up to your levels of polite middle-class rural chemists, but I don't smell and I'm not a skunk.

AIDAN. It's a poem.

NUALA. What is?

AIDAN. A poem. Y'know? What poets write. It's an image in a poem, by an American poet, it's on the leaving cert. course for Christ sake, he describes his wife rooting in a drawer like a skunk. Jesus Nuala, it's affectionate. I'm trying to be affectionate.

NUALA. You're trying to be affectionate? Aidan, skunk is not a nice word to call your wife. You don't describe the way your wife smells, to a skunk.

AIDAN. Who's talking about the way you smell?

NUALA (*slings the last few items of personal clothing onto the bed, and prepares to exit*). Poets writing about their women in bed. Or in the toilet maybe. Great. 'I am a poet. My wife is a skunk.' Fucking marvellous. Here. (*From the bundle she flings the pants at him.*) There's your pants. Don't lose them. And don't let any ould fella be rubbing you. You might be very tempting in them things. Scout.

She goes out and pushes the clothes on to other beds, and puts some things into a hot press in the corridor.

AIDAN *exits after* NUALA.

Back in the sitting room ANGELO *stands.* UNA *is standing in the doorway to the kitchen with a mug of tea.*

ANGELO. And that's how it started. I was sitting down here, and heard the entire episode.

UNA. I'm not impressed.

ANGELO. You're not impressed. I'm not trying to impress you.

UNA. Everybody has arguments. Fights. You lock yourself off from the world for thirty years, you might not realise that. You're in somebody's house for the first time in your life, and you overhear an argument.

Before I went down home. When I was studying, and then teaching, here, in Dublin, I lived in flats or houses with thin walls. You get used to some fella at three in the morning, next door, kicking his head off the wall and shouting over and over at his wife; (*Imitates Dublin accent.*) 'Ye bitch. Ye bitch. I'll bleedin' burst ye.' Over and over, until you hear the crack of stick, or a thud against the door; and then everything goes silent; and you go back to sleep, because you know the punishment is over, and that even the victim is relieved.

ANGELO. What can one say?

UNA. Yeah. And then, the next day, you go out to work, not even remembering it, until maybe the following evening, when you're at home making the dinner, and the noise comes through the wall again; 'Ye bitch. Ye bleedin' bitch.' Dublin is a funny place. A ball of laughs. You don't know what you're missing.

ANGELO. Oh but I do. I know all about them. I told you. I'm a professional.

UNA. Yeah? Well don't go telling me that just because you overheard them fighting that it's sufficient explanation.

ANGELO. You have a very cynical view of marriage.

UNA. Do I?

ANGELO. You're not married yourself?

UNA. I know that women sometimes get the shit knocked out of them.

ANGELO. And women, I suppose, can do no wrong.

UNA. I know that men have tempers. It's part of what he thinks he is. And if a man gets into a temper then you're supposed to live with it.

ANGELO. You don't have a husband.

UNA. I had a father – Father.

ANGELO. Ahhhh. (*Pause.*) I see.

UNA. What do you see?

ANGELO. I see you have strong views. And your views have a story behind them.

UNA. Now look here, with all respect I'll ask you not to unload any of your psychological codswallop on me. I'm not defending Aidan. I know he has a temper. I know what that's about, and I know the way that little boys are tolerated, by their mammies and wives. But I do want to find out what happened to Aidan. He wouldn't hit Nuala. Things were beginning to go well for them. And a squabble in the bedroom didn't cause what happened.

ANGELO. I'm only saying that was the start of it. There was more.

UNA. There was more?

ANGELO. There was more.

UNA. The first night?

ANGELO. There was much more. You see, you think the woman can do no wrong. But that is not true.

UNA. Go on.

ANGELO. She blew. Flipped. Went cuckoo. She just went bananas.

UNA. How?

ANGELO. I don't know. They were on the landing. (NUALA *and* AIDAN *appear on the landing.* ANGELO *moves towards the hall to remember.*) I couldn't hear, because they had begun talking very low. I think he whispered something at her, came on down the stairs, and, I remember she was standing just there, like she was possessed, and then, snap, like that, she blew. I was sitting over there; I could see straight through that door. She said something. Something; like I'll kill him.

UNA. No. I don't believe that.

ANGELO. I'll never forget the scream she let out.

NUALA *screams off-stage.* AIDAN *enters and crosses into the kitchen.*

Pause.

Then NUALA, *sobbing, enters and follows* AIDAN *into the kitchen. We hear her crying.*

UNA. I don't believe it.

ANGELO. Of course, I could be wrong.

AIDAN *enters, and sits opposite* ANGELO. *Both stare at the ground for a long while as the crying finally quietens. As always in these shifts, by putting on glasses,* ANGELO *becomes the elderly* FATHER SIMEON.

AIDAN. Sorry about that.

ANGELO. OK. OK. OK.

AIDAN. No, it's really terrible Father. You'll just have to excuse us. Y'see, Nuala, well, is going through a very difficult time. Y'see, she can't have babies.

ANGELO. Ahhh. I see.

AIDAN. It's just we're having a tough time. But it's . . . it's not serious.

He flicks on the TV. The Pope is delivering a sermon somewhere. He flicks it off.

NUALA *enters, looking subdued, embarrassed, and red in the face.*

NUALA. Would you like something to drink, Father?

AIDAN *smiles devotedly at her.*

UNA *looks on at the scene.*

ANGELO (*to* UNA). I knew the way she said it. There was something very sinister about it.

NUALA. Aidan. Will you take some tea love?

AIDAN (*joyful with her apparent change*). OK pet. Yes. I will. Here. (*Rises.*) I'll give you a hand.

NUALA. No.

ANGELO. There was something very sinister about it. I knew that.

UNA. Yeah. So what happened next.

ANGELO. That was all. She brought in the tea. We drank it. And then you and Liam and your mother returned.

UNA (*smiling*). That was all.

ANGELO. That was all.

UNA. What did she say?

ANGELO. When?

UNA. When you were drinking your tea.

ANGELO. Nothing. Nothing in particular.

UNA. Oh no you don't Father.

ANGELO. I beg your pardon?

UNA. You're not to be trusted.

ANGELO. She was just sinister. That's all.

UNA. I know. She told me.

ANGELO. It was outrageous.

UNA. It was a joke.

ANGELO. She was letting Aidan down. She wanted to humiliate him. Let him down in public. Destroy him.

UNA. Come on. What did he do to her five minutes earlier.

ANGELO. It was a joke worthy of a teenager.

UNA (*smiles*). You're embarrassed.

ANGELO. I suppose.

UNA. So what did she say? Go on tell us. 'What, do, you, do with, it.'

NUALA (*giggling*). Excuse me.

ANGELO. It's good to be light-hearted.

NUALA. I was just thinking of something ridiculous.

AIDAN. Oh well, don't keep it to yourself.

NUALA (*laughing*). It's . . . too . . . dirty.

ANGELO. Ha.

NUALA (*seriously*). I was just wondering what you do with it all. In a monastery.

ANGELO. All what?

NUALA (*laughing*). All the sperm. In a monastery. You could have a sperm bank.

AIDAN. Jesus Christ Nuala.

NUALA. Well Father isn't afraid to talk about sperm banks. We've no children Father. Aidan says I'm infertile; but how does he know it's not him. I go for tests. Everyone pokes around at me. Why won't he go for a test?

AIDAN. This has got nothing to do with Father Simeon, or the Pope, and you know it. (*Stands.*) Why are you doing this to me?

NUALA. Why are you taking yourself so serious?

AIDAN. You have no right to do this to me. No right. Here. (*He pours the tea over her.*) There's your tea. Now you will have to go up and change. Won't you. Won't you. Won't you. Won't you. Won't you.

He drags her upstairs to the bedroom as she protests.

NUALA. No Aidan. Ah no, please Aidan. It was only a joke. I'm sorry. Don't be cross Aidan. Please. Don't be cross. I was wrong Aidan. Please. Don't lose your temper. Aidan.

They disappear into the bedroom.

UNA *and* ANGELO *remain in the sitting room.*

UNA. The bastard. She didn't tell me everything then.

ANGELO. Apparently not.

UNA. Did he hit her?

NUALA. Aidan I'm sorry. Please. You'll be sorry.

ANGELO. It wasn't my business. I don't know. I don't think so. You couldn't hear much from down here.

A sound of thumping from upstairs.

ANGELO. Anyway. You were all back from the church in a few minutes.

Enter LIAM *and* MRS KEVITT *into the sitting room from front door.*

MRS KEVITT. Well, that was only gorgeous.

LIAM. Yes Ma.

MRS KEVITT. Such a nice young priest.

LIAM. Yes Ma.

MRS KEVITT. Oh, the sermon he gave after the Rosary.

LIAM. Only gorgeous.

MRS KEVITT. Only gorgeous.
Father Simeon, do you think, in all earnestness, that this visit will do any good? I mean; will it bring the young people back to Mass?

LIAM *groans.*

ANGELO. I would have every confidence, Mrs Kevitt, in the Holy Father.

MRS KEVITT. Oh now, it's not right nor proper. There's too much Father. Too much of everything; when there was less, people were far happier.

UNA. Where is Aidan and Nuala?

ANGELO. Eh, they're getting the beds ready.

MRS KEVITT. Hmmm. (*Pause.*) Do you know Father, I know, for I see it with my own eyes.

ANGELO. I beg your pardon?

UNA. Mother, isn't it time we went to bed, if we're going to be up at six in the morning . . . ?

MRS KEVITT. You see Father, at home, I supervise the flowers in the church. I always kept a good home for them all; Aidan and all; he was used to the very best Father; and I suppose I had that, what would you call it, talent, for flowers, and so forth; and then of course my late husband, Gerald, was very friendly with his Lordship. So they asked me to, y'know, look after the flowers.

ANGELO. How fascinating.

MRS KEVITT. Well I see it with my own eyes in that church; little hussies, Father, swanking round in the best of clothes. Do you think they have any respect? Not the slightest. (*To* UNA.) I caught that Freeny one smoking, if you don't mind, up on the altar, last Saturday, when she was putting up the Dahlias for the Maguire wedding. Cheeky little strap.

ANGELO. I'm not entirely following you Mrs Kevitt.

UNA. Mother, it's time for bed.

MRS KEVITT. It's like this Father. When we receive Holy
Communion, we're receiving the body of Our Lord – on the
tongue. And Communion in the hand is not proper. And
people like me didn't spend our lives kneeling – kneeling
before the Blessed Sacrament just to see some Joan Freeny
treating the House of God like – like – like a cafeteria.

LIAM. You see Father, me mother thinks this Joan Freeny is
having it off with one of the curates.

UNA. Liam. Will you have manners. (*She goes for him as he makes his
exit.*)

LIAM (*laughing*). Sorry, sorry, sorry. I'm going to bed.

MRS KEVITT. Where is Aidan. Aidan.

AIDAN (*from above*). Yes. Com-ing. (*Rushes down.*) Com-ing. Coming. Ahhh, well, you're all back. How did it go?

MRS KEVITT. Where's Nuala?

AIDAN. Ah. She's tired. Went to bed. Eh. I think she has the 'flu.

MRS KEVITT. Oh dear.

AIDAN. Yes, well. The rooms are all ready for you. Liam is
bunking in the front bedroom with Father. If that's alright?

ANGELO. Anywhere at all. Anywhere at all.

MRS KEVITT. Mmmm. Well if she's gone to bed, then she's gone
to bed. Father, it's been a pleasure meeting you, and please
God, we'll be meeting again in the morning. God willing.

ANGELO. With his help. Good night. Good night. Good night.
(*Turns to* UNA, *when* MRS KEVITT *is a little way up the stairs.*)
And that was it. You all went to bed, and I sat here with Aidan.
Your mother slept well I trust?

UNA. Eventually. When she had given a full critique of the
shoddy room and the dampness of the bed.

ANGELO. That wasn't far wrong.

UNA. Yeah? Well, get on with the story. You and Aidan. What
did he tell you?

ANGELO. I'm sorry. It's confidential.

UNA. Don't give me that.

ANGELO. Private. I'm not at liberty . . .

UNA. Bloody bullshit. It wasn't confessions. It was talk. And he's dead.

ANGELO. Really?

UNA. You know damn well he is. And I want to know what was going on in his head.

ANGELO. You're so sure of yourself, aren't you? Look, I'll make a deal with you. I'll tell you, if you promise to tell me what Nuala said to you.

UNA. Nuala said nothing to me.

ANGELO. You're lying.

UNA. How do you know?

ANGELO. Because you already told me she mentioned the joke. (*Approaches her.*) Funny how that sperm keeps popping up this evening, isn't it. Sperm. I've a good memory you know. Excellent.

UNA. Nuala and I talked the next day. When mother said she would go with the scouts to the Park, and you agreed to go to Galway with Liam for the following day, I decided to stay here and mind Nuala.

ANGELO. Why?

UNA. She had the 'flu.

ANGELO. She hadn't.

UNA. I didn't know that at the time. And she never told me about the fight. Look, you're getting a bit too clever now. What did Aidan tell you?

ANGELO. Oh Aidan told me a lot.

UNA. I'm sure.

ANGELO. But it's a secret. You wouldn't like to be hearing Aidan's little secrets, now?

UNA. I would.

ANGELO. No you wouldn't.

UNA. Get on with it.

ANGELO. You'll regret it.

UNA. I want to know.

ANGELO. Well don't blame me if it opens a can of worms.

UNA. What?

ANGELO. He thought she was . . . sick . . . mad . . . sort of possessed. (*Pause.*) He thought she was a witch.

UNA. What?

ANGELO. Your brother. Thought his wife was a witch. A witch.

UNA. You're lying.

ANGELO. I'm not. He probably thought you were a witch too. (*Approaches* UNA.) Maybe you are?

AIDAN (*rises from chair and gets* ANGELO's *attention*). Father. Before you go to bed.

ANGELO. Yes?

AIDAN. I want to talk . . . please.

They both sit. UNA *watches from the door.*

AIDAN. That little incident . . .

ANGELO. Yes?

AIDAN. Earlier . . . I kind of lost me temper.

ANGELO. Oh that.

AIDAN. Yes. But it wasn't what you think.

ANGELO. I had forgotten about it.

AIDAN. You see, in the beginning, everything was fine. When we got married. She was great then. Her uncle is in the hospital, and when he moved out of here, we moved in, before the corporation could bat an eye.

ANGELO. I see.

AIDAN. I was teaching. Everything was fine. I mean she just adored me. Then she couldn't have babies. I think that affected her. I was disappointed, but I told her it didn't matter. We could keep trying. We could adopt. No. She was going . . . going strange. It's as if she grew up into something different.

ANGELO. Was she very young when she married?

AIDAN. A teenager. Oh she was beautiful. She was everything I dreamed of. Y'know, it's funny, but I used to think of going on for the church. I was five years teaching before I put it out of my head.

ANGELO. Is that a fact?

AIDAN. Then I noticed Nuala. I taught her from her first year in school. I knew her inside out. I felt I could see into her. And then one day, about a year after she had left, she phoned me and asked would I go to the school reunion with her. God she was beautiful.

ANGELO. You talk like she was dead.

AIDAN. She is, in a way. She just changed.

ANGELO. How?

AIDAN. About two years ago. Stopped going to Mass. Wouldn't eat meat. Started tossing up all that bloody rice and lentils, and raw carrots.

ANGELO. Goodness.

AIDAN. Jesus, I'm sick of the smell of those damned lentils all over the house. She changed Father. (*Pause.*) Something got into her.
    Then one day, last May, in school, I went into the girls showers – I was looking for a schoolbag, one of the students reported was stolen – they're always doing that, hiding each others bags – I thought the place was empty. But of course there had to be one of the fifth years in there, showering. Bloody old fashioned bitch. And there was a hullabalu. I had to stay out until the thing was cleared up.

ANGELO. Bless us and save us.

AIDAN (*aggressively*). But that evening I came home to her. In bits, Father, in bits. And do you know what she said? My own wife – she asked me did I do it on purpose? My own wife, and she suspected me. Oh she said she believed me but she didn't.

ANGELO. Keep your voice down.

AIDAN. You could see it in her. She was delighted to see me caught out. And all the time since then, she has that smirk on her face, and it's there, at the back of her mind. I can't look at her without thinking about it and feeling guilty. She's evil, Father. She's torturing me.

ANGELO. She's your wife.

AIDAN. No. She's not.

ANGELO. Please keep your voice down.

AIDAN. Do you know what I believe?

ANGELO. What?

AIDAN. Right – do you know?

ANGELO. What?

AIDAN. There's no women priests, right?

ANGELO. Right.

AIDAN. And you're a celibate, right?

ANGELO. Right.

AIDAN. You're in your monastery – to be close to God – and to be close to God you stay clear of women – right?

ANGELO. Nooo.

AIDAN. And I'm telling you that my wife is a witch. My wife is dead. That is a shell upstairs. Possessed by something that wants to destroy me.

ANGELO (*erupts*). You're mad. You're insane. You ought to be locked up. (*He rushes over to* UNA.) That's what I said to him. That's what I told him. I understand these things. I knew what was going on. I'm a psychologist. He didn't know that. He thought I was some dopey old Friar from the Middle Ages. No way.

AIDAN (*shouts over to* ANGELO). She reads Astrology books. And Tarot Cards. And hands – and dreams – I'm telling you Father, all that shit, she takes serious. And it is serious.

ANGELO (*to* UNA). Your brother was a fucking lunatic.

UNA. Please stop. That's enough.

AIDAN. I'm sorry for unloading all that on you Father. I'll see you in the morning. (*Goes towards the door.*) I didn't touch her. Tonight. I didn't. (*Exit.*)

ANGELO. He didn't lay a finger on her. He said that.

UNA. The bloody eegid. I suppose it took him thirty-four years to work up the courage to get married. He couldn't handle anything going wrong.

ANGELO. Do you know what my opinion was; I thought that someone should recommend suicide to him. After all, he had the Pope and his mother sitting on his shoulder, he wasn't likely to look for a divorce.

UNA. You take a funny attitude for a man of the cloth.

ANGELO. Your brother was sick. I don't mince me words. Excuse me, I need to relieve myself. (*He exits to the downstairs toilet.*)

UNA *sits down and flicks on the TV. Images of Phoenix Park.*

Upstairs NUALA *wakes and comes down in her dressing gown, wondering who is in the house.*

NUALA. Aidan . . . ? Aidan . . . ?

UNA. In here Nuala, it's me.

NUALA. Una. Why didn't you go to the Pope?

UNA. I didn't want to leave you alone.

NUALA. Yeah?

UNA. Aidan said you had the 'flu.

NUALA (*looks at the TV*). Is this him now?

UNA. Yep. That's him. Just landed. The airplane waved at everyone.

UNA *and* NUALA *watch the TV in silence. They flick off the sound after a few moments and continue to watch. Slowly a giggle rises in both of them.*

NUALA. He's a lovely man, isn't he?

UNA. A bit on the old side for me.

NUALA. A yeah, but he's nice.

UNA. How's your 'flu?

NUALA *does not reply. Both giggle again.*

UNA. Oh now, he's a great man.

NUALA. He always looks very worried. Doesn't he. Suppose he has a lot of worries.

UNA. He has in his hat. If he had half the worries that you and I have he'd have something to worry about.

NUALA. No, he has worries. He has. I mean, supposing he is right about everything. Suppose he's having visions, and God is appearing to him and he knows he's right. It must be very depressing for him when people don't listen. I mean, nobody listens to him, really.

UNA. D'ye think he has visions?

NUALA. Dunno.

UNA. Come on, do you?

NUALA. Maybe.

UNA. Do you?

NUALA. He might have, yeah. I'd say a man like that would have visions. (*Long pause.*) I have visions.

UNA. You have visions?

NUALA. I have visions.

UNA. Don't tell anybody that.

NUALA. I told Aidan. Nearly scared the shite out of him. I had this dream one time. About Aidan, in a boat, and he had no oars, y'know? And there was this hand coming up out of the water. And I was watching this. And I knew that the hand was going to grab his willie, and I woke up real scared.

(*Pause.*)

It was real vivid, y'know?

UNA. Did you tell him?

NUALA. I was going to, and then I didn't. I was going to say, to be careful, y'know, that day. I kept me mouth shut. Well, be janey, didn't he come in that evening and tell me that he was in a terrible argument in the staff room, with the domestic science teacher, and he was real upset, because the domestic science teacher is a real oul faggot. So I says, Aidan, I had a vision last night, that something was going to happen you today.

UNA. And what did he say?

NUALA. He flew off the handle and told me I was a eegid. An

effin eegid, he says. He's a terrible mouth on him, your brother, when he looses the rag.

UNA. I know.

NUALA. Here, look at this he's giving his sermon. Turn him up a bit.

Voice of homily up for a few moments.

Ah here, turn him down.

UNA. Well the mother is in that crowd somewhere.

NUALA. That mother of yours is a terrible targer too Una.

UNA. Nuala, you can't think we're all bad?

NUALA. She'll have Liam as bad as Aidan be the time she's finished.

UNA. There's something up with you and Aidan, isn't there?

NUALA. Huh. There hasn't been anything up for months, as far as I can figure out. Would you get married?

UNA. Sure. Don't you know I'm nearly engaged.

NUALA. Yeah? Mr Right I suppose?

UNA. Maybe. I'm not sure.

NUALA. I married Mr Right. I thought he was God Almighty. The only thing I didn't realise was that he thought he was God Almighty too.

UNA. Come on Nuala.

NUALA. I was too young. Too romantic. I think you'd be better off living together. I mean he has his own friends. He doesn't like any of my friends. None of them. No time for them.

UNA. Oh Nuala, you're being very harsh.

UNA. You're really very angry Nuala; what's the matter?

NUALA (*rises*). I'm fed up, Una. Fed up. He bosses me, y'know bosses me all the time. He never buys me flowers. Ever. Never. If he has friends in the house I can't open me mouth without getting me head bitten off. And that frigger on the box. That yeti.That misogynist.

UNA. Nuala. Stop it.

NUALA. Whatever hope there was of getting on with Aidan is rightly shang-hied be that Santa Claus.

UNA. Nuala, that's crazy. Stop it.

NUALA. Is it? Is it? Aidan is out there walking round the Phoenix Park in a pair of short pants, like a ten year old, and that fella is like Big Daddy to the lot of them.

UNA. But you said yourself that you liked the Pope. You're getting bitter.

Pause.

UNA. You miss not having a child, Nuala. Is that it?

NUALA. Oh cop yourself on Una. You're older than me and you have no child. Don't fantasize about marriage. I have a child. That's the problem. He's called Aidan; I wanted a man.

We hear the toilet flush. NUALA *exits.*

The phone rings and UNA *answers it.*

UNA. Hullo? Who? Yes this is Una Kevitt. Who's that? Who? Who? Father Simeon? (*Looks towards the toilet.*) Yes that's right, I sent a message. Yes. To be here. That it was urgent, that is correct. But, but, but, Father – were you never in this house – yes – my mother – but you were never – not even for the Pope's – you were in Maynooth to see the Pope – Yes – Do I what? – I do please – come round immediately – could you make it sooner? – no, sorry – OK. Please. It's very urgent.

ANGELO *returns to the sitting room smiling. They stare at each other.*

ANGELO. You seem nervous.

UNA. No.

ANGELO. Why?

UNA. Because I know you're a liar.

ANGELO. I told you what your brother said. You haven't told me what Nuala and you talked about.

UNA. I'm beginning to think that it's none of your business.

ANGELO. Oh. Very well then. The matter rests. You demanded I come round here and rake up the dead with you. I've answered your questions. So – why don't you offer me a drink before I leave?

UNA. I think I'd prefer if you left immediately.

ANGELO (*sits*). Not a chance.

UNA (*moves to go*). Then I'm afraid I'm going. You can let yourself
out when you like . . .

ANGELO. There's someone coming over to see you; I heard you
on the phone. You can't leave now.

UNA. Please let me go.

ANGELO. Don't you want to know the whole story?

UNA. I know the story. He was sick. The marriage was a disaster.
He took the gutless way out by drowning himself – sorry –
electrocuting himself – that's all – now please let me go.

ANGELO. Oh no. That's not at all what happened. That's not it
at all.

UNA. You're not Father Simeon.

ANGELO. The penny has dropped.

UNA. You're not my father's cousin. You walked in here and
spent two nights in this house, and none of us ever doubted
you. You're an imposter. I'm frightened of you. (*Breaks up a bit.*)
I'm frightened you're going to . . .

ANGELO. Rape you?

UNA. Please don't touch me. Please don't.

ANGELO. No, no, I won't touch you. You're wrong about that.
You're wrong about a lot of things. You see there are things
you don't understand. Things. Don't you really want to know
what happened the following night. Things. Things you are
afraid to look at.

UNA. I know all that. The hairdryer. Bathroom. I know.

ANGELO. No you don't. You know nothing. Nothing.

UNA. Who are you? Who are you?

ANGELO. That's what you really want to know. And that's what
I'm going to tell you.

ACT TWO

Late on the second night of the Pope's visit.

Everybody is in bed: MRS KEVITT, NUALA, AIDAN, UNA. *Noises off-stage.*

LIAM *is at the front door, drunk. He attempts to open the door but has lost the key. Eventually, he finds the key, opens the door and falls into the hallway.*

LIAM. He's got the whole world in his hands etc.

Falling, laughing and staggering; he bursts into the sitting room.

LIAM. Habemus Papem! Boys and girls – it's the Pope! the Pope! the fucking Pope! Gone. They're all gone to bed, the shites. Ye think they would have waited up. For a first-hand account. Of the Holy Father . . . and the young people (*Sings.*) He's got the whole world in his hands, she's got the whole world, in his hands, he's got the whole world in his hands.

People emerge from their beds.

LIAM. Young people of Ireland . . . I . . . love . . . you. (*Collapses.*)

AIDAN, MRS KEVITT, NUALA *and* UNA *rush downstairs.*

AIDAN. Liam, Liam. For Christ sake Liam.

NUALA. What's up with him?

UNA. He's pissed . . . again. That lad is taking a dangerous liking to the bottle.

MRS KEVITT (*exploding at the door*). Sacred heart of Jesus, has there been an accident. Liam . . . Liam, pet. Is he dead? Liam. I knew this would happen. I said it. I said it. He'll be the death of me.

UNA. Ah he's just drunk.

AIDAN. Una.

UNA. What? He is isn't he?

MRS KEVITT. He'll be the death of me, that child. He's turning out like his father. Drunk, and him supposed to be in Galway seeing the Holy Father.

LIAM *is recovering. He starts to sing.*

AIDAN. Liam, wake up.

NUALA. I'll put on some coffee.

LIAM (*sings*). He's got the whole world in his hands . . .

MRS KEVITT. Liam. Where have you been.

LIAM. Oh hullo Mother. Hullo Una. Aidan. I've been to Galway to see the Holy Father. And have me beads blessed. Ah ha.

MRS KEVITT. You're an ignorant blaspheming whelp.

UNA. Easy mother.

MRS KEVITT. Where is Father Simeon . . . ?

LIAM. He went away.

AIDAN. What?

LIAM. He went away; disappeared. I got back on a bus. I don't know where Father Cinnamon is.

MRS KEVITT. You left this house with my relation, you ought to have come back with him. Where did you get drunk anyhow?

LIAM. There was more than me had drink. Ha ha. Why do ya think everyone was so excited? In Galway. Did ya see me on the television. I was carried out, be the ambulance men. It was just like a rock concert.

NUALA (*comes back in with some coffee*). Here Liam, drink this.

LIAM. What's this.

NUALA. Coffee.

LIAM. I don't want any of your coffee. (*Spills it roughly.*)

MRS KEVITT *is in tears.*

LIAM (*to* NUALA). Ye can't cook you can't have babies, you couldn't even pass the leaving. How the fuck do you expect me to drink your coffee?

AIDAN. Liam, shut your mouth.

UNA. Get him to bed Aidan.

AIDAN. I am I am, gimme a chance.

LIAM. Ye wouldn't have a drink in the house, be any chance?

MRS KEVITT. Oh it had to come to this. I'm not surprised.

LIAM. Ah shut up. You're always whinging.

AIDAN. Liam. You're not to talk to your mother like that. OK. I'll not warn you again.

LIAM (rises and becomes cantankerous, even dangerous). What the fuck are you on about! You say damn worse yourself: just because everyone is here looking on, we should keep our mouths shut.

MRS KEVITT. You've been to Mass with the Holy Father. It's not very nice for you to be cursing . . . in front of . . .

LIAM. Fuck the . . . in front of who? In front of Nuala? Ye don't want me to let down the family in front of Nuala? It was you said she couldn't cook; that she must have been dragged up . . . not reared.

UNA. That's enough Liam.

LIAM. It was you said she never washed her hair.

UNA. That's enough Liam.

LIAM. It was you said she never flushes the toilet!

UNA. That's enough Liam.

LIAM. And Mammy says I shouldn't leave money lying around this house.

MRS KEVITT. Ye bloody little guttersnipe ye . . . (Goes for him.)

Enter FATHER SIMEON (To them.) ANGELO (To us.)

ANGELO. Hello, hello, hello.

AIDAN. Ah. Father Simeon. We didn't expect you back.

ANGELO. I got lost. In Galway. Yes. Lost our young friend. Ah, I see he arrived back safely, thank God. I was very worried. Well, I suppose he's been telling you all about the very beautiful experience we all had in Galway.

LIAM. Yis are all full of shite about the Holy Father. The fact of the matter is ye can't stand the sight of one another. I'm going to bed . . .

MRS KEVITT *sits and weeps.*

AIDAN's *head twitches as if he could kill.*

ANGELO *breaks into a false laugh.*

ANGELO. Ha ha ha ha. Ah yes, young people; they're so . . . expressive.

AIDAN. Sit down Father. Would you like some tea?

NUALA (*to* MRS KEVITT). Maybe, Mother, you'd like a sandwich or something?

MRS KEVITT. No thank you very much Nuala.

AIDAN. Well I'm having a drink. (*Fetches a bottle.*) Will you take a glass Father?

ANGELO. Eh . . . (*Looking at* MRS KEVITT.) No thank you.

MRS KEVITT. I'll have a small drop Aidan. Just to settle my head.

ANGELO. Eh . . . perhaps I will have just the tiniest drop Aidan.

MRS KEVITT. We've had a bit of an upset. Father.

ANGELO. Oh?

MRS KEVITT. Apparently little Liam, when he got lost from you was very worried, in the big crowd and all, and, not having anything to eat. He was very upset, poor child. So Aidan there gave him a drink to settle him, but, ha ha, I'm afraid it went to his head. Poor Creature.

ANGELO. Oh quite. Yes. Yes. Well he'll sleep now.

MRS KEVITT. Sure they think they're grown up Father. But sure they're not. It's the youthful energy.

ANGELO. Quite.

MRS KEVITT. I don't think he'll really settle now until he gets home tomorrow. I'll look after him tomorrow – when I get him home.

NUALA (*with a tray*). Would you like a sandwich Mrs Kevitt, Mother?

MRS KEVITT. No thank you dear; I don't eat anything at night.

NUALA *offers sandwiches to* AIDAN *who refuses them. She sits with the tray and begins eating. She eats steadily then more compulsively until she has turned the action into a grotesque ritual.*

While she is eating the following takes place.

ANGELO. A pity about the rain today in Knock. I thought that must have spoiled things a little on the invalids. Of course there can never be time for everything.

AIDAN. That's enough Nuala. Stop it.

ANGELO. No indeed. Never enough time for everything. If the poor man had time enough for everything he'd be exhausted.

AIDAN. Nuala.

ANGELO. And then on the other hand he seems to have time for everyone. Especially the children.

MRS KEVITT. Ah yes Father, the children. I thought he was wonderful today with the children. And the way he spoke. My goodness.

AIDAN. Nuala I said that's enough. You're upsetting me.

ANGELO. Well of course if we haven't time for the children then who do we have time for.

MRS KEVITT. Just what I'm always saying Father.

AIDAN. Nuala. Stop it.

MRS KEVITT. Suffer little children. Isn't that what it says?

ANGELO. And come unto me.

AIDAN. Nuala.

NUALA *has become streaked with food on her face, mouth etc. She breaks.*

NUALA. I'm sick father, I'm sick, I'm about just up to here sick of it. Good night everybody. (*She exits in tears.*)

Pause.

ANGELO. Yes. Yes. It was a pity about the invalids alright.

MRS KEVITT (*sinks to her knees and begins*). The angel of the Lord declared unto Mary . . .

ANGELO *kneels with her. Both recite.* AIDAN *stands.*

AIDAN. It was Liam. It was Liam. Liam. The little sparrowfart. The little bastard. (*He repeats this three times then exits suddenly.*)

The Angelus is concluded.

ANGELO *stands up.*

MRS KEVITT (*kisses* ANGELO's *hand, whispers*). Thank you. (*She exits.*)

UNA. So that was the end of it?

ANGELO. That was the Pope's visit to Ireland. Everybody on the streets cheering, and crying, and watching the television. But all the time, inside the houses, the bickering and fighting went on and on. Just like any other night.

UNA. Don't lecture me on the subject.

ANGELO. And you think that the woman can do no wrong?

UNA. I didn't say that.

ANGELO. No. But you think that. You think that between the pair of hens, your unfortunate brother was pecked to death?

UNA. Just like that. What are you saying?

ANGELO. He came back. To me. Here. He was livid. You could see it in his eyes – he was gone off the head.

Enter a demented AIDAN.

AIDAN. Father, I want to talk to you.

ANGELO. You do?

AIDAN. I do.

ANGELO. About?

AIDAN. Her.

ANGELO. Your mother?

AIDAN. My wife.

ANGELO. Your wife?

AIDAN. Yes. My wife.

ANGELO. Good.

AIDAN. What do you mean, good . . . ?

ANGELO. It's about time you talked to someone. I've been

thinking about what you said two nights ago. And if you think the way you do, then you ought to do something about it.

AIDAN. I should?

ANGELO. Yes, you should.

AIDAN. She's sick.

ANGELO. I know. You told me that last night.

AIDAN. But she's more than sick.

ANGELO. If she's sick then she needs a doctor.

AIDAN. She needs more than a doctor.

ANGELO. How do you mean?

AIDAN. She's possessed. That woman up there – is not – my wife. My wife would not look at me the way she does. My wife never looked at me like that. I tell you Father, she is – a witch. A witch.

ANGELO. You're crazy.

AIDAN. Prove it.

ANGELO. How?

AIDAN. Do something to her. You could do it. Pray over her or something. Exorcise her. Cure her. I want my little Nuala back.

Pause.

ANGELO. Nuala is upstairs.

AIDAN. Do you not see what she's done these three nights? Do you not feel the vibrations in the house? It's affecting everyone. Making people do strange things Father. And she hates the Pope. Hates him. She told me that.

ANGELO. Nuala is upstairs.

AIDAN. Go up to her Father. Comfort her. Ask her what the matter is. Oh she'll talk to you, because she's afraid of you. And you'll see. You'll see it in her eyes.

ANGELO. I've heard what they say. It's on the Catholic Radio every day. The one great success the Devil has scored in our time, is that people no longer believe in him. Isn't that right?

ANGELO (*leans forward, melodramatic stare*). You're not suggesting . . . ?

AIDAN. It's the one great success the Devil has scored. Isn't that right?

ANGELO. That is right.

AIDAN. You go up there now and say a wee prayer over her. You just go up there. And we'll see what happens. I say . . . we'll see . . . what happens.

Pause.

ANGELO (*to* AIDAN). What room is she in?

UNA. No.

ANGELO *looks over at* UNA.

UNA. I don't believe it. You're sick.

ANGELO. Oh I went up to her alright.

UNA. You bastard.

ANGELO (*to* AIDAN). Go into the bathroom. Have a good long bathe. You need it to relax. It'll give me time to have a little chat with her.

UNA. I don't believe you could have done that.

AIDAN *goes to the bathroom.*

UNA. You went into her bedroom?

ANGELO. In a professional capacity. A sort of counsellor.

UNA. It's psychological rape.

ANGELO. A sort of surgery . . . psychologically speaking. Yes.

UNA. No. No you couldn't.

ANGELO. I did.

UNA. She was terrified of you.

ANGELO. Just like you are. But you want the whole story, don't you? You want to take everything out of the cupboard and look at it. No more pretending for Una. No. Everything was not hunky dory in the past was it. So you want to know. And I'm here to show you. You want to know. You will.

UNA. Who are you?

Ring at the door.

ANGELO. Well I'm certainly not Father Simeon. Because I do believe that's him at the door. Shouldn't you answer it?

Ring at the door. ANGELO *exits.*

Another ring at the door and UNA *answers it. A priest is there.*

UNA *is distraught.*

PRIEST. Are you Una Kevitt?

UNA. Father, please come in.

PRIEST. We spoke on the phone? You're distressed, child?

UNA. Thank you for coming Father. I'll be alright now.

PRIEST. You said it was urgent. Actually, I rarely leave the cloister. But then you and I are related, yes?

UNA. My father, I believe was your cousin.

PRIEST. Ah yes. Poor Donal. Poor Donal. I think he was a bit of a black sheep. How is your mother?

UNA. Father, I must ask you something terribly important.

PRIEST. Yes?

UNA. We've had a death in the family. My mother is still very upset about it.

PRIEST. Yes, Lord bless us, and so young. Tragic. Tragic.

UNA. It wasn't just an accident Father. It was suicide.

PRIEST. God is merciful.

UNA. You were never in this house before?

PRIEST. I told you over the phone. Never. In fact I never even met poor Donal's wife.

UNA. The tragedy happened, on the morning of the Pope's departure.

PRIEST. Ah Lord bless us. Yes. It was a pity I thought about the bad weather, at Knock. But, but, excuse me . . . your poor mother, how did she cope with such a tragedy?

As UNA *speaks,* ANGELO *comes down the stairs.*

UNA. There's something else happened that weekend. In this house. Something very curious. And I think you should know about it.

UNA *now stares at* ANGELO *who is in the doorway.*

PRIEST. Well go on. Go on child. You can tell me.

ANGELO. He won't believe you.

UNA *is speechless.*

PRIEST. What's the matter child?

ANGELO *laughs and sits down between them.*

UNA. Father.

PRIEST. Yes?

UNA. There's only you and me . . . in the house . . . now.

PRIEST. Yes. If you say so. I don't know. Now tell me what happened.

As ANGELO *scrutinizes the* PRIEST, UNA *breaks down.*

UNA. I'm sorry Father . . . I just . . . need help.

PRIEST. There there . . . you'll be alright.

ANGELO. I don't believe it. I don't believe it. Look at him.

UNA (*pulls herself together*). Excuse me. Now. Would you like a cup of tea Father?

ANGELO. 'Would you like a cup of tea Father?' – I just don't believe it.

UNA. What do you not believe?

PRIEST. Pardon?

ANGELO. I just don't believe this fella is real. I mean look at him. Barry bloody Fitzgerald.

UNA. He's been in a monastery.

PRIEST. Pardon?

UNA. I'm saying Father, you're in the monastery.

PRIEST. Yes. Yes. All my life really. The Order of the Two Crosses.

UNA. The Order of the what?

ANGELO. God . . . he's not even a Jesuit.

PRIEST. Two Crosses. Yes. Either side of Our Blessed Saviour on

Calvary. You see Saint Augustine said – Do not despair, for one thief was saved. Do not hope, for one was lost.

UNA. Yes. I see.

ANGELO. You see damn all. You don't know what that means no more than he does.

ANGELO *may rise and move freely about the space now.*

UNA. Are you jealous?

PRIEST. Pardon?

UNA. Tell us. Tell us what that means. What Saint Augustine said.

Pause.

PRIEST. Do you know I've never been quite sure. I'm just a simple priest, child.

ANGELO. Oh not this drivel again.

PRIEST. Aye. I was never very good at the books Una. I just said me prayers.

ANGELO. Get him out.

UNA. Why?

PRIEST. Eh?

ANGELO. Just get him out.

UNA. Why?

PRIEST. Why do I pray? Ah sure we all pray.

ANGELO. Dandruff. Shiny elbows. And a nose as red as a beetroot.

UNA. I think he's nice.

PRIEST. What?

UNA. The Pope. I think he's nice.

PRIEST. Ah yes. He's nice alright.

ANGELO. He's got darning in his underwear. Can you believe that? It's the nuns do it for them.

UNA. How do you know?

ANGELO. I can see through his clothes. And yours.

PRIEST (*his puzzlement slowly turning to annoyance*). How do I know what Una?

UNA. Nothing.

PRIEST. You're very upset child. You're distracted.

ANGELO. Get rid of him.

PRIEST. Are you feeling alright?

ANGELO. Get rid of him.

ANGELO *disappears into the kitchen, where he kicks up a rumpus with cutlery, to distract* UNA.

UNA. If I could try and talk about it Father. You see, the morning after the Pope's visit, actually, it was the last day . . . he was leaving that day . . . yes. Well . . . we had this terrible tragedy. Now I knew that Aidan and Nuala were having difficulties, in the marriage. Though Nuala, and himself kept things fairly much to themselves. Anyway, I had my suspicions. You see Aidan was normal. He might have hit her once or twice. But other than that . . . He even wanted to be a priest at one stage.

PRIEST. Did you talk to his wife? Woman to woman.

UNA (*very confused*). Yes. No. That is, she went away. It was in the bathroom Father. That morning. The whole body was blue . . . like it was lying there for ages . . . and the lungs all inflated . . . like the chest was like a balloon floating on the water.

During this last speech, ANGELO *makes a fleeting appearance from the kitchen in full pontificals gesturing like the Pope, but smoking a cigar.* UNA *cracks into hysteria, laughing and crying at the same time.*

ANGELO *returns to the kitchen. A long pause in which* UNA *recovers. Meanwhile, the* PRIEST *is patient with what he perceives as a young woman in shock.*

PRIEST. You're not on tablets, child, are you?

UNA. No Father.

PRIEST. Honest?

UNA. Honest. No.

PRIEST. Mmmm. That itself. I mean . . . sometimes . . . when someone has an upset . . . they . . . sometimes go for these remedies.

ANGELO (*back to normal dress, whispers from the kitchen door*). You didn't tell him that yis found the body stark naked, except for a pair of black panties and a suspender belt. Oh, the things people get up to in the privacy of their own bathrooms.

UNA *almost laughs again.*

PRIEST (*looks over his shoulder suspiciously*). You haven't left a kettle on or anything?

UNA. No. Why?

PRIEST. Well it's just you keep looking over my shoulder. Towards the kitchen. As if there was something in there. Or someone. There is no one in there, is there?

UNA. No.

ANGELO (*pokes his head out of the kitchen door*). Oh ye can't cod a cod that was codded before.

PRIEST. Ye can't cod a cod that was codded before y'know.

ANGELO *slips from the kitchen to the hall and now speaks to* UNA *from the hall door to the sitting room. The* PRIEST *rises and pokes his nose into the kitchen.*

ANGELO. Get rid of him. And I'll tell you everything.

UNA. Everything?

ANGELO. Everything. If you really want to know. Just get rid of Sagart Aroon here.

PRIEST (*wanders about inspecting the kitchen, hall and sitting room*). Ah yes, it was a lovely home. Lovely. How long were they married?

UNA. Five years.

PRIEST. Five years. Five years. No children. Ah well. It's sad though. You know, it's a funny thing, funny thing; but when you go into houses nowadays, you don't seem to see as much sign of prayer as you used to. Mmmm? No Sacred Heart Picture. Or Our Blessed Mother. St Martin de Porres, he was very popular. St Brigid. Blessed Oliver Plunkeet. St Patrick. St Joseph.

ANGELO. He's not going to go through the lot of them is he?

UNA. Shut up.

PRIEST (*astonished*). I beg your pardon?

UNA. I'm sorry. I'm sorry Father. I'm not feeling very well.

PRIEST. No. Ah you've been through a lot, poor creature.

UNA. I shouldn't have brought you out.

PRIEST. No. Probably not. But I am some sort of a relative; and I am a priest; and sure something in you thought I might help. Might understand. You reached out, unknown to yourself. (*He places his hands on her shoulders, and* ANGELO *gestures violin music on the stairs.*) Out of that terrible darkness, wanting to touch some Light . . . some spark of hope. From this valley of tears that you are in, you reached out. Your phone call itself, was a prayer. A cry from the dark mountain of Calvary.

ANGELO. Will ye make up your mind, is it a mountain or a valley? No wonder she doesn't know where she is.

PRIEST. You reached out . . . like the thief on the cross; and you mustn't despair.

UNA. Every word you say is true Father. And I'm really grateful for you coming around. Really.

PRIEST. I'll pray for you. Will you be alright now; on your own?

UNA. Oh I will Father.

PRIEST. And you're not on tablets?

UNA. No.

PRIEST. No. Good. Right then. Good night. And remember me to your mother. Good night.

UNA. Good night Father.

ANGELO. Safe home Father. God bless. Mind the dustbin.

PRIEST *exits, and we hear a crash off-stage.*

ANGELO. Thick.

ANGELO *returns and sits on the sofa.*

UNA *joins him. She is a little crazed, but determined.* ANGELO *winks at her.*

ANGELO. Pity about the weather. In Knock.

UNA. OK.

ANGELO. OK.

UNA. OK.

ANGELO. OK . . . settle.

UNA. OK.

ANGELO. I'll tell you everything.

UNA. OK.

ANGELO. I'm sort of like, eh, in fact, out of this world.

UNA. I could have said that from the beginning.

ANGELO. Not mortal.

UNA. Not human.

ANGELO. Hold on now. Just hold on. I had my reasons.

UNA. For imposing yourself on my family.

ANGELO. I was sent for. I'm only doing my job . . . I work
y'know . . . I work for . . . the top management.

UNA. What?

ANGELO. Top Management.

UNA. The Pope?

ANGELO. Hmm. Not at all. The Vatican, is what we call . . .
middle management.

UNA (*Pause*). Are you telling me that you work for . . .

ANGELO. Yes.

Pause.

UNA. D'you want a drink?

ANGELO. Love one.

UNA (*pours into two tumblers*). I need a drink.

ANGELO (*lights a cigar*). Mind if I?

UNA. Not at all. They're not good for you though. Here.

ANGELO. Thanks. You see, Aidan was an idiot. A cretin.
Thought his wife was a witch. Phew. Did you ever hear
anything as ridiculous. He beat her. He did. He may have
interfered with children.

UNA. You're a liar. Wherever you came from, you certainly didn't

come down from 'top management' as you call it; in fact I
think it's more likely that you came out of the fucking
basement.

ANGELO. Now don't take that tone. And don't curse in my
presence.

UNA. I'll curse where I like and when I like.

ANGELO. So you don't believe me.

UNA. No I don't believe you.

ANGELO. Will I tell you a joke?

UNA. I beg your pardon . . . ?

ANGELO. A joke. A joke. Will I tell you a funny story?

UNA. You want to tell me a joke. I'm standing here in a haunted
house, talking to who might be the Devil and he wants to tell
me a joke.

ANGELO. So when this fella gets to become Pope he's allowed to
ask three questions. And he gets answered. From upstairs.
Direct, see? So what does he ask?

UNA. I dunno what he asks.

ANGELO. He asks will there be women priests? And the boss
says, 'not in your lifetime, Holy Father.' And then he asks
another question. Will there be married priests? And the boss
answers him; 'Not in your lifetime, Holy Father.' And then –
what does he ask? What does he ask? – Will there be another
Polish Pope? And the boss smiled at him and said; 'Not in my
lifetime, Holy Father.'

Pause.

UNA. Are yous Protestants?

ANGELO. You're so narrow minded.

UNA. I'm asking you a bloody question.

ANGELO. Don't curse.

UNA. I'm not cursing.

ANGELO. It's bad language.

UNA. So bloody what. There's no one here only me. (*She takes
another drink.*)

ANGELO. Oh you're wrong. You're wrong there. I'm the only one you might be able to see – but we're all here, y'know.

UNA. What did you do to Nuala?

ANGELO. I gave her a fright.

A scream from NUALA *in bed.*

ANGELO. She screamed.

UNA. I'll bet.

ANGELO *takes the poker from the fire and hops up on a chair. He strikes an angelic pose.*

ANGELO. I was like this. On the pedestal beside the bed. (*He grins.*)

NUALA *screams again.*

UNA. What are you doing with that poker?

ANGELO. I'm not very used to this stuff. I'm told this is the way you do it in Europe. You kind of appear suddenly, with a lance or something in your hand. It gives you authority. That's the idea.

UNA. But that's a poker.

ANGELO. I know it's a poker. OK. So it's a poker. I'm only giving you the general gist. As a matter of fact I wasn't dressed like this at all.

UNA. No?

ANGELO. No.

UNA. So what were you wearing? Ostrich feathers?

ANGELO. Do you mind if I finish . . . ? Do you mind if I finish my story?

UNA. What were you wearing? I'm only asking.

ANGELO (*gets down from the chair and discards the poker, in a huff*). Fine. Fine. Fine. I'm going. You wanted to know what happened. I'm telling you what happened . . . and then you won't let me speak. I knew I shouldn't have taken this job.

UNA. Hey Father.

ANGELO. I'll end up debilitated.

UNA. Father Simeon.

ANGELO. I'm not your father. I'm not Father Simeon. I'm something entirely different.

UNA (*approaches*). What's your name?

ANGELO. Angelo.

UNA. Angelo.

ANGELO. Angelo.

UNA. Angelo.

ANGELO. Angelo. It's Italian. Little Angelo. Little Angelo.

UNA. You're an Italian Angel?

ANGELO *breaks down and sobs, very childishly.*

UNA. Are you upset?

He nods. His nose runs. She offers him a hanky which he takes and uses.

ANGELO. There's no point. You wouldn't believe it.

UNA. Try me.

ANGELO. No.

UNA. Angelo.

His upset increases on hearing his name.

UNA. Look, tell me what's wrong.

ANGELO. I'm . . . very depressed. (*Blubbers.*) I've made a mess of everything. And if I told you you wouldn't believe me.

UNA. I would.

ANGELO. You wouldn't.

UNA. I would.

ANGELO. You wouldn't (*Turns.*) would you?

UNA *nods.* ANGELO *gathers himself together.*

ANGELO. You see, we take a long term view of everything. Well, we've been having problems with middle management for a while. In or around a thousand years. Well, about a hundred years ago, things were getting real bad. They were getting out of control. Are you listening?

UNA. I'm listening.

ANGELO. Started bringing all their own fancy ideas – like infallibility. That was a bit cheeky. Well. It was decided to infiltrate.

UNA. Infiltrate?

ANGELO. You won't believe me.

UNA. I will. Now go on, infiltrate what?

ANGELO. Infiltrate down here. It was a big operation. I was sent down as a baby, to become Pope, and clean up the plant. Well it was very difficult trying to become Pope. By the time I got there I was too old to do any of the things I was supposed to.

UNA. Pope John the twenty-third?

ANGELO (*cheerful*). That's right.

UNA. No I don't believe you.

ANGELO (*almost recovered*). I lost a bit of weight since then.

UNA. No sorry.

ANGELO. I was too slow. I botched. When I got back upstairs.

UNA. I'm sorry – no – you can't cod a cod that was codded before. (*She goes for more drink,* ANGELO *follows her.*)

ANGELO. I like the Italians. They don't rush. I didn't rush. They play all the time, even when they work. These guys in the Vatican now, they work too hard. They make everyone nervous. It's not nice to be nervous. Who likes to be nervous.

UNA. Are you nervous?

ANGELO. I'm nervous. I'm nervous. I'm nervous. I'm nervous. Can you imagine what it's like to be Pope?

UNA. No.

ANGELO. It's nice. It was a big job, y'know? I botched it up. Now I only get little jobs.

UNA. Why do you say you botched it?

ANGELO. Don't you see. It took me eighty years. I was supposed to do a thousand things. But I couldn't. If I had lived on till I was a hundred and twenty people might have got suspicious. I left it too late. I didn't realize that can be a danger for humans. Leaving things, until it's too late.

UNA. He was a good man – John the twenty-third.

ANGELO. When the word came that I was to return immediately, I wrote a little letter, to everybody. Peace on Earth. A letter to the whole world. Not just to Catholics, or Christians. But to Buddists and Hindus, and Atheists, and everybody – the whole world – to all people. That was the last thing I did. *Pacem in terris*. It was silly I suppose. It's out of print now.

Pause.

UNA. Angelo.

ANGELO. Mmm?

UNA. I believe you. Or maybe I believe in you.

ANGELO *returns the hanky.*

UNA. No, keep it. Have another drink.

UNA *goes to fill the glasses, thus turning her back to* ANGELO. *He sits on the couch, looks uneasily at the hanky in his hand then throws his eyes to heaven, and wipes the sweat off his brow.*

ANGELO. What about you?

UNA. Nothing to tell.

ANGELO. Lies.

UNA. Truth.

ANGELO. Lies. I can see these things. Like I can see your black panties.

UNA. Father Simeon.

ANGELO. I'm not Father. Why do you call me Father when you're embarrassed . . . ?

UNA. It sounds better.

ANGELO. But it's not true. Why not call me Your Holiness.

UNA. Look, hold on a second. I don't know if I can accept all this.

ANGELO. All what?

He has regained his confidence. She her unease.

UNA. You, being who you say you are. It's outrageous.

ANGELO. You're not married, are you?

UNA. No.

ANGELO. Aidan married though. Eventually. When he decided he couldn't be a priest. He settled for second best. That's what they think, y'know. That marriage is second best.

UNA. How could you be who you say you are if you're being so unfair to Aidan?

ANGELO. Angels have been known to fall before. But that's not the case with me. I'm just being truthful. You're just too concerned with Aidan. Why are you not married?

UNA. None of your business.

ANGELO. Why are you living at home with your mother, sitting in the house night after night, smoking, withering away, when you could be alive, out in the world?

UNA. I don't like going out.

ANGELO. You wear black panties. Of course you'd like to live.

UNA. I have a very full life.

ANGELO. Full – full – full? Full of yellow little holy pictures, and dusty statues in your bedroom, that you pray to and beg for the grace to endure your little life of solitude. How do I know that, eh, if I'm not who I say I am. Eh?

UNA. Anyone could know that. Anyone could guess that about . . .

ANGELO. About? About, about what? Say it. About a woman in her thirties, educated, beautiful, whose dreams about what life might be like are almost forgotten memories.

UNA. I'm going out with Stephen O'Rourke. As a matter of fact we plan to get married this year.

ANGELO. Oh. (Pause.) And who is Stephen O'Rourke?

UNA. He's in the bank.

ANGELO. A banker. A banker. You're going to marry a banker. How's your back?

UNA. It's not so bad – How did you know about my back?

ANGELO. So you're going to marry Stephen O'Rourke, the banker from Bally Drum Inver. The pity of it.

UNA. Look, you've no right to speak to me like this; Stephen is . . . a good . . .

ANGELO. A good catch – your mother might say. What with a farm of land, and a bank job, sure you're on the pig's back.

UNA. How did you know about my back?

ANGELO. The whole world knows about your back. Why did you put off the wedding with Mr O . . . twice in the past three years . . . ?

UNA. Because . . . there were financial reasons.

ANGELO. Yeah? Financial reasons. Financial reasons. A little bungalow. Is that the reason?

UNA. Yes.

ANGELO. Bullshit. You just can't stand the thought of going to bed with him, that's all. He makes your skin crawl. The thought of that white arsed passionless old horse, with barely a hair left on his head, wheezing away on top of you like a mechanical pump, makes your skin crawl.

UNA. No.

ANGELO. Why?

UNA. No.

ANGELO. Because he doesn't love you, nor you don't love him.

UNA. Stephen adores me – he worships me – he'd do anything for me.

ANGELO. He wouldn't put the land in a joint account for you though, would he . . . ?

UNA. The land is his mother's; he can't just dispose of it like that.

ANGELO. And you're walking on dangerous ground my lady, the day you plant your little bungalow on her territory.

Pause.

UNA. You are evil.

ANGELO. No. Just showing you what you're afraid to look at yourself. Sometimes, when people are afraid of the truth, they call it evil – to protect themselves.

UNA. I'm not protecting myself.

ANGELO. Does he take you out? Does he?

UNA. Yes.

ANGELO. Where? Where?

UNA. Places. Plenty of places.

ANGELO. To the rugby club? To the bankers' dinner dance? To visit his mother? Where?

UNA. We came to Dublin last year. (*Breaks down.*) To the horse show.

ANGELO. To the horse show. And how did he behave, at the horse show?

UNA. Well. Very well.

ANGELO. Yeah? Una, your fiancé would feel the flank of a prize Charolais in public, quicker than he'd feel you. You need someone to show he loves you. To understand how you feel – to be tender – and affectionate – you need to feel that the whole world is looking on and thinking; there goes a woman who is loved – and you need someone who will love you with all the razzamatazz of his body. Not some pious wimp who . . . adores you.

UNA. I don't know where you came from, but life is not like that. Neither Stephen nor I are teenagers.

ANGELO. Oh but you're so wrong. Life is like that. Life can be like that if you make it.

UNA. Stop it.

ANGELO. Go on, bury yourself in your new bungalow, and your teaching, and, and, breed turkeys or something, but nothing, nothing will be a compensation for being tethered to a man who is not in love with you.

UNA. No.

ANGELO. Yes. And you think you can carry on for thirty years polishing his television. Hoovering the carpet on some drawing room that's never lived in? Without wanting more?

UNA. Yes.

ANGELO. His mother will probably give you three delft ducks as a wedding present, and you'll put them on the mantelpiece, and watch them, as you wither, and they'll still look back at you, even when you've turned into a dry brittle stick.

UNA. Stop it. Stop it.

ANGELO. Who was it? Who was it? Who was it Una? (UNA *is in tears now.*) Who frightened you when you were little. Your father? Aidan? Was it Aidan used to touch you? Who is shaping you into the image of this dry juiceless stick? Because it wasn't God. And it wasn't me. And it wasn't yourself.

UNA *is in bits.*

ANGELO. I suppose it doesn't matter.

UNA. I studied . . . so . . . hard . . . all the time . . . I dreamed . . . I'd escape . . . Aidan never touched me . . . no . . . not like that . . . but he teased me . . . he knew he was Daddy's little pet. He knew he could throw his weight around. He said I was . . . stupid . . . and he said stupid girls grew moustaches. One day . . . he caught me . . . in the bathroom . . . looking for hairs . . . and he just laughed . . . he laughed . . . and laughed . . . and laughed.

(*Enraged.*) I'm not stupid . . . I'm not I'm not I'm not stupid. (*Pause. The rage goes.*) Oh God . . . why am I so depressed . . .

ANGELO. Now you're making sense.

UNA. No I'm not. I'm a woman . . . I need . . . someone . . . to look after.

ANGELO. You need someone to love you.

UNA. Whatever. One way or another. But I'll tell you, the glamour of the city wears off when you're in a flat for ten years and still going to night clubs. In the hope that out of all the shit someone will come for you. I did that. Queuing outside the same toilet, ten years after. And no one came for me. It's not fair.

ANGELO. So you sank back into the same world you were so desperate to leave.

UNA. It's not fair.

ANGELO. And now all the neighbours wonder 'when will Una be giving us the big day.'

UNA. 'She must be hard to please.'

ANGELO. 'She's no chicken now.'

UNA. And so I take what I get . . . because I have no choice.

ANGELO. More fool you. You have a bad back. You dress like a nun. You're going to enter what can only be described as a legal arrangement with a man you have no feeling for – for the rest of your life?

He'll kill you of course. You know that. Or else you'll have to kill him.

UNA. I have no choice.

ANGELO. You have.

UNA. How?

ANGELO. You could be so passionate.

UNA. With the right person. With a real man. I could I could . . . I could . . .

ANGELO. Open the floodgates . . . burst. Your body is like a dry land. It needs rain. Monsoons. It needs to be washed back to life.

UNA. What am I saying? What are you saying?

ANGELO. Come away with me.

UNA. What?

ANGELO. Come away with me – leave now – we'll get a ticket to America – South America – write to your mother – write to Stephen O'Rourke – write to your school principal – tell them to go fuck themselves.

UNA. But you're an angel. God will want you back.

ANGELO. I don't want to go back. We could go to Rio de Janeiro.

UNA. I could teach English as a foreign language.

ANGELO. I could work in a circus.

UNA. What about Aidan?

ANGELO. Forget Aidan. Who cares about him? Look, you came to this house to find out something for yourself. It's not Aidan you're really interested in. You came to find something you were always afraid of.

UNA. Yes. Yes. Ohhh yes.

ANGELO. What are you smiling at?

UNA. I was just thinking . . . when I was little . . . I used to be afraid of the Pooka Man. But when I was in Dublin, with a one-bar heater and a smelly carpet . . . I used to dream of someone coming for me. Bursting the door down. I used to listen to voices of people laughing in the flats below me, and I'd say – 'I wish some pooka man would come and get me.'

ANGELO. The Pooka Man.

UNA. The Pooka Man.

They kiss.

UNA. It would be a bit like marrying the Devil though.

ANGELO. It could be fairly enjoyable alright.

They kiss again.

UNA. No.

ANGELO. No?

UNA. No. I won't.

ANGELO. You won't?

UNA. I can't.

ANGELO. You can't?

UNA. I won't.

ANGELO. You won't?

UNA. Stop.

ANGELO. Stop what?

UNA. I'm going mad.

ANGELO. You're going mad.

UNA. I'm going to fall over the edge.

ANGELO. You're going to fall over the edge?

UNA (*screams*). Please for God's sake stop.

(*Pause.*)

My mother.

Enter MRS KEVITT.

UNA. And Liam.

Enter LIAM.

UNA. I couldn't do it to them.

ANGELO *and* UNA *now find themselves on the edge of activities. They butt into the conversation when required.*

MRS KEVITT. U-na. U-na . . . Is that you?

LIAM. No . . . it's me.

MRS KEVITT. What's keeping Una. She was to drive me to the shops. She said she'd be back by now.

LIAM. She phoned.

MRS KEVITT. Oh, is she bringing Stephen round? Well that's good. I can put on the dinner then so, Stephen adores stuffed hearts.

LIAM. She won't be round with Stephen.

MRS KEVITT. What?

LIAM. I said she won't be round with Stephen. (*Aside.*) God, why does it have to be me. She's coming round with that cousin of dads; the monk.

MRS KEVITT. Father Simeon?

ANGELO. Actually, eh, I'm not really Father Simeon.

UNA. No Angelo. Leave that.

ANGELO. I have to tell her I'm not Father Simeon.

UNA. I don't think she could swallow that; Just tell her what we're doing.

ANGELO. Mrs Kevitt, your daughter and I are going to South America. Forsaking chastity, poverty and obedience, I intend having a passionate affair with your lovely child.

MRS KEVITT *shrieks.*

ANGELO. And by my love, devotion, and the prowesss of my razzamatazz to keep her . . . in good health.

MRS KEVITT. Jesus Mary and Joseph, Una, what's he talking about?

UNA. It's true mother. Angelo and I are going to Rio de Janeiro. Angelo has an offer from a circus.

MRS KEVITT. Angelo. Angelo. (*Smacks* UNA.) You slut. Hussy. Bitch. (*Retreating to the door.*) I always knew it. Defiance. That's what it is. I always knew it. I seen it in you from the start. From the day I caught you with the lipstick. Whore. (*Exit.*)

LIAM. Of course, it's the women are to blame. Luring a poor innocent monk to Rio de Janeiro.

UNA. Angelo is not a monk. He's an angel.

LIAM. Ah I see . . . he's . . . an angel. He's not a monk he's an angel. (*Retreating to the door.*) And you're probably not a teacher . . . no . . . I suppose . . . you're his little squirrel. Well mind your Angel doesn't fly away when he gets his nuts. Because when she's gone (*Points after* MRS KEVITT.) and this house is mine, and you come back here a second time with your tail between your legs, it's me you'll be looking to, for a key to the door. Remember that. (*Exits.*)

AIDAN *enters, looking a bit ghostly.* UNA *is startled and moves away.* AIDAN *goes quite close to* ANGELO.

AIDAN. That's a dirty business that. Father.

ANGELO. What?

AIDAN. You and me sister. You and me sister, doing the bold thing in Brazil. A dirty business.

ANGELO. Well actually Aidan, ahem, you see, there is something you ought to know.

AIDAN. Oh I know alright. I know you're not be blame. A man like you, pure as the driven snow. She's a slut Father. I know she's me own flesh and blood, and I love her, but she's a slut. Excuse me language Father, but whore is too good a word for her.

ANGELO. No, it's not quite like that, I'm afraid. You see . . . I'm . . . I'm . . . I'mm . . . (*Sighs and looks over towards* UNA.)

AIDAN. A slut father. That's the way they work. I told you that about Nuala. They're all the same. All after the one thing. They want to drag you down, and tie you down.

ANGELO. I'm sorry Aidan, but you're talking horse shite. You're a sick twisted idiot . . .

AIDAN. Yes Father that's right. All that's very fine talk Father, and I agree with every word you say. Every word. But I'm just saying to you, that Nuala, Una and the rest of them; they're not to be trusted. Never. (*Exits.*)

UNA. I thought he was dead.

ANGELO. Yeah, I'd say he's been dead for years.

UNA. But I thought he was dead, Angelo. Dead.

ANGELO. Dead. Yes. He's dead. He's been dead since he was twenty-eight. (*Moves towards her, with urgency.*) Look Una, get out of here. With or without me. Go. – Leave the country. Contact Aer Lingus, Ryanair, Sea Link, anybody; but get out.

UNA. You've tried every trick in the book to evade the truth. Now. I want . . . to know.

ANGELO. The truth can be what you make it.

UNA. I want to know what happened in this house. Now stop avoiding that, and tell – me. You promised.

ANGELO. No. You don't want to know – you want a life – a lover – a big pool of ecstasy. A good ride.

UNA. No.

ANGELO. Yes.

UNA. No.

ANGELO. Yes.

UNA. No – no – no.

Pause.

It is a show-down situation. She outstares him.

ANGELO. OK, OK, OK, OK. Sweetheart. You want to know what happened . . . ?

UNA. I really want to know what happened.

ANGELO. Right. You want to know what happened. I'll tell you what happened. You're sure you wouldn't consider Brazil.

UNA. I'm sure.

ANGELO. A couple of Brazilian nuts, is, as they say, out of the question?

UNA. Get on with it.

ANGELO. You're a fool Una. You're walking into it.

UNA. I know what I'm doing.

ANGELO. OK, OK. You're the boss in the final analysis. It's your life Una. Your one, single, precious life. You could still get out you know. (*Shouts.*) Una, you could still get out that door.

UNA (*shouts back*). I don't want to get out.

She puts her hand to her mouth, and steps back, and there is a moment of silence. From now the tone of a killer enters the POOKA MAN's *voice.*

ANGELO (*coldly*). I went into her room. I stood on the pedestal beside the bed.

NUALA *screams in the bedroom.*

ANGELO. Shhhhh.

NUALA. Father . . . what are you doing. (*Giggles.*)

ANGELO. I appeared to her in a dressing gown. She thought I was her father. That's why I had the poker. Her sweetest recollection of her father was sitting by the fire, while he sent little sparks up the chimney with the poker. (*To* NUALA.) Don't be afraid.

NUALA. I'm not.

ANGELO. I told her she was asleep, and that I knew everything about herself and Aidan.

NUALA. It's terrible Daddy. He hurts me. He beats me.

ANGELO. You want out. You want to go away.

NUALA. I do . . . next summer . . . definitely. I'm leaving. If things don't improve.

ANGELO. Things won't improve pet. But don't leave it till next year. Go soon. Go to America. To your sisters. They'll mind you.

NUALA. Daddy . . . I love you.

ANGELO (*gets down off the chair*). So I went away. Leaving you and your mother in bed. Liam in a coma from drink, Aidan in the bathroom, and Nuala content with her prayers. And the real Father Simeon back in his body.

UNA. You mean the one that was here that week, was the real one.

ANGELO. Yes.

UNA. And what about the other fella?

ANGELO. Another trick of the mind Una. A face that once passed before your eyes. A hand that once held your hand . . . a shadow. You couldn't sleep. You had a curious fantasy about Aidan; drowning in the bath. It upset you, and you decided to come downstairs for a glass of water.

UNA *grows frightened and moves to the foot of the stairs.*

UNA. No. No.

ANGELO. You stood there, looking up at the bathroom door. You could see from the light under the door that there was someone in there; and yet no sound. Could it possibly be that your brother was lying in there? (*Moves up to the landing.*)

The bathroom door opens and a pale and damp AIDAN *emerges in a dressing gown.*

UNA. You died in there.

ANGELO. A death alright. But not Aidan's. There was a body found in the bath. A naked body, except for a pair of black panties and a suspender belt.

UNA. Angelo, Angelo, please help me.

ANGELO. I can't help you now Una.

AIDAN. What's up with you sis? (*Rubs his head with a towel.*)

UNA. Nothing. Do you not use the hairdryer?

AIDAN. Nope. (*Going.*) Never used a hairdryer in me life.

ANGELO. Never used a hairdryer in his life. (*Leans over the landing.*)

AIDAN. There's plenty of hot water if you want a bath Una. (*Exits to the bedroom.*)

UNA. No. No thanks.

ANGELO. Oh but you do. You do want a bath Una. You're fascinated by the thought of having a bath.

UNA. No Angelo. Please help me. Please save me.

ANGELO. You had your choices Una. And you failed.

UNA. Please Angelo. Little Angelo. Please save me. Please save me. They were wrong. They were wrong about me. I was nice. I just wanted to please people. I wanted him to like me.

ANGELO. But they never really knew you Una. You were in your own little play – acting the part.

UNA. I was afraid.

UNA *goes into the bathroom and closes the door.*

The POOKA MAN *clicks his fingers.*

Pause.

The other characters enter and watch the bathroom door.

The DOCTOR *emerges from the bathroom.*

DOCTOR. I'm very sorry Mrs Kevitt. She must have been dead since last night. (*Looks towards the kitchen.*) You haven't left a kettle on or anything?

MRS KEVITT. Oh yes, I was going to make you a cup of tea. Doctor. Aidan, plug out the kettle.

DOCTOR (*confidentially to* AIDAN *as he passes*). Eh, you are the brother?

AIDAN. Yes Doctor. But I didn't really know her that well. You know? Since I got married – living up here in Dublin – we sort of drifted apart.

DOCTOR. She wasn't on tablets, or anything?

AIDAN. No Doctor.

DOCTOR. No?

AIDAN. No Doctor.

DOCTOR. Well that's good. I mean, sometimes, in these cases . . .

MRS KEVITT. It was a terrible accident Doctor.

AIDAN. Will you have tea Doctor?

DOCTOR. No, no thanks.

AIDAN *returns to his seat.*

AIDAN. Does anyone want tea?

NUALA. No.

MRS KEVITT. No pet. I'm saying Doctor, that it was a terrible accident to happen.

DOCTOR. Mrs Kevitt, as you'll understand, I have to make a report. Now if I found that the remains was blue, and the lungs inflated, then I might say it was an accident. Or a bruise on the head. Perhaps, consistent with a knock that might have caused her to slip. But I'm afraid I didn't find that. That girl electrocuted herself.

MRS KEVITT (*asserts herself*). Doctor, we are all family here. We just came up from the country to see the Holy Father. It was a terrible accident.

AIDAN. It was. Wasn't it Doctor? It was a terrible accident.

LIAM. A terrible accident.

DOCTOR (*after surveying all of them*). The ambulance will be round in half an hour. I suggest you throw out what remains of that hairdryer.

AIDAN. Of course, Doctor.

DOCTOR. Good day to you all. And sorry again for your trouble. Don't worry. There'll be no inquest.

MRS KEVITT. Good morning Doctor.

AIDAN (*goes to the door with him*). Thanks again Doctor. And sorry for dragging you out so early. (*He slips him the money.*)

AIDAN *returns, and they continue to stare into the middle distance, but they are more paranoid now.*

MRS KEVITT. Of course the O'Rourkes will have to be at the funeral.

AIDAN. Yeah.

MRS KEVITT. I always said he was no good for her. Aidan, you'll have to deal with the undertakers.

AIDAN. Yeah.

MRS KEVITT. And you're to go to Brennans. I'll have no truck with Comerfords again. Not after the way they treated us before.

LIAM. I thought they were alright? The Comerfords.

MRS KEVITT. I don't want to discuss it Liam, thank you.

AIDAN. Should we tell the O'Rourkes . . . what happened.

MRS KEVITT. You say nothing. Nothing; it's none of their business.

LIAM. I suppose the school will want to be in on it; guard of honour and all that crack.

MRS KEVITT. Oh nothing would do her but she'd go to college. That's where the trouble started. Instead of staying at home. (*Breaks down.*) I never had a day's trouble with her up to that. Not from the day she was born.

AIDAN (*breaks down*). Jesus Mary and Joseph protect us. It's terrible.

ANGELO *motionless since he clicked his fingers, saunters down into the sitting room, observed with amazement by* NUALA. *He comes behind her and places his hand on her head. She tightens with the touch then relaxes as he caresses.*

ANGELO. You won't forget what I told you?

NUALA. I won't forget.

ANGELO. Good. Good. That's my good girl. (*He pets her and heads for the front door.*)

LIAM *and* MRS KEVITT *stare into the middle distance,* AIDAN *watches his wife suspiciously, while* NUALA *smiles to herself.*

Curtain

LOOSE ENDS ■ STUART HEPBURN

On leaving school at sixteen, Stuart Hepburn spent a long time
trying to convince himself that he was a lab technician. After six
years he admitted defeat and enrolled at the University of Stirling,
where, as well as becoming the President of the Students' Union
and sitting on the National Executive of the NUS, he graduated in
1982 in Politics and Sociology.

He spent the next three years acting, writing, directing and
driving the minibus for his own theatre company, 'Badinage'. He
wrote revues, street theatre shows and pantos. The most
successful of these were probably the 'Lord Kagan' series of
revues at the Edinburgh Festival Fringes of 1982 and 1985.
Throughout this period he supported himself and his family
through professional acting but by 1985 decided to spend more
time on writing.

His television work includes *The Macramé Man*, episodes of *Winners
and Losers* and *Taggart*, a screenplay, *Don't use the Handles*, and a
BBC Scotland documentary, *See Glasgow, See Culture*. For the stage
he wrote a revue and a Christmas show for the Tron Theatre,
Glasgow. *Loose Ends* was his first commission from the Edinburgh
Traverse; it has been recorded by both Radio 4 and BBC 2 for
transmission in 1990. He has just completed a new commissioned
work for the Traverse entitled *The Turkey that Fought Back*.

Characters

SPUD VALENTINE, a street trader from Glasgow
CALLUM SHAPIRO, young runaway from Skye

Loose Ends was first staged at the Traverse Theatre, Edinburgh on 27 May 1989. The cast was as follows:

SPUD	Stuart McQuarrie
CALLUM	Forbes Masson

Directed by Ian Brown
Designed by Ian McNeil
Lighting by Ace McCarron

A grubby bedsit, a bed, a couch, a chair, Calor gas heater and a sink full of dishes. Discarded clothes, empty beercans, hamburger boxes, Kentucky Fried, Rainforest and Pot Noodle containers litter the floor. An ancient Decca eight track cartridge player completes the furnishings.

The flat has recently been modernised and divided into 'flatlets', although the off-white woodchip wallpaper has not aged well. Hanging from the door by the letter box is a piece of string with a luggage label attached.

Night. The flat is dark and empty. We hear the echoing sound of two sets of footsteps ascending the stairs outside the front door.

SPUD (*sings*). They tried too sell us Egg Foo Yong. Foo yong, tooo reeely be in looove . . .

A hand comes through the letter box and feels for a key on a string. Left, right . . . The hand withdraws a luggage ticket with a note on it.

. . . whit's this?

Silence . . . The door is suddenly kicked from the outside. Frustration.

Aw whit, I don't believe it. The bastard's changed the lock.

He kicks the door again, in frustration.

Shit . . . I'll just have to use the spare keys. Here, gie's that.

A shinty stick smashes through the panel of the door and is withdrawn. The hand comes through again, and undoes the snib on the Yale lock, the door opens, and in walks SPUD VALENTINE.

He is dressed in a shabby ill-fitting suit. He looks like what he says he is: a street trader at the lower end of the market.

Behind him enters CALLUM SHAPIRO. *He carries several bags, including a large sports bag and a carry-out of four lager cans. He is dressed in jeans, baseball boots, sweat shirt, and a grubby combat jacket. He is younger and better dressed than* SPUD, *but looks as if he hasn't washed for three days.*

SPUD *switches on the lights and smiles at* CALLUM. CALLUM *looks desperate.* SPUD *realises the problem.*

SPUD. Oh right. Through there.

SPUD *indicates the toilet door and* CALLUM *crosses stage left and exits, leaving his bags.*

SPUD *produces dozens of pairs of socks concealed about his person, and hides them.*

SPUD *(surveys the flat).* Jesus Christ, look at the place . . .

He frantically starts to shovel the cans into a black plastic bag, and some of the rubbish under his bed into the bin. He takes up a particularly disgusting looking Pot Noodle and sniffs it, then reels back in disgust.

Mind you, better than when I cooked it.

He throws the Pot Noodle into the bin. He rearranges the mess more than cleans it up. Coming to a pile of newspaper clippings, he picks them up and carefully hides them under an old suitcase. Finally he looks in the mirror, and tarts himself up a bit.

A bit worse for wear Spud.

He spits on his hand and smears down his hair, then makes a final check of the rubbish-strewn flat. Suddenly he spots the carry-out. He picks up the cans and is just about to open one when the toilet flushes and CALLUM *returns, catching* SPUD *redhanded.* CALLUM *takes the place in.*

SPUD. Fancy a can?

CALLUM *gingerly sits on the couch.*

SPUD. Take a pew.

CALLUM *half gets up then finally sits.*

SPUD. Aye . . . ah like good can of lager. *(Expansive.)* How about yourself Callum, are you a lager man or an export man?
    Maybe you're a whisky man. *(Winks.)* I think you're a whisky man. Am I right or am I wrong? Aye a whisky man . . . a whisky man . . . shame we've only got this pishwater eh?

Drinks

Silence. SPUD *waits for* CALLUM *to speak. Pause.*

SPUD *(knowingly).* Aye, whisky . . . By Christ you saved my bacon the day, even if you didnae know whit you were doin . . . if the busies had caught me wi' that box o' socks that would've been me, eh? . . . Fortnight's B&B at the Bar L, eh? . . . if you hadn't been standing in that shop door, eh? You must have thought I was mental . . . I mean it's no' everyday you get a box of assorted gents sports socks shoved up yer parka, eh? . . . And they never even gave you a second look . . . Want tae huv seen their faces when they caught up wi' me . . . want tae huv seen them . . . 'Where's sat box?' the big yin says . . . 'Whit box?' says I, 'I've nothin' on me but a pair o' braces'. . .

Couldnae believe it, but . . . want tae huv seen them . . . (*Smiles to himself.*)

Pause.

. . . want tae huv seen their faces . . . want to have seen them . . .

He goes over to the window and stares out.

Pause.

. . . aye . . . (*Sniffs. Turns back to* CALLUM.) Aye, you're not saying much, Callum . . . I mean stop me if I'm monopolising the conversation, know what I mean.

Pause.

. . . still waters run silent, eh?

He goes back to the window.

(*To himself.*) Heh heh . . . nothin' but a pair o' braces . . .

Pause.

You're secret's safe with me big man . . . eh?

Pause.

I'm starving too, I could eat a biled baby with pimples . . . you hungry Callum?

Goes over to the cupboard.

What we got here . . .

He goes over to the old suitcase and suddenly notices a Pot Noodle, and hurriedly hides it inside.

. . . not a sausage, bad case of the Mother Hubbards, Callum my old sport. Ach, never mind, the cup that cheers eh?

Drinks, and sits down opposite CALLUM *studying him.*

Pause.

So, Skye eh. I'm saying you're from Skye . . . I've never been
to the Highlands . . . I had an auntie in Aberdeen. I always
wanted to go, but I never . . . (*Breaks off in mid-sentence and
shrugs.*) . . . must be great living out in the country, eh? All that
. . . country and that . . . aye, must be great . . . aye . . . Heh,
I've got it, how about a bit of music, eh?

He goes over to the eight-track and begins fiddling with it.

Picked this video up for a song at the barras . . . guy wanted
a fiver . . . I told him to take a wander, gave him two pound
fifty . . . he threw in these cassettes . . . well, when I say
cassettes . . . ah well, they're not really cassettes . . . they come
in before cassettes, more . . . classy, know what I mean . . .
most of them are shite right enough, but there's one good
one . . . where is it? Oh right . . . just listen to this . . .

*He reverentially picks up a cartridge and puts it in, we hear a very
scratchy sounding Roy Orbison singing 'Blue Bayou'.*

Big Roy . . . that's what I call music . . . Big Roy. Are you a
music fan yourself, Callum? . . . don't tell me . . . don't tell
me . . . Bobby Darren? Eh . . . what a voice eh, old Bobby
Darren, eh . . . 'Mac the Knife' . . . 'Chicago' . . . 'Lazy
River' . . . aye ye can keep your Frank Sinatras and your Mel
Tormes . . . gie me Bobby Darren anyday . . . Oh but big Roy's
the man for the song writing, eh? . . . 'Only the low-oonely,
Bum bum bum bum shabby doo wah . . . '

We gradually become aware that CALLUM *is softly sobbing . . .* SPUD
is at a loss. He decides to ignore it.

Aye, ah like a can of lager . . . don't get me wrong export's all
right but you can't beat a . . . a lager . . . So anyway, . . . you
fancy a can? Oh no, you've got that one . . . So . . . how you
doin' and that eh? . . . Skye, eh? . . . Do you er . . . (*Casts
around for something to discuss. His gaze alights on the eight track.*)
They're great these things they just keep playing over and over
. . . cartridges they call them . . . cartridges . . . it's a loop . . .
bit like a . . . bit like a CD. (*With conviction.*) Aye, a CD . . . CDs
were based on these . . . the loop, like, . . . it just keeps . . . just
keeps playing like . . . they don't make them any more either. I
wonder how they never caught on, I mean you'd think folk
would go a bundle on them, non-stop music and that,
supermarkets and . . .

SPUD *is finally able to contain himself no longer. His demands build in volume.*

Gonny stop it. (CALLUM *sobs.*) I'm saying . . . (CALLUM *sobs.*) . . . gonny can it.

He switches off the eight track and shouts with real venom and the threat of violence.

Would you fucking shut up . . .

CALLUM *stops crying in surprise, they stare at one another.* SPUD *breaks the moment.*

Aye, funny the cartridges never caught on.

Pause.

. . . I like a can of lager . . . (*Drinks.*)

Pause.

SPUD *goes back to the window.*

Aye, the drunks are out in force the night . . . it's not so bad on a Tuesday . . . See, Friday night when the discos come out . . . the noise . . . it's like the battle of Bull Run oot there . . . they're too drunk to hit each other mostly . . . nothing like a good night out on the town eh?

SPUD'*s eye lands on the shinty stick. He goes to it and picks it up. He feels the weight in his hand and thumps his palm with it.*

Like the hockey eh? . . . I'm not much of a sportsman myself . . . mare a looker on than a joiner in . . .

CALLUM (*quietly*). It's a shinty stick.

SPUD. What's that?

CALLUM *gets up and takes the stick from him, then sits down cradling it.*

CALLUM. It's not a hockey stick, it's a shinty stick.

SPUD. Oh it's not a hockey stick . . . it's a shinty stick. Pardon my ignorance . . . a shinty stick . . . teuchter hockey . . . eh? (*With contempt.*) Shinty . . .

He turns back to the window . . . Laughs, attempting to cheer CALLUM *up.*

Could do with one of them doon there on the mean streets, eh? You'd win a few arguments with that, eh?

Pause.

Aye, I like a lager . . .

He leaves the window and sits down again.

Long pause.

. . . was it the music?

Pause.

. . . I mean if you didn't like it . . . Roy Orbison's not everybody's cup of tea . . . I've got Chet Atkins? . . . No? . . . Los Trios Paraguayos?
    I don't like them so much . . . but I mean you only had to say . . . (*Pause.*) Collector's item this is, you know . . . thirty bob at the barras . . . guy wanted a tenner too . . . I'm no mug you know . . . no flies on me . . . it's not everybody's cup of tea . . .

CALLUM *sniffs.*

SPUD. What?

    CALLUM *shakes his head.*

SPUD. . . . you only had to say . . .

    A note of indignation creeps into his voice.

(*Aside.*) A man can't play his own choice of music without . . . upsetting folk . . . thought it might cheer you up . . .

CALLUM. It had nothing . . .

SPUD. I mean how was I to know?

CALLUM. It had nothing to do with the music . . .

SPUD. Eh?

CALLUM. It wasn't that.

SPUD. All I'm saying is you only had to say, that's all I'm saying. (*Mutters under his breath.*) Man cannay play his own music . . .

    Pause.

So what was it then?

CALLUM. Sorry?

SPUD. If it wasn't the music what was it?

CALLUM. What was what?

SPUD. What was it that made you greet?

CALLUM. I . . . It's difficult . . .

SPUD. What is?

CALLUM. To tell . . . it's private.

SPUD *is scandalised and gets up.*

SPUD. Oh private now . . . Private . . . very good eh? . . . I bring you in out of the cold, offer you the comfort of my home and suddenly we're talking private . . . oh very good, eh? . . . good job this flat isn't private eh?

CALLUM. If you . . .

SPUD. Good job the lavvy wasn't private, eh?

CALLUM. If you want to know I was . . .

SPUD. Bloody gratitude that is.

CALLUM. I am grateful.

SPUD. Charming that is. Bloody charming. Ask a man in and that's all you get from him . . .

As SPUD *witters on* CALLUM*'s lines come in softly and then louder so that by the end of the sentence he has shut* SPUD *up by simple volume. 'Kindness' is belted out.*

CALLUM. I was crying . . . I was crying because you're the first person down here that's shown me a bit of kindness . . .

SPUD. What's that?

CALLUM. Kindness.

SPUD. Kindness? What you on aboot, kindness . . . I was never kind in my puff, pal. I've had it hard, son, hard. Not like some I could mention. Hmmph, kindness . . .

CALLUM. Call it what you like . . .

SPUD. I will, I will . . . Kindness.

Goes to the window.

CALLUM. Where I come from, if some one needs a hand, you help them . . . that doesn't seem to happen down here . . .

SPUD (*turns. On the attack*). Damn right it doesnae . . . get your retaliation in first, do unto others before they do unto you, that's name of the game here. Dog eat dog.

He turns back to the window . . . Mutters.

SPUD. Kindness . . . (*Pause. He turns and looks at* CALLUM.) Aye you'll be missing Granny's Heilan hame, eh?

CALLUM. I've been . . . it's been a bit lonely down here.

Slight pause. CALLUM *takes a sip of his can.*

SPUD. Lonely, Lonely! You count your blessings . . . Christ, I wish I'd the time to be lonely. Hmph. Lonely.

He swigs down the last of his can, turns and picks up another.

SPUD. Aye, I like a can of lager.

CALLUM. Sorry?

SPUD. I'm just saying . . . I like a can of lager . . . (*He takes the can out of the bag.*)

CALLUM. Feel free.

SPUD. What's that?

CALLUM. Have a can.

SPUD. You begrudge me a can?

CALLUM. I just said *have* a can.

SPUD. It was the way you said it.

CALLUM. I don't begrud . . .

SPUD. . . . begrudge me a can of lager. This! . . . I don't even like it.

CALLUM. Have it all, have it all.

SPUD. Fucking hate the stuff, as well. Begrudge me a drink.

CALLUM. I don't begrudge you it.

SPUD. A can of lager . . .

CALLUM. But . . .

SPUD. Aye, right enough, that's what they say about you teuchters . . .

CALLUM. What's that?

SPUD. What?

CALLUM. What do they say?

SPUD. What does who say?

CALLUM. What do they say about us teuchters?

SPUD. Well, they say you're tight-fisted.

CALLUM. Who says?

SPUD. What?

CALLUM. Who says we're tight-fisted?

SPUD. (shrugs). 'They' say it . . .

CALLUM. Who's they?

SPUD. Well . . . everybody.

CALLUM. When?

SPUD. What?

CALLUM. When do they say it?

SPUD. Well . . . they say it all the time.

CALLUM. I've never heard them . . .

SPUD. Well you wouldn't.

CALLUM. Why not?

SPUD. Well they wouldn't say it in front of you would they? . . . I mean they'd wait till you'd gone . . . then they'd say it. (Confidentially.) That's the sort of two-faced bastards they are . . . (Conciliatory.) I mean, they're maybe saying it about me too.

CALLUM. You never know.

SPUD (considers for a beat). No . . . they wouldn't.

CALLUM. How do you know?

SPUD. What?

CALLUM. How do you know they're not saying you're tight-fisted?

SPUD. What do you mean?

CALLUM. If they were saying it behind your back you wouldn't know, would you?

SPUD. But they wouldn't say I was tight-fisted.

CALLUM. Why not?

SPUD. Because I'm not!

CALLUM. Could have fooled me.

SPUD. What?

CALLUM (*conciliatory*). And you've had your money's worth tonight.

Pause.

SPUD. Sorry?

CALLUM. Mmm?

SPUD. Had my money's worth? What's that meant to mean? . . . I'm saying what's that meant to mean?

CALLUM. Nothing!

SPUD. You can't come marching into my place and make comments about me being tight-fisted.

CALLUM. I never came marching in.

SPUD. . . . marching in here . . . tight-fisted? . . .

CALLUM. I never said . . .

SPUD. . . . . tight-fisted . . .

CALLUM. I never said you were tight-fisted.

SPUD. You did.

CALLUM. I didn't.

SPUD. Who did then? . . . Who did?

CALLUM (*shrugs*). They did.

SPUD. Did they?

CALLUM. They did!

SPUD. And who are they?

CALLUM. Everybody.

SPUD. Everybody?

CALLUM. Everybody.

SPUD. Including you?

CALLUM. Yes . . . no!

SPUD. Your balls in a sling it doesnae . . .

CALLUM (*utter frustration*). Oh why not!

SPUD (*triumphant*). There you are! You did say I was tight-fisted. Not only do you come in here and abuse my hospitality but you're a lying bastard with it!

CALLUM. Jesus Christ.

SPUD. What do you think I am, eh?

CALLUM. I don't know.

SPUD. Marching in here . . . calling me tight-fisted . . . me?

CALLUM. Look, I didn't . . .

SPUD. Just what sort of a mug do you think I am?

CALLUM. Right. Right, I'll tell you.

SPUD. Oh will you?

CALLUM. Yes I will.

SPUD. Oh aye? And what sort of mug am I then? Eh? . . . Eh?

CALLUM. You're the sort of 'mug' who uses a total stranger to dodge the police and save your own neck, then takes him to a pub and sticks to him like shite to a blanket until you've drunk all his money, even down to getting him to pay for the carryout which you then take back to your flat and get rid of at double quick time. That's the sort of mug you are . . .

Pause.

SPUD. You calling ma a shite?

CALLUM. What?

SPUD. Shite to a blanket, that's what you said, eh? . . . You're the blanket and I'm the shite, I suppose . . . Eh? . . .

CALLUM. I didn't mean . . .

SPUD. A shite . . .

CALLUM. No . . .

SPUD. Oh aye, I'm the shite, right enough . . . I'm the stupid shite for asking you here . . . well you needn't stay any longer . . . there's the door . . . I never forced you up here . . . you accepted my invitation . . . then you burst oot greeting, call me tight-fisted, and suddenly I'm the shite . . .

At this CALLUM *jumps up.*

CALLUM (*shouting*). I never called you a shite, I never called you tight-fisted . . . I was speaking metaphoric. You're a metaphoric shite, and I'm a metaphoric blanket . . . right!

SPUD. No need to get upset.

CALLUM. I'm not upset.

SPUD. What were you greeting for then.

CALLUM (*shouts*). I mean I'm not . . . (*Realises he's shouting and quietens down.*) I'm not upset with you.

SPUD. Well you've a funny way of showing it.

CALLUM. Sorry.

SPUD *readjusts his clothing and clears his throat, eyeing* CALLUM *suspiciously. He breaks off eye contact muttering.*

SPUD. Call me a shite . . .

CALLUM. I never . . . (*Gathers himself.*) Look I'd better go . . .

He starts to collect his things.

SPUD. Who's stopping you?

CALLUM. I didn't want to . . .

SPUD. Aye, right. Go then.

CALLUM. Right then.

SPUD. Right . . .

Pause, during which CALLUM *has collected his bags and is about to leave.*

SPUD. What you got all they bags fur?

Silence.

CALLUM. They're just bags.

SPUD. Just bags? . . .

CALLUM. They're just bags.

SPUD. I can see they're just bags . . . I didn't think they were a
set of golf clubs . . . I mean if you were off for a fortnight in
Dunoon I wouldn't bat an eyelid, but what I'm saying is, what
I'm saying is . . . it's a bit unusual to be carrying around such a
large amount of casual luggage at one o'clock in the morning,
know what I mean?

Pause.

Have you got somewhere to go?

CALLUM. Yes . . .

SPUD. Aye?

CALLUM. Yes! . . . Well no . . .

SPUD. No?

CALLUM. Yes . . . no . . . I don't know, I'll . . . I'll find
something . . .

SPUD. Fair enough . . .

CALLUM. Right . . . (*He turns to go.*)

SPUD (*mutters*). Stay here if you want . . .

CALLUM. What?

SPUD. . . . nothing . . .

CALLUM. Right . . .

SPUD. I'm just saying . . . Well . . . You could . . . can, er stay
here if you want . . .

CALLUM. Here?

SPUD. Aye.

CALLUM. I don't think so.

SPUD. Fair enough.

CALLUM. Right.

SPUD. No skin off my nose . . . suit yourself . . . (*Sniffs.*) . . . Just
for the night I mean, like.

They look at one another.

CALLUM. Just the night? . . .

SPUD. Forget it . . .

CALLUM. I don't know.

SPUD. Right then.

CALLUM. Because if . . . you know . . .

SPUD. Forget it!

Pause.

But you could.

CALLUM. Could I?

SPUD. Only if . . .

CALLUM. . . . you sure?

SPUD. Sure . . . maybe . . . Och sit down for fuck's sake.

CALLUM *has put down his things. They look at one another.*

SPUD. But just er . . .

CALLUM. Just the night then.

SPUD. Right . . .

Pause.

SPUD. You hungry?

CALLUM. Starving . . . but you haven't got . . .

SPUD. Shut your eyes . . . go on . . . shut your eyes.

As CALLUM *does so,* SPUD *nips over to an old suitcase and takes out a Pot Noodle. He puts the kettle on, and ritually gets out a single plate and two forks, carefully laying them out. He checks the kettle and waits for it to boil.* SPUD *looks at the sports bag which has* CALLUM's *name on a luggage label.*

SPUD. That a tally name?

CALLUM *still has his eyes shut.*

CALLUM. What?

SPUD. You can open your eyes . . . Shapiro . . . that a tally name . . . ?

CALLUM (*slight hesitation*). Yes . . . sort of . . . I'm half Scottish, half Italian, half Jewish.

SPUD. That's three halfs.

CALLUM (*wistfully*). Story of my life.

SPUD. You think you've got problems? I've got five American faithers . . .

CALLUM. How'd you manage that?

SPUD. I'm the result of a passionate, but alas short lived liaison between my mother and a group of American airmen on St Valentines Day 1950 . . . that's where I get my name.

CALLUM. Spud?

SPUD. My whole name's William George Alexander Hiram Valentine Bremmner.
   My ma was dead romantic that way.
   A few years later she was just dead . . .

They drink. CALLUM *starts to unwind.*

In this next section, when the kettle boils, SPUD *takes the top off the Pot Noodle, and pours in the water.*

CALLUM. Why did you have to break the door?

SPUD. Ach, me and the Landlord are having a wee difference of opinion, at the moment . . . storm in a teapot, so to speak . . . (*Pause.*) So, eh?. . . Skye eh? . . . So your da' kicked you oot?

CALLUM. . . . I left before he could . . . I crashed his car into a Police Land Rover.

SPUD. I can see he wouldn't be pleased.

CALLUM. It was empty though . . . the Land Rover . . . but it seemed the right time to bale out . . . things were . . . it was a bit difficult at home . . . (*Drinks.*) I got the bus down here . . .

SPUD. When was this?

CALLUM. Three months ago . . .

SPUD. Streets paved with gold eh?

CALLUM (*shakes his head*). I just wandered around for a while . . .

SPUD. That'll be the culture shock . . . Ach but there's loads of you teuchters around. Did you not meet any?

CALLUM. Just because I lived north of Drymen doesn't mean to say I know everyone else who does.

SPUD. Aye right enough.

CALLUM (*smiles*). I saw this bloke playing the pipes, kilt, the whole bit . . . he was playing . . . oh I can't remember what . . . anyway . . . (*Remembers.*) 'Macrimmons Lament' he was playing, so I went up to him and I asked him if he knew 'The Hen's March To The Midden' and do you know what he said to me? . . . He said 'Search me mate, I'm from Bishop's Stortford.'

SPUD. Bishop's Stortford . . . Jesus Christ . . .

CALLUM. Where is that?

SPUD (*still scandalised by the ignorance*). I've heard it all noo . . . Bishop's Stortford . . . Whit?

CALLUM. Where is Bishop's Stortford?

SPUD. Errr . . . doon Carlisle way . . . near Newcastle . . .

CALLUM. Anyway, I had the address of someone in Partick, but they'd moved . . . I don't know where.

SPUD. What you need is a crash course in city living.

CALLUM (*surveys his bags and the present situation*). I think I've had it.

SPUD *serves out the Pot Noodle. He gives* CALLUM *the plate, and takes the pot himself. He presents it with a flourish.*

SPUD. Aye, right enough. Anyway, there you go . . . haute cuisine . . . well, mair biled watter cuisine . . . you can have sweet and sour or sour and sweet.

CALLUM. Thank you . . . (*He notices some of the discarded Pot Noodle cartons.*) You eat a lot of this stuff?

SPUD (*assuming he's talking about the flavour*). You must be kidding, it's vile . . . I usually get the curried chicken. So, did you find a gaff?

CALLUM (*speaking through a mouthful of noodles*). What?

SPUD (*speaking very deliberately*). Did you find somewhere to stay . . . when you came down?

CALLUM. Oh, yes . . . I got a list of digs from the council . . . Mrs McLeod.

SPUD. McLeod? . . . There you are then, home from home.

CALLUM. Not really. You had to ask for the bath plug. I wasn't even allowed to cook in my room.

SPUD. Name o' Christ, I don't know what I'd do withoot the old kettle.

CALLUM. I didn't really get on with her.

SPUD. Did you sign on?

CALLUM. I couldn't believe it . . . I got a job right away, in a garage.

SPUD. . . . mechanic?

CALLUM. Yes . . . Well . . . not just the mechanic . . . I got to sell the petrol as well . . . well it was mostly the petrol, actually . . . than the mechanic . . . at night . . . I lasted three weeks.

SPUD *looks at him questioningly.*

CALLUM. . . . bad timekeeping . . . well Mrs McLeod didn't like you hanging about . . . I had to start work at eight o'clock at night . . . the pub was the only place I could . . . well . . . I don't find it easy meeting people.

SPUD (*cheering him up*). Well, you met me, didn't you?

CALLUM. Yes, yes I did.

SPUD *burps in appreciation of the meal, and puts his feet up, and does his Uncle Spud act.*

SPUD. It's hard for me to put myself in your position, know?
    You see, Callum, . . . how can I put it? . . . in my business, my occupation, I'm meeting people all the time, know what I mean . . . see I make friends easy . . . Hmph . . . people.
    Christ, sometimes I just come back here for a bit of peace, from all the people . . . know what I mean . . . you see, what I've found is, if you like people, they'll like you. That's my philosophy, that's my philosophy on life, and it's never let me doon yet.

CALLUM. I wish I knew the secret.

SPUD. There's no secret. You like people, they'll like you . . . and the burds, Jesus Christ! Not got a girlfriend yet Callum.

CALLUM. At home, not here.

SPUD. I'll bet you have, eh? Good-looking lad like you . . . this place is crawling with them . . . know what I mean, I've had a few nights up here.

CALLUM (not listening). I used to see this girl waiting for the bus . . .

SPUD (dismissively). Hmph, birds . . .

SPUD. . . . I used to sit three seats behind her . . . she got off two stops ahead of me . . .

SPUD. Don't talk to me about birds . . .

CALLUM. . . . I just wanted to talk to her . . . but . . .

SPUD. Well, when it comes to the women, you've either got it or you havenae, know what I mean. (Pointing at the Pot Noodle.) You finished with that?

CALLUM. What? Oh, yes.

SPUD takes it off him and devours the last noodle.

SPUD. So where's Mrs McLeod, then?

CALLUM. No rent, no room. The woman at the Social Security said I was intentionally homeless . . . I've been on the streets for three days.

SPUD. Where'd the money come from, then? (Indicates the cans.)

CALLUM. Pawned my watch. I got it for my twenty-first . . . God know what I'll say to my mum . . . anyway, there's nothing left.

SPUD (absolutely straight). Boracic . . .

CALLUM. Pardon?

SPUD. Boracic lint . . . skint . . .

Pause. SPUD has finished his meal and gets up.

Christ, nae wonder you were greeting, eh . . . I wish I'd time for greeting . . . I wish I'd time . . .

CALLUM. I'm sorry if I embarrassed you.

SPUD (goes to the window). Me? . . . Christ disnae bother me son . . . seen it all, me . . . oot there . . . you see it all . . .

Pause.

So, no job, eh? What, er, particular line of work were you considering?

CALLUM. Line of work? I've got O level Art.

SPUD. More than some, Callum. I mean, this is the land of opportunity son, the enterprise culture, jump oot there and grab it before some other bastard does.

CALLUM. I've never been very good at that sort of thing.

SPUD. Well you'd better learn, son, or you'll get left behind. You've got to run to stand still these days. I mean look at me. I don't let the grass grow under my feet. Keep moving, bobbing and weaving, a bit of this, a bit of that, a bit of the other, know what I mean, that's the gemme.

CALLUM. I sort of hoped I could get a job helping people.

SPUD. Get tae fuck. You help yourself first son, that's my advice.

CALLUM. I want to do both.

SPUD. You can't do both. You've got to choose. You want tae help folk, away back with the Monarch of the Glen and live on a shortbread tin in Skye. Am I right?

CALLUM. I don't know.

SPUD. Of course I'm right. It's common sense.

Pause.

I've got a proposition for you.

CALLUM. What?

SPUD. An offer.

CALLUM. And what's that?

SPUD. Well, I've been thinking about expanding the business . . . branching out, diversification, so to speak . . . but I need the right personnel. How no come in with me?

CALLUM. What? . . .

SPUD. I can recognise a man with potential when I see one . . . What do you say?

CALLUM. Selling socks?

SPUD. But that's just the beginning. Razor blades, giant balloons, squeaky dogs. I mean, look how Reo Stakis started . . .

CALLUM. Who?

SPUD. Just take your time . . . no rush . . .

CALLUM. It's just that I don't know how long I'll be staying here.

SPUD. Ahhhh . . . the mountains are calling you home . . . back to the solitary whitewashed croft.

Pause

CALLUM. I lived in a Portakabin beside a leaky septic tank.

SPUD. You whit?

CALLUM. It's not back up there I want to go, it's south. I want to go to London.

SPUD. London? (*He takes this as a personal affront.*) London, eh? . . . Well excuse me, Callum, excuse me, but if you canny get to the top of your own wee midden heap, what's the point of trying to climb an even bigger one doon there, know what I mean . . . Plenty cheap digs doon there, eh? . . . plenty friendly folk doon there. (*Unaware of the irony.*) . . . Christ the place is crawling with beggars . . . nick the sugar oot of your tea . . .

CALLUM. You ever been there?

SPUD. Oh aye, great place London . . . they wouldn't give you a reek of their shite . . . What?

CALLUM. You ever been there?

SPUD. Well, no, but . . .

CALLUM. Well what are you on about, then?. . . My brother's down there. He'll fix me up. (*In hope rather than with certainty.*) I've just got to find his address, that's all.

Pause. They settle down again.

SPUD. Aren't they temporary lavvies?

CALLUM. Pardon?

SPUD. Portakabins?

CALLUM. You said it . . . Och it's not as bad as that . . . My dad

runs the 'Skye Fryer Fish Restaurant and Souvenir shop' . . .
(*Sadly.*) He's not very good at it though.

SPUD. Strikes me you'd be better off up there than doon in
London.

CALLUM. Oh yes, bundle of fun . . . serving frozen deep fried
breaded haddock and reconstituted crinkle cut chips to tourists
that don't know a fish supper from a . . . a Pot Noodle.

SPUD. You no' like it then?

CALLUM (*drinks*). I hated it . . . och that's not true . . . I sort of
liked it . . . och I can't explain . . . I had to get out, that's all.
Everything was closing in.

Pause.

SPUD (*reverie*). I got this letter once . . . telt me I'd won the
chance to buy a two lavvy log cabin time-share in Arrochar . . .
all I had to do was turn up and I'd get a drink and a fabulous
free gift. The photo looked great, too, like something out of
Heidi . . . I lost the letter, but . . .

CALLUM (*not listening*). And then I come down here and as soon
as I open my mouth it's like, like I was a foreigner . . . that girl
on the bus . . . she looked at me as if . . . 'where's Skye, is that
near Rothesay?' she said . . . (*Drinks.*) . . . at least in London
there's plenty other foreigners.

They are getting drunker.

SPUD. But you'll not get an offer like mine.

CALLUM. What offer?

SPUD. That's what I'm saying, that's what I'm telling you . . .
come in with me . . . I could use a bit of muscle.

CALLUM. Is there much money in it?

SPUD. I can make up to a hundred a day.

CALLUM. Pounds? . . . Doing what?

SPUD. Punting . . . you name it . . . I've sold it . . . I could sell
Ian Paisley a crucifix . . . Look I'll show you . . . Try to sell me
that hockey stick.

CALLUM. Shinty.

SPUD. What? . . . Aye well try to sell me it . . . I'm walking doon the street right, this is me . . . you take the stick.

SPUD *walks past* CALLUM.

Well stop me . . . Here, I'll walk past again.

He walks past again.

CALLUM. Excuse me would you like to buy . . .

SPUD. Piss off!

CALLUM *shrugs in meek acceptance.*

SPUD. No no no . . . you don't give in so easy . . . Look at you . . . See it's your body talk is all wrong, standing there like a fart in a trance . . . stick your chest out, heid up . . . and fix me with your eyes . . . This is a class piece of merchandise you're offering . . . erra antique walking stick, as seen on TV . . . only two pounds now . . . that's the way it's done . . . Believe in it, believe . . . see when I'm out on the street, Callum, I'm moving through the crowds like a tiger on vaseline, I'm up on my toes, I'm gliding . . . erra gents sports socks . . . erra cuddly toy . . . erra four sheets o' Christmas paper for a pound now . . . ready for anything . . . 'thanks darling, that's one pound fifty' . . . 'change a fiver? . . . certainly Jim' . . . no bother . . . At one with myself and my environment . . . but you've got to believe, you've got to.

SPUD *is exultant.*

CALLUM. So how come you're living in a . . . place like this?

SPUD. What?

CALLUM. If you're making all this money, how come your staying here?

Pause.

SPUD. . . . maybe you'd prefer to be walking the streets.

CALLUM. No, no . . . but it does seem a bit strange.

SPUD. Aye . . . well . . . it's a tax dodge . . . this way, nobody realises what I'm up to, I have to maintain a low profile . . .

CALLUM. And in the meantime you're stealing socks from 'What Every Woman Wants'.

Pause.

SPUD. Three days on the streets eh? Lucky it's no' too cold.

CALLUM. What? . . . Aye . . . you get soup in George Square.

SPUD. It's an expanding business, the lost generation . . .
alcoholically jobless, intentionally homeless, congenitally
hopeless . . .

CALLUM. You didn't use words like that when you're sober.

SPUD. Beneath every inarticulate sober Scotsman lurks a drunken
poet.

CALLUM. That's very good.

SPUD. I'm so glad.

CALLUM. No, but . . . but you never struck me as the kind of
bloke that . . . well, what I mean is . . .

SPUD. What you mean is you thought I was thick.

CALLUM. Yes . . . well no . . .

SPUD. . . . I suppose naebody from Dennistoun can tell a
conjugated verb from an iambic fucking pentameter?

CALLUM. Dennistoun?

SPUD. What?

CALLUM. You told me you were from Dalmarnock.

SPUD. Dennistoun, Dalmarnock . . . I've a weakness for
alliteration.

CALLUM. You've done it again.

SPUD. Done whit?

CALLUM. Used big words.

SPUD. Is there a law against it?

CALLUM. No, I never said there was.

SPUD. Well shut it then.

CALLUM. I'm sorry I spoke.

CALLUM *moves to the window.*

SPUD. Well then.

Long pause.

CALLUM. Your putty's falling out.

SPUD. What?

CALLUM. The window, your putty's coming away.

SPUD. Putty?

CALLUM. Sorry?

SPUD. Putty! . . . (SPUD *joins him at the window*.) Is that all a window means to you?

CALLUM. It's a window.

SPUD. Aye but look oot the window, what do you see?

CALLUM. The window ledge . . .

SPUD. Further, further.

CALLUM. Lights?

SPUD. Dreams, man, dreams.

CALLUM. Dreams? I've nothing against dreams . . . about the only thing that kept me sane up North.

SPUD. What did you dream about?

CALLUM. Getting away.

SPUD. Anything else?

CALLUM (*holding up his can*). Fiona . . .

SPUD (*dismissing the gag*). But did you ever have a real dream? Something you wanted so much you could smell it when you closed your eyes.

CALLUM. That was the septic tank.

SPUD (*fierce*). Don't laugh at me . . . (*Beat*.) . . . I'm serious . . . you must have had a dream when you were young . . . eh?

CALLUM. No.

SPUD. Come on, you must have . . . eh?

CALLUM. Well . . .

SPUD. Aye? . . .

CALLUM. Well, when I was wee I wanted to build . . .

SPUD. Go on . . .

CALLUM (*warming to the theme*). I wanted to be a boat builder . . .

SPUD. Boats?

CALLUM. . . . ocean going yachts. Sail to the Bahamas, Tenerife, Caribbean . . . I was an apprentice at the boat yard but it closed . . . that's why I was working for my dad.

SPUD *is stunned by this news.*

SPUD. What did you say?

CALLUM. My dad, that's why I was working . . .

SPUD. Not that, before that . . . the boats, the yachts.

CALLUM (*dismissively*). Building boats? . . . It's just a dream, man.

SPUD *is panting with emotion.*

SPUD. But you worked in a boatyard.

CALLUM. Sweeping up and scraping paint . . . for six months, that's all . . . Why, what's wrong? Are you all right?

SPUD (*straight*). Can I trust you, Callum?

CALLUM. . . . depends what it is.

SPUD (*desperately grabbing his shoulders*). Can I *trust* you?

CALLUM. . . . yes.

Pause.

SPUD (*whispered*). Ferries.

Pause.

CALLUM. Ferries.

SPUD. Ferries . . .

CALLUM. Ferries?

SPUD. Aye Ferries! You know, boats for people and cars . . . Christ don't tell me you've not got ferries where you come from?

CALLUM. Of course they have. My uncle works on one.

SPUD. What?

CALLUM. What?

SPUD. Your uncle? . . . What does he do?

CALLUM. Ehm . . . engineer, he's an engineer.

SPUD. Christ almighty, I don't believe it . . . Don't move.

SPUD *is on the verge of tears of excitement. He rushes to where he hid the clippings, and withdraws an old copy of the National Geographic . . . He rushes back to* CALLUM.

SPUD. There it is . . . 'A Trip Down the Yangtse Kiang'. Look at that . . . black and white . . . well, colour.

CALLUM. It's very nice, but I don't . . .

SPUD. It says here they're crying out for ferries in China . . . they can't get enough of them.

CALLUM. You've lost me.

SPUD. Can you not see? (CALLUM *can't.*) You just think of all the ferries that are getting laid up in Europe . . . I've got all the details here.

He brings out masses of newspaper clippings, all concerning ferries: travel brochures, photographs, diagrams, the lot. He has obviously been saving them up for some time.

I've done all the research, all the hard work . . . look at this, and this . . . you buy them for pennies, sail them to China, sell them and you're made for life.

CALLUM. Well it seems a bit . . .

SPUD. Its the chance of a lifetime, and I'm asking you to come in on it . . .

CALLUM. Me?

SPUD. It all fits . . . the boatyard, your uncle, I can't believe it.

CALLUM. But how much is all this going to cost?

SPUD. Thousands . . . but we stand to make millions . . .

CALLUM. And where are you going to get the money?

SPUD. I've already put out the feelers . . . I've got the backing of the Chinese government. I've just been waiting for the right partner. What do you say?

CALLUM (*wanting to believe it*). I don't know what to say. Sounds a bit risky to me.

SPUD. It's a stone cold certainty . . . Are you in?

CALLUM. But what do I have to do?

SPUD. Just come in as my partner . . . you're perfect for it . . .
perfect.

(Walks off.) . . . first the letter, then you.

CALLUM. Letter?

SPUD. . . . from the Chinese government.

*Cautiously, he goes to the suitcase and brings out his most treasured item.
A copy of the Daily Record. He shows an advert to* CALLUM.

CALLUM. They're asking for tenders for a fleet of ferries.

SPUD. Correct . . . that confirmed the first message . . . and then
you arrive, a boat builder, with ferry engineering contacts . . . I
can't believe it.

CALLUM. But it's just an advert.

SPUD. It's in code of course . . . well you can't be too careful.
Can you?

For the first time CALLUM *is suspicious of* SPUD.

CALLUM. Are you serious?

SPUD. Of course I'm serious . . . I've already written back . . . in
code too.

CALLUM. Code . . .

SPUD. You see it was in the messages, here . . . same place as the
messages . . . (*Indicates the box of clippings.*) . . . and now you've
arrived, it's all slotting into place . . .

CALLUM. Are you all right?

SPUD. Never felt better . . . never felt better . . . we're going to
do this, eh Callum? . . . eh? You and me, what a team . . .
(*Smiles.*)

CALLUM. I'm not too sure about all . . .

SPUD. Not bad for a boy brought up in a single end in
Baillieston . . . well, . . . not so much single end as singled
oot . . . I was the only kid in oor street with more names than
the Celtic First team . . . you see I was the result of a brief but
ashas lort . . . alas ssshort liaison . . . short lived liaison
between my mother (*By this time* SPUD *is panting almost
uncontrollably.*) and a group of American airmen on St Valentines

day . . . Nineteen sixty, er fifty . . . you and me . . . all the way
to China . . . all the way to China . . . this calls for a
celebration . . . where's the drink? Where is it? There's none
left, there's none left . . . Where is it?

*He is turning the place upside down, and collapses in despair on his
knees. He is on the verge of mental collapse.*

Long pause.

CALLUM. Look . . . I think . . . maybe you should see a, get
some help . . .

SPUD. A doctor? (*Shouts.*) A doctor . . . I already go to the doctors
. . . (*Defiant.*) Every Wednesday I have to go to the doctors . . .
every fucking Wednesday . . . (*Defeated.*) Wednesday . . . (*He
calms down.*)

Silence.

I get better then I get a jag. (*Shivers.*) It's when I feel cold and
it's still warm, before the voices though . . . I haven't heard
them for ages . . . and I . . . I talk a lot and use the big words . . .
then I have to get my jag . . . then it's all right . . . stops you
being depressed . . . stops you being happy too . . . sort of . . .
evens you out . . . flat . . . (*Smiles.*) But now you could stay
'cause it'll be all right . . . and the ferries . . . I could teach you
things about the messages . . . I used to be a teacher . . . but I
got awful cold one day . . . awful cold, my head was tight . . .
(*Brighter.*) I used to get the kids to call me by my first name . . .
(*Duller.*) that was before the voices . . . Then when I was cold
when my mummy died I just started crying . . . and they said I
had to go . . . just for a rest, like . . . to Gartloch . . . just for a
rest . . . the jag helps you to rest . . . slows you down . . . then
you don't use the big words . . . alliteration . . . (*Laughs.*)

CALLUM. You were in hospital?

SPUD. I'm not a loony, you know, I just needed a rest, I was
there for five years . . . but there was no room left . . . I go
up there to see my friends most days . . . just for the company
like . . . but, eh . . . (*Pause. Bright.*) I worked in the gardens . . .
we grew great tomatoes . . . I go and sit in the gardens . . .
some of my friends aren't there any more . . . at night I come
back here . . . home . . . see there wasn't enough room . . .
some of them are in the doss house, or the streets . . . we had
to leave . . . it would be good if someone could stay here with

me though . . . at home . . . home . . . here . . . the social
worker said she would see . . . said she would see . . . I wish
they'd let us stay but . . .

He turns to CALLUM *and smiles.*

I get my jag on a Wednesday . . .

Pause.

I was just remembering what you said . . . (*Through tears.*) . . .
about being lonely . . . I don't want you to go.

CALLUM. I'm not going anywhere . . .

SPUD. No, listen, I meant what I said . . . just one night.

CALLUM. Don't worry, I'm not going.

SPUD. And the ferries . . . you'll help me? You canny walk the
streets this time in the night . . . morning . . . eh? . . .

CALLUM. It's all right . . . It's all right, I'm not going anywhere.

SPUD. You'll stay?

CALLUM. I'll stay.

SPUD. Even though . . .

CALLUM. Don't worry . . . I'll . . . take care of you . . .

SPUD. Just the one night like . . . but you could . . .

CALLUM. It's all right . . .

SPUD. That's my man . . . eh? That's my boy . . . you hungry?
I'm not very good at cooking. (*Sniffing back the tears and composing
himself.*) They taught you how to cook when they let us out but
. . . I'll put some more music on.

CALLUM. Don't bother.

SPUD. It's no trouble . . .

CALLUM. Well actually, I've got a wee bit better sound system
here.

CALLUM *retrieves from his bag a Hitachi Super Woofer ghetto blaster.*

SPUD. Jesus Christ man . . . where did you get that?

CALLUM. Same way as you got your socks.

SPUD. And you had that in your bag when the cops were after me? Jesus . . . how did you not tell me?

CALLUM. I wasn't sure if I could trust you . . . then when I came up here . . . I didn't want to embarrass you.

SPUD caresses the magnificent machine. Taking in the battery of dials, leads, etc.

SPUD. It's beautiful man . . . beautiful. You got any cassettes?

CALLUM. No. It's got a radio. Here.

He switches it on. The strains of 'I'm not alone any more' by Roy Orbison are heard.

SPUD. It's Roy . . . it's Roy Orbison! You did have a cassette.

CALLUM. No, it's the radio.

SPUD is not listening.

SPUD. . . . oh man . . . sounds great . . . oh I could just lose myself in that voice.

He lies down on the couch and closes his eyes, listening to the sound of the music, letting it wash over him. The track ends and we hear the voice of the DJ.

DJ. That was 'I'm not Alone Any More' by Roy Orbison, a fitting epitaph for one of the all time greats of Rock And Roll, who sadly died last night at 11.35 at the Corpus Christi Hospital in Memphis, Tennessee. His hits spanned almost two generations of music, from the late fifties to the present day, and we'll play you out today with one of his loveliest songs 'Blue Bayou'.

SPUD has sat up and is stunned by the news.

SPUD. Big Roy . . .

CALLUM. It's all right. It's all right. Just you lie down and rest.

SPUD is sobbing.

SPUD. Big Roy . . .

CALLUM covers SPUD with an old blanket and sits by him. He looks at SPUD lying on the couch. He hesitates before picking up his things and going out quietly, leaving the radio where it is. As the door closes, SPUD stands up and looks at it. As 'Blue Bayou' finishes, the lights go down.

End of Play

VALUED FRIENDS ■ STEPHEN JEFFREYS

Stephen Jeffreys was born in London. After working variously as a paint deliverer, teacher, art college lecturer and in the Jeffreys family business (making billiard tables), he became a full-time playwright in 1978 after the success of *Like Dolls or Angels*. This study of a stuntman on the skids was followed by a two-year residency at the Brewery Arts Centre, Kendal, where he helped set up the touring company Pocket Theatre Cumbria, who premiered several of his plays including *Watches of the Night* (1981), *Futures* (1984) and an adaptation of Dickens' *Hard Times* which has been given many productions in Britain and abroad. His Spanish Civil War play, *Carmen 1936*, won an Edinburgh Festival Fringe First for Communicado in 1984 and enjoyed a successful run at the Tricycle Theatre, London. He followed this with *Returning Fire* (Paines Plough), and *The Garden of Eden*, a play for a cast of 150 about nationalised beer in Carlisle.

He has been involved for many years with the National Student Drama Festival and was Arts Council Writer-in-Residence with Paines Plough (1987–9). At the time of going to press, his latest play, *The Clink*, a Jacobean Revenge Comedy, is scheduled for presentation by Paines Plough in autumn 1990. *Valued Friends* won him the 1989 Evening Standard Most Promising Playwright Award.

Characters

SHERRY, late twenties
HOWARD, early thirties
PAUL, early thirties
MARION, early thirties
SCOTT, thirty
STEWART, early forties.

Setting

The action of the play takes place in the basement flat of a large
late Victorian house in Earl's Court. A sitting room. One door
leads off to a bedroom, another to the rest of the flat and a pair
of French windows looks on to a small concrete garden. At the
start of the play, the flat is cosy and cluttered.

Valued Friends was first staged at the Hampstead Theatre on 9 February 1989. The cast was as follows:

SHERRY	Jane Horrocks
HOWARD	Peter Capaldi
PAUL	Tim McInnerny
MARION	Serena Gordon
SCOTT	Martin Clunes
STEWART	Peter Caffrey

Directed by Robin Lefèvre
Designed by Sue Plummer
Lighting by Gerry Jenkinson

ACT ONE

Scene One

Early June 1984. We hear the Searchers' 'Needles and Pins'. Lights up.

The sitting room of the flat, just before midnight. HOWARD *has commandeered the table, sitting at his typewriter surrounded by papers, books and card index systems.*

SHERRY *is standing next to him. She wears a short dress, an absurd floppy hat and a huge shoulder bag. She has just come in and speaks with great excitement and volume.*

SHERRY. The train is packed, Howard, I mean I've trodden on faces to get a seat. We're somewhere between Knightsbridge and South Kensington, there's this just incredible smell of sweat, you know, not stale sweat, excited summer sweat. Suddenly there's this guy, lurching towards me through the pack and he is *crazy*, there are are no questions about this, the man is *gone* and he has singled out *me*, no one else will do. He shoves aside the last remaining body and looms over me, hanging from the strap, swaying like a side of beef, I mean he's *enormous* and he starts stabbing his finger at me: 'How much do you *care?* How much do you *care?*' That's all he's saying, over and over. 'How much do you *care?*' Everyone's looking at me. *He's* crazy but they're staring at *me*. They want to know how much I care too. About what, nobody's saying, so I take a chance, put my hand on my heart and say: 'Very deeply, very deeply indeed,' thinking this might get the crowd on my side, but no, nobody applauds, nobody cries, nobody even *laughs*. They're just waiting for the crazy to come back at me, and, Howard, he does. 'What about? What do you care so much about?' And they all *stare* at me again. I can feel the mood of the train switching against me. We get to South Ken. but nobody gets off. They all live there, I know they do, but they're saying to themselves: 'We'll walk back from Gloucester Road.'

The doors shut, the train starts. 'What about? What do you care *about?*' Howard, I can't think of anything. In a calmer moment I might have said: 'The early films of Ingmar Bergman, my mum and being the greatest stand-up comedian the world has ever seen.' But I can think of *nothing*. The silence is just incredible. I mean I'm not ignoring the guy, I'm racking my brains. The whole carriage is racking my brains. Eventually I look the guy in the face, admission of defeat, and he just says: 'You see, you see.' And the doors open and he gets off at Gloucester Road. All those people who really live in South Ken. are now saying to themselves: 'What a glorious evening – we'll walk back from Earl's Court.' Howard, they're prepared to stay on till Hounslow Central, gawping at my embarrassment. We get to Earl's Court, I'm so paranoid I can't face them all in the lift, I have to climb the emergency stairs to escape. Have you *any* idea how many emergency stairs there are at Earl's Court?

HOWARD. Eighty-four.

SHERRY. Are there really?

HOWARD. I counted them.

SHERRY. What a nightmare. Are you going to make some tea?

HOWARD. No.

SHERRY. I put the kettle on when I came in.

HOWARD. I don't want any tea.

SHERRY. Oh. Did you go out collecting tonight?

HOWARD. They phoned me up. I told them I was ill.

SHERRY. Howard!

HOWARD. I've been out twice. What's the point? Collecting for the miners in the Royal Borough of Kensington and Chelsea? I was stood two hours outside the tube on Monday with me plastic bucket, copped one pound forty and I put the quid in meself. If I'd been up in Glasgow I'd not have been able to hold the thing up after five minutes.

SHERRY. So you're writing the book instead?

HOWARD. That's it.

SHERRY. Going well?

HOWARD. No.

SHERRY. Oh.

Pause.

Are the others in?

HOWARD. I'm sorry.

SHERRY. No, I didn't mean you were being –

HOWARD. I'm just tired, I'd like to go to bed.

SHERRY. – boring or anything. Well go to bed.

HOWARD. I can't, I need to speak to Paul and Marion.

SHERRY. Where've they gone?

HOWARD. Concert. The Searchers.

SHERRY. Oh yeah. More sixties nostalgia. Is it healthy I ask? I mean, you can't imagine these destruction metal bands getting together for twenty-first anniversary gigs.

HOWARD. Destruction metal?

SHERRY. Very big in Germany. These guys, they hire a warehouse and smash the stage up with drills and amplified sledgehammers. It's pretty loud. Paul did a piece about it in the NME.

HOWARD. You mean, they use, like, manufacturing tools for –

SHERRY. Yeah, cement mixers and stuff –

HOWARD. – signalling the decline of manufacturing culture, that's . . .

He makes a note.

SHERRY. Apparently it gets pretty dangerous. I mean you're standing there listening and the walls fall in on you, it's meant to be great.

HOWARD. Well it would be.

SHERRY. You gonna put that in your book?

HOWARD. Might make a nice little footnote. The section on de-industrialisation.

SHERRY. Howard. You couldn't lend me some money could you?

Pause.

HOWARD. How much d'you want?

SHERRY. Just . . . a tenner. Is that all right? Brian at the Queen's Head owes me for my last three gigs – and he wasn't around tonight, bastard, and there's a few –

HOWARD. I'll lend you ten quid, Sherry.

He reaches in his pocket. Sound of people arriving through the front door.

Did it go all right, the Queen's Head?

SHERRY. Pretty dead audience. Got a couple of laughs towards the end. I don't think they understood what I was doing at all.

He hands her a ten pound note.

Oh . . . that's great, ta.

HOWARD. Well as long as you're getting the bookings, getting the experience.

SHERRY. Yeah, well. I'm getting the experience. But the audiences don't seem to be learning much from it.

She scrunches the money up and hides it in her hand as she hears PAUL *and* MARION *approach.*

PAUL *comes on, car keys in hand, closely followed by* MARION.

PAUL. You're still up.

MARION. They're still up.

HOWARD. Good were they?

PAUL. Merely stunning.

SHERRY. Didn't get their pacemakers wired up in their wah-wah pedals, then –

PAUL. It's easy to be cynical. They did not look one day older. Twenty-two years on the road and they looked like a set of fresh-faced youths.

MARION. And they hadn't learned any new songs either.

PAUL. You know what I admire? I admire the sheer stamina, the slog, the perseverance. All this bullshit you hear about the rock 'n' roll heroes, the ones who destroy themselves with drugs, or chuck lawsuits at each other or get killed in plane crashes. That's not heroic, that's the soft option. You know what true heroism is? It's twenty-two years in a Ford Transit staring at the cat's eye lights on the way back from the Club-a-go-go, Lowestoft.

MARION. Does anyone want tea?

HOWARD. Love some.

SHERRY. It's just boiled, I put it on.

MARION. My ears are ringing.

She turns to go. SHERRY *follows her.*

SHERRY. Marion. I had this really weird thing happened to me on the tube. There we were, between Knightsbridge and South Ken. . . .

PAUL *holds up a cassette.*

PAUL. Look at that, eh, magnetic gold.

HOWARD. You got an interview?

PAUL. Fifteen minutes' worth. Frank and John. Classic. Cut some old favourites into it and I've got a nifty programme. Syndicate it globally.

He slumps into a chair. HOWARD *tidies papers.*

(*Suddenly remembering.*) And! And – You'll never guess.

HOWARD. What?

PAUL. The support band.

HOWARD. The Swinging Blue Jeans.

PAUL. More obscure.

HOWARD. The Downliners Sect?

PAUL. More talentless.

HOWARD. More talentless that the Downliner's Sect? I give in.

PAUL. The Blue Scarecrows.

HOWARD. Never heard of them.

PAUL. You won't have heard of them. They've only been together for six months. But you will have heard of the bass guitarist.

HOWARD. Jack Bruce down on his luck is he?

PAUL. Dennis Combes.

HOWARD. Never.

PAUL. The man himself.

HOWARD. Dennis Combes.

PAUL. Bass guitar, vocals and insulting the audience.

HOWARD. Making a go of it then, is he?

PAUL. No. Had a few words with him. Christine – remember Christine – they're married now, just about – she's got a good job, likes to get him out of the house of an evening.

HOWARD. Can see her point. Was he good?

PAUL. Same as ever. Played a fretless. Still trying to sound like Charlie Mingus.

HOWARD. He was all right, Dennis. The two of you were good together.

PAUL. Well . . .

HOWARD. You were, should have stuck at it.

PAUL. Like the Searchers.

HOWARD. Could have been where they are today.

PAUL. The thing with Dennis, the real problem, was that he never accepted the idea that the bass guitar is a background instrument. There you are, up on the stage singing the crucial line of the lyric, and Dennis turns up his amp and starts playing semi-tone runs, crawling up and down the fingerboard like a demented spider.

HOWARD. Great days. Remember the big gig. The Old Refectory.

PAUL. I've still got the ticket. It was pink. October 27th 1973. Southampton University's own band, Centrifugal Force, supporting Leonard Cohen.

HOWARD. Shrewd piece of booking. Everyone cheered up when Leonard came on, he seemed quite chirpy in comparison.

PAUL. Lennie Cohen. Remember how old we thought he looked.

HOWARD. Great days.

PAUL. Great days. Old Dennis.

HOWARD. You were mad to jack it in.

PAUL. I still play –

HOWARD. You know, in a *band*. I reckon if you'd have stuck at it you could really have –

PAUL. Yeah, shut up will you Howard.

Pause

Interviewing Bronski Beat for the NME tomorrow.

HOWARD. Oh yeah?

PAUL. Oh *yeah*.

MARION *and* SHERRY *are back.* MARION *carries a tray. On it are a traditional earthenware teapot and four distinctive mugs, a bottle of milk, a sugar bowl and a packet of biscuits.* SHERRY *is talking as they come in.*

SHERRY. . . . . all those people who actually live in South Ken. have decided, 'What a stupendous evening, we'll walk back from Earl's Court,' I mean, they're prepared to walk back from –

HOWARD. Hounslow Central.

SHERRY. Howard –

PAUL. What's this?

SHERRY. I was telling Marion –

HOWARD. She had to climb the emergency stairs by all accounts –

SHERRY. Shut up, Howard –

PAUL. – Will somebody tell me –

SHERRY. This guy I met, on the train between –

HOWARD *suddenly stands up.*

HOWARD. Look, I want to go to bed.

The other three are puzzled by his vehemence. A pause.

PAUL. Well, go to bed then.

HOWARD *sits down again.*

HOWARD. I waited up to tell you something. Some news. It affects all of us. I thought I should wait until we were all together.

MARION *is pouring tea and handing it round.*

MARION. If we've got mice again, I'm leaving.

HOWARD. We've got a new landlord.

Pause.

PAUL. Is that it?

SHERRY. We're always having new landlords.

PAUL. Seven in ten years.

SHERRY. Eight now.

PAUL. Yeah, eight now.

HOWARD. The rumour is, this one's different.

PAUL. Says who?

HOWARD. Tracey from the top flat. She came down earlier on. asked if I'd heard anything.

PAUL. And?

HOWARD. Well I said no, and Tracey said the guy on the second floor, the bald geezer –

PAUL. – the one with the Renault Five –

HOWARD. Yeah, he'd gone, cleared off 'cos the landlord had found something dodgy in his lease, and he'd said that the people on the ground floor had been offered three grand each to leave.

SHERRY. Three thousand pounds, just to clear off?

HOWARD. That's the story.

PAUL. And is that the lot?

HOWARD. So far.

Pause.

PAUL. Tracey says that the bald Renault driver, now departed, says that the ground floor have been offered three grand each to go. It's not exactly Reuters we've got here, Howie.

HOWARD. All right, next time I'll keep it to myself.

SHERRY. Three thousand pounds. Be handy, wouldn't it?

They look at her doubtfully.

PAUL. We had the same story, exactly the same, two years ago when that Swedish woman sold out.

HOWARD *stands.*

HOWARD. OK. OK. Sorry I mentioned it. I can go to bed now. Sorry it wasn't more interesting. Put my tea on the side and I'll heat it up for breakfast. Goodnight.

He goes.

SHERRY. Goodnight.

PAUL *goes to the door, looks, then follows* HOWARD.

PAUL. (*off*). Howie!!

SHERRY. Marion?

MARION. Yes?

SHERRY. You couldn't lend me ten quid could you?

MARION. Ummm . . . ohhh . . . I expect so.

SHERRY. It's just that Brian, the bastard, owes me –

MARION. You know we've got to pay the phone bill this week.

SHERRY. Is it a lot?

MARION. Well. Your share is.

SHERRY. Oh shit.

MARION. Paul's worked it out. It's on the hall table.

SHERRY. Oh. (*Pause.*) I'd still like ten quid.

MARION. Tomorrow?

SHERRY. That would be . . . lovely, yes.

MARION. I suppose it must end somehow. Why not like this?

SHERRY. What?

MARION. Living together. It's been ten years. Life's not meant to happen that way. After a while you go your separate ways, buy squeaky clean places with freezers and get surrounded by cats and children. I've met people who've done it.

SHERRY. Well, this might be your chance. You could go and do all that with Paul.

MARION. Would he want that?

SHERRY. Probably. I know he likes freezers.

MARION. Would I want that?

SHERRY. Yes I should think so.

MARION. And what would you do?

SHERRY. Kip on floors, I don't know.

MARION. You're getting a bit big for that, Sherry. Floors, that was a long time ago.

PAUL *is back.*

PAUL. He's all right. He was just pissed off cos he's got to get up early to pick up some leaflets at the printers for his NATFHE branch.

SHERRY. It was silly staying up. I don't see why he didn't get me to tell you.

PAUL. Did you see the breakdown of the phone bill?

SHERRY. No I haven't. Stop hounding me.

PAUL. It's the first time I've mentioned it.

SHERRY. It's always money now. You used to be able to get some really good conversation in this flat. Burning issues and moral dilemmas and things. Now all everyone talks about is money.

MARION. I should get time to go to the bank at lunchtime.

SHERRY. Sorry? Oh right. The money.

She gets up and heads for the door.

See you in the morning.

SHERRY *goes.*

PAUL. What money?

MARION. She's broke.

PAUL. You shouldn't lend to her, it makes her worse.

MARION. I said I was going to read those reports for Jeremy tonight, oh well.

PAUL. Picks up forty quid a week if she's lucky, then splurges out eighty in the Portobello Road on an antique wedding dress that doesn't fit her.

MARION. She'd be happy. If we got money to go.

PAUL. Don't talk about it or she'll spend all the cash on the offchance.

MARION. I was talking to Jackie today. Marketing Jackie. She hadn't realised how old I was. She thought I was about twenty-five. She went all quiet.

PAUL. Even if it did happen and the landlord came up with a heap of money I still wouldn't go. It's ideal, living here.

MARION. Marketing's funny. They all sit round and say things like: 'In five years time, every home will have a computer like every home has a toaster.'

PAUL. What happened to our toaster?

MARION. It broke.

PAUL. You don't look thirty-one. Twenty-six, twenty-seven at the outside.

MARION *bends over and kisses him.*

MARION. I'm going to bed.

Jennifer's having a baby.

PAUL. Jennifer.

MARION. Roger and Jennifer.

PAUL. Oh.

MARION. We could buy a place. If he came up with enough.

PAUL. The four of us?

MARION. No, silly, you and me. Renting doesn't make sense.

PAUL. We've been renting for years. When did it stop making sense?

MARION. Sometimes it feels a bit cramped. Anyway, everything changes eventually.

PAUL. I don't like change. I like things that go on and on.

MARION *breaks away from him and goes towards the bedroom door.*

Marion?

MARION. Bring me a glass of water when you come, will you?

She goes into the bedroom.

PAUL *sits for a moment. Then remembers the interview tape. He gets up and puts it in the cassette machine. Goes to the drinks cupboard. Pours a brandy. We hear* PAUL's *voice on the tape.*

PAUL. I'm backstage at the Albany Empire, Deptford after a tremendous gig by that great band of the sixties and indeed the eighties, the Searchers, and I've got bass guitarist Frank Allen with me. Frank, you've got that distinctive Searchers sound, I mean the high harmonies and twelve string guitars, that's had quite an impact on rock and roll history.

FRANK. It has, I mean the Byrds got a lot of credit for that, but in fact the Byrds used the twelve string sometime after us and I believe they were influenced, certainly Tom Petty has admitted being influenced by our twelve string sound and Bruce Springsteen. He was using 'When you walk in the room' on his stage show for quite some time. And Marshall Crenshaw came to see us in New York . . .

Fade to Blackout. We hear the Searchers singing 'When you walk in the room.'

Scene Two

December 1984

The room is much tidier. Christmas cards adorn every available surface. There is a small, genuine Christmas tree with lights.

MARION *is hoovering. She's wearing a suit and gives the impression of being older and richer than she really is.*

She switches the hoover off, looks around, houseproud.

PAUL *comes in. He's clearly anxious.*

PAUL. Are we going to offer him a drink?

MARION. No.

PAUL. Are you sure?

MARION. We want him in and out quickly. We want to make him feel like an intruder. We want tension and hostility.

PAUL. So no drinks, not even coffee.

MARION. Not even coffee.

PAUL. It's cold out there, he'll be cold.

MARION. The psychology is: no coffee.

PAUL. Right.

Pause.

They're not going to get here in time, I knew we should have made it later.

MARION. It doesn't matter.

PAUL. It does matter. We don't want Howard lecturing him on economics and we don't want Sherry saying anything.

Noise of front door.

MARION. I talked to them last night. They know what to do.

SHERRY *comes in at the run. She wears a heavy coat.*

SHERRY. Oh God. He's not here yet.

MARION. No.

SHERRY. Christ it's so cold.

She goes to the sideboard and pours herself a large brandy. PAUL *is stupefied by this.*

I had this really amazing thing happen to me on the bus –

MARION. Not now. You know what to do?

SHERRY. Yes I say nothing. Absolutely nothing. I leave it to the smooth-tongued among us. When he speaks to me I say: 'Signor Landlord, I know nothing, nada, absoluto zilcho –'

PAUL. Do you often drink my brandy?

SHERRY. What?

PAUL. Elton John's manager gave me that.

SHERRY. Paul, it's really so cold outside, you have no idea –

PAUL. If it's my birthday. Or I have something to celebrate. Or I'm in the depths of terminal depression. Then I have some of my cognac –

MARION. Please.

PAUL. Then and only then –

SHERRY. It's only a drink –

PAUL. If you just wanna get warm, there's a bottle of sherry I got off Bananarama –

MARION. Please!

Pause

He'll be here any second. Howard will probably be late. The important thing is this: we will give away nothing, no information at all. Our financial standing, our mutual relationships, our careers, these will remain a closed book to him, all right? He's the landlord, make him feel like one. If there's any official statement required from our side, Paul will make it and there will be no dissenters, right?

SHERRY. Right.

MARION. And above all: if he mentions a sum of money, whatever it is, as compensation for our giving him vacant possession, we look incredibly depressed.

SHERRY. Depressed, right.

A ring at the doorbell.

SHERRY. Oh shitbags.

MARION. I'll go.

She makes for the door, then turns for a moment.

Sit down. Look as if you live here.

She goes. PAUL *and* SHERRY *sit.*

SHERRY. Suppose he offers us the four grand Tracey and the others got –

PAUL. You look depressed –

SHERRY. I'll try –

Pause.

PAUL. Think of something to say –

SHERRY. I can't –

PAUL. Quick before he comes in –

SHERRY. Oh Christ, oh internal megadeath –

MARION *comes back leading* ANTHONY SCOTT. *He's a go-getter, only just thirty, younger than the inhabitants of the flat though he doesn't realise this. Public school manner, clean, clear-cut, confident. Despite themselves,* PAUL *and* SHERRY *stand when he comes in. He holds some papers, recently extracted from his briefcase. He's talking as he comes in into a micro tape recorder.*

SCOTT. . . . substantial areas of wasted space, corridors and so on, then large reception room, French windows, opening to garden, rear, good evening, so you two are . . .

He looks at SHERRY, *checks papers.* SHERRY *doesn't know if she should speak.*

PAUL. Paul Cameron.

SCOTT. Excellent. Anthony Scott.

They shake hands.

So therefore, the other one's called Howard, you must be Sherry Martin.

SHERRY *is immensely relieved.*

SHERRY. Yes, pleased to meet you (*They shake hands.*) although my Equity name is Sherry St George.

PAUL *and* MARION *are appalled,* SCOTT *puzzled.*

SCOTT. Equity? Do you deal?

SHERRY. It's just you can't have the same name as somebody else, and somebody else already had my name, although . . . obviously it *was* her name, so I had to find another and my aunt's maiden name was St George so I thought . . . rather stylish and . . .

SCOTT *looks at her as if she were mad.*

. . . as a stage name . . .

SCOTT. *That* Equity. Sorry didn't cotton. Different worlds.

He sits down.

Are you all in that line of business?

SHERRY. No, Paul's a freelance broadcaster and Marion's in computers. Howard's not here yet, he's a lecturer at . . .

She realises she's said too much.

. . . the moment. That's why he's not here yet.

Pause. PAUL *and* MARION *are looking daggers at* SHERRY.

. . . but he'll be here soon. When he finishes his lecture.

Pause.

It's about the re-birth of German industry in the nineteen fifties.

Pause.

So he won't be long. Can I make you a cup of coffee?

SCOTT. I – no I really musn't stay long. Should we wait for this –

PAUL. Howard. Howard Unwin.

SCOTT. Perhaps we'll give him a moment or so. You're an actress then?

SHERRY. Well I'm more of a performer, really. I'm breaking into the alternative comedy scene.

Sound of front door.

SCOTT. Television? Lot of money in that.

SHERRY. Yes. On a good night, you can take home twenty quid.

SCOTT. Ah.

HOWARD *comes in.*

HOWARD. Sorry I'm late. Howard Unwin.

SCOTT. Anthony Scott. (*They shake hands.*) For a man who's had to explain an economic miracle, I'd say you were a shade early.

HOWARD *can't work out how* SCOTT *knows.*

SCOTT. The Krauts, your lecture. Lot to learn from them.

HOWARD. Well, yes.

HOWARD *searches the faces around him for clues. Then gives up.*

I'll sit down.

SCOTT *immediately leans forward. He's well prepared and he gets going in a cards-on-the-table-manner.*

SCOTT. Now you've been living here as tenants for quite some time, five years, isn't that right?

PAUL. Ten.

SCOTT. Ten.

He seems momentarily depressed.

Long time. Well. You will not be unaware of the situation. My line of business is property. My interest is primarily, I would say, a creative one. I like to seize opportunities and make the most of them. Six months ago I bought this property as part of a portfolio of similar . . . units. You'll be aware I bought it sight unseen, tenants and all because I have a particular interest in the area and . . . well a good price is a good price.

Pause.

I should, perhaps, apologise for having taken so long to contact you, but I was aware you were tenants of long standing and I decided to . . . approach the other occupants first. Now, you're here in the basement. The second floor and the ground floor are both vacant. The top floor will be vacant by the end of January, the first floor by the sixteenth of February. You will be the sole remaining tenants. I want to be quite clear about this: I have no intention of being a landlord. That's not my . . . thing at all. I . . . that is my company Anthony Scott Developments . . . refurbish properties – substantial buildings in promising locations renovated with a degree of wit and imagination . . . and then sold. To an increasingly clamorous market. Earl's Court . . . becoming an interesting part of the world. Conservation area, nice London square, convenient for the city, handy for the airport, lots of brownie points . . .

He looks around.

Needs a bit of work. As with much rented accommodation, the landlord tends to let things slip. Actually, needs an awful lot of work.

Pause.

What I'd like to do is gut the whole house, shove in a central wall, re-arrange the accommodation on to different levels, so you have seven or eight different units, one bedroom, two bedroom flats, making the whole property more space efficient.

PAUL. They did that to the one on the corner.

HOWARD. Yes they did, they put in a . . .

PAUL. . . . central wall, yes.

SCOTT. Yes.

Pause.

This work will be much easier to accomplish if you are no longer living here.

Pause.

So. There are a number of routes available. A number of routes. All of which we are at liberty to explore. One of which we will choose to travel on.

Pause.

Route one, and this is the route I absolutely prefer and which I cannot recommend to you too highly . . . I will pay you a sum of money for vacant possession. Which you would dispose amongst yourselves as you thought fit. And we would name a date for your vacation of the premises.

He looks around. They look back at him.

Should we . . . for any reason . . . not be able to avail ourselves of this route, then we may have to get into re-housing. This could be rather a messy route. Under the terms of your tenancy, I would need to find you accommodation of an equivalent nature to that which you are now enjoying. Now obviously it can't be *exactly* the same and we might find ourselves quibbling over a French window here and a lavatory pedestal there . . . if you catch my . . . it's a big wrangly, a bit nit-picky as processes go, which is why I'm not madly keen to set foot down this particular . . . boulevard. But of course if we can't agree on option one, then re-housing it may have to be. I may not be into being a landlord, but I have a colleague who is and he has a whole *sea* of flats not a biscuit's toss from this very spot and, should it come to the push, I have little doubt that the courts will rule one of these to be as damn near equivalent as equivalent can be . . .

He waits for comment, but there are still no takers.

Failing that . . . I could in the very near future turn this place into a building site. A lot of work could be done around you, scaffolding, brickdust, rough labouring chaps working funny hours with their jovial badinage floating in through the windows . . . and in the meantime I can hardly fail to note that the rent you're paying is way below the going whack for this area. If I were to make a concerted push at the Rent Tribunal to bring you into line, you could well find yourself paying twice or thrice the current sum . . . but . . . this is not a pleasant option, not by any means a scenic route. It's possible that we'll have no problems whatever reaching an agreement, in which event, it may be possible for me to offer you one of the newly created units on this very spot in the not too distant future, possibly at a highly competitive price . . . so . . . that's it.

Pause.

That's where we stand.

Pause.

PAUL. You mentioned a sum of money.

SCOTT. Yes.

PAUL. For vacant possession.

SCOTT. Yes.

PAUL. What sort of sum are we talking about?

SCOTT. Well, this would be a figure on which we would have to agree.

They wait.

But I would have to say, at this juncture, that the absolute ceiling on such a sum, working as I am within tight budgets, the absolute ceiling would be around twenty thousand, twenty-five thousand, say around six thousand each.

MARION, PAUL *and* HOWARD *instantly look incredibly depressed.*

SHERRY (*a yelp of joy.*) Yahhh!!

Suddenly she realises she has to suppress her feelings.

Well, that's not very . . . I mean that's . . . well . . . as a sum . . . that's . . .

Pause.

SCOTT. And I think I ought to say, right from the start, that we are not in a negotiating situation here. You are not about to make a killing out of me. We are not talking telephone numbers. We will be looking to settle amicably, speedily and sensibly.

Pause.

PAUL. Well we obviously can't make any decision here and now. We'll need to consult among ourselves –

SCOTT. Surely, surely.

PAUL. But there is one point I would very much like to make. This is our home. It has been our home for some considerable time. We would none of us be at all happy to have to leave it.

SCOTT. Well, this is a point of view, yes. But the world moves on, times change and so forth –

PAUL. It's a pleasant area, convenient for all our working arrangements, we get on extraordinarily well together, almost like a family –

Scott *is becoming embarrassed and makes up his mind to get out.*

SCOTT. Well. (*Looks at his watch.*) I have to be going, I have another . . .

He leans forward.

I think you should talk through this very clearly amongst yourselves.

He searches for a possible ally and fixes on SHERRY.

SCOTT. I would greatly appreciate an early response.

He stands.

Look, what are we now, the fifteenth of December. If you can give me vacant possession by the . . . fifteenth of February, I shall pay you thirty thousand pounds. Thirty thousand. All right. And I think you can consider yourselves damn lucky.

He hands SHERRY *a business card.*

Telephone me. In a few days. When you've talked.

He goes out, MARION *following him.* SHERRY *is about to let out a whoop of joy, but* PAUL *claps his hand over her mouth at the last moment.* HOWARD *monitors* SCOTT's *progress along the corridor.*

HOWARD. They're passing the phone now, just edging into the kitchen, up to the fridge, past the fridge, he's lingering there in the doorway, a quick word, another quick word and he's . . . GONE!

PAUL *removes his hand from* SHERRY's *mouth*

SHERRY. Thirty thousand! Thirty thousand pounds, yeah! (*Pause.*)
How much is that each?

PAUL. You're getting nothing.

SHERRY. No really –

HOWARD. Seven thousand five hundred –

SHERRY. Seven thousand five hundred! Pounds!

PAUL. Sherry –

SHERRY. Yes, I know, I know –

PAUL. I mean, you all but screwed up the whole thing –

MARION *is back.*

MARION. Could you I ask myself have managed to divulge more
information?

SHERRY. I'm sorry –

MARION. I seriously doubt it –

HOWARD. All that about Germany, how did he know that –

PAUL. Sherry broke down under questioning –

SHERRY. I know, I'm sorry, I'm sorry, I just got unnerved by the
quiet, but we got the result, eh? Seven and a half thousand
each!

They look at her.

PAUL. Well. It's not a bad starting point.

HOWARD. He was definitely worried by the end –

SHERRY. Starting point? But he said . . . didn't he . . . that to get
the money we had to be out by . . . when was it?

HOWARD. The fifteenth of February.

SHERRY. Right, otherwise the offer would be off, that's what I
thought.

PAUL. Well he would say that, wouldn't he?

Pause.

SHERRY. You mean . . . we're not going to take it?

She looks at all of them, then sits, despondent.

We're not going to take it, are we?

PAUL. (*explaining.*) *We* are holding all the cards. *He* is setting up an artificial deadline in order to panic us into a decision. *We* are not going to be panicked.

MARION. Just look how much it went up just by sitting here staring at him. He started at twenty. We made ten grand in five minutes just by keeping our mouths shut.

HOWRD. Paul was magnificent. All that sob story stuff –

MARION. 'Our lovely home.'

HOWARD. 'Couldn't bear to leave it –'

MARION. 'One big happy family.'

MARION *and* HOWARD *are in a great state of mirth,* PAUL *is a little puzzled.*

PAUL. Well. It is a nice flat, isn't it? We do like living here.

Slight pause.

HOWARD. Sure, yes, it was just, I mean, the way you said it, sort of laid on with a trowel –

SHERRY. But look, he pointed out, you know, all the things he could do . . . turn it into a building site –

PAUL. Oh balls –

SHERRY. Put the rent up –

HOWARD. In point of fact, the rent, because it's a controlled rent, can only go up by small increments. Even if he argues to the Tribunal that the facilities here have been vastly improved, which quite patently they haven't –

No one is listening to him.

PAUL. He can't turn it into a building site, because if we're still here, he can't develop it. The guy actually said, he wanted to put in a central wall –

SHERRY. So what are we doing? We're not taking the money, what are we doing?

PAUL. We're going to sit it out, we're going to stay here until he pays us a decent price.

SHERRY. You mean, even more than thirty thousand . . .

PAUL. Sherry, think it through. You're given seven and a half grand. You're out on the street, what do you do?

SHERRY. Take a taxi to the Ritz.

PAUL. If we play our cards right, we could get enough out of him to buy a place.

SHERRY. What, the four of us?

PAUL. Well. Not necessarily the four of us. But . . . some of us . . . at the end of this process . . . should be in a position to buy . . .

Pause.

SHERRY. All right then. We're not taking thirty thousand. We're going to sit here, getting in Scott's way. So when does it stop? What do we take?

HOWARD. I don't see that we have to put a figure on it. I mean, we're in the basement, so we're in possession of the drains, now the drains, it seems to me are a key feature if you're wanting to make dinky flatlets out of the whole –

MARION. Sixty thousand.

Pause.

That's what we want. Fifteen thousand each. The golden rule when dealing with these people is to take the first sum they offer you and double it. So. He offers us seven and a half each. I personally, will not move from this place until I have a cheque for fifteen thousand pounds in my hot little hand.

Pause.

SHERRY (*disbelieving*). Fifteen thousand? Each?

PAUL. She's right. Aim high. It's there for the taking.

MARION. Howard?

HOWARD. Well, I think the principle is . . . right, I'd put it, in practical terms just a shade lower, you know, maybe forty, forty-five . . .

SHERRY. Supposing he tries to re-house us.

PAUL. We keep objecting. It has to be equivalent accommodation. We just keep saying . . .

MARION. The kitchen's smaller . . .

PAUL. It's further from the tube . . .

MARION. The rent's higher . . .

PAUL. He won't want to take us to court. He wouldn't want the hassle.

Pause.

SHERRY. So we just. Sit. Until he offers us . . . sixty thousand.

MARION. That's it.

HOWARD. And if he doesn't?

MARION. Then we just . . . sit. Until he does.

They contemplate this.

Slow fade to blackout. In the darkness we hear Bob Geldof singing 'I don't like Mondays.'

Scene Three

July 1985

Some books, ornaments and pictures are now missing. They have been packed into the cardboard boxes which stand prominently in a corner.

PAUL *is at the table, seated. He's speaking clearly into a good quality microphone.*

PAUL. . . . but now standing here in the vast emptiness of Wembley Stadium, it seems impossible to believe that in a few days time, Bob Geldof's dream will be transformed into reality.

SHERRY *comes in, then, seeing* PAUL *recording, stops in her tracks, trying to look unobtrusive.*

Before my eyes, teams of blue-overalled workmen are just starting to assemble ton upon ton of scaffolding . . .

SHERRY *is perplexed.*

into the enormous stage which will be graced on Saturday by some of the most prestigious names in rock music today. And the giant video screen, at present just a skeletal framework, will be carrying images, not only of the super-celebrities who are to perform here, but also of the silent millions on whose behalf they will play. This is Paul Cameron from Wembley Stadium for the ABC.

Pause.

This is Paul Cameron from Wembley Stadium for Radio Free Europe.

Pause.

This is Paul Cameron from Wembley Stadium for RTE.

Pause.

This is Paul Cameron from Wembley Stadium for Radio Zagreb.

He switches the tape off.

SHERRY. You certainly get around.

PAUL. The tapes get around. I'm always stuck here.

SHERRY. Is Howard in?

PAUL. No.

SHERRY. You said you were going to record my act and put it in a piece on the alternative comedy scene.

PAUL. Sherry, this stuff goes out to Tasmania and Warsaw and places. It won't increase the audience for your three minutes of random obscenity at the Queen's Head on a Sunday night.

SHERRY. Be nice to have a reputation, even if it's only an international one.

She makes to go.

PAUL. Sherry. What do you want to do?

SHERRY. I don't know.

PAUL. Somehow we've got to find a way out of the deadlock.

SHERRY. I would love to find a way out of the deadlock. Only I don't seem to have much clout around here. Marion makes up her mind what she wants, you go along with her because you're a couple, and Howard goes along with you so he can be in a majority. It doesn't seem to matter much what I think.

PAUL. OK, I see that. Now tell me what you want to do?

SHERRY. In an ideal world?

PAUL. In an ideal world.

SHERRY. OK I would like all this to end. Just stop. I would like Anthony Scott's scaffolding and rubble and workmen to disappear. I would like to be able to answer the phone without the fear of him shouting at me and calling us a lot of bastard ingrates. I would like it very much if other people stopped packing my belongings into cardboard boxes just to give Scott the impression that we're actually about to move. And . . . yes, I would like Marion to stop screaming 'Fifteen thousand each or die' every time I try to discuss the situation. (*She's made herself quite upset.*) Paul, I just want to take the ten thousand Scott's offered and go. And I honestly don't care what happens afterwards.

Pause.

PAUL. Right. OK. I understand that.

SHERRY. Now. You tell me what you want. Not Marion, *you*.

PAUL. I want to stay here –

SHERRY. Paul, we can't stay here, that's the whole –

PAUL. And Marion would like to have some children.

SHERRY. I know that, I didn't ask about that –

PAUL. But it's relevant. Marion would like us to buy a place together and have children –

SHERRY. Well, I don't see why you don't do just that. You'll have ten grand each, that's plenty, she's just got promoted, what's all the fuss about the extra five grand? Take the money and breed.

PAUL. Ah, well. There's one problem we have here. And it's rather a large one.

Pause.

Marion and I are no longer a couple. Any more. Which I . . . regret. We may look like a couple. On account of sleeping in the same bed. But that's a matter of convenience. We have to do that until we get Scott's money. And when we do, we're going our separate ways.

Pause.

SHERRY. Everybody knows this, don't they.

Pause.

Everybody knows this except me.

PAUL. Who's everybody? I know obviously. Marion knows.

SHERRY. Howard?

PAUL. Well, Howard knows, but Marion doesn't know that Howard knows.

SHERRY. You told Howard.

PAUL. Yes.

SHERRY. On account of Howard being a boy and boys talk to boys.

PAUL. I suppose.

SHERRY. Then how come girls haven't talked to girls. Girls always talk to girls.

PAUL. Well I suppose . . . Marion at the moment is . . .

SHERRY. I get it. She wants the two of you to look like a united front. If I'm kept in ignorance then there's less chance of me thinking I can scream the place down for taking the ten thousand and going.

PAUL. Well now you know.

SHERRY. This is awful. When you started going out together, she cycled four miles to tell me. What's happened, Paul, I don't understand.

PAUL. It's a perfectly rational decision. She wants to have children. And I don't. That's the way it's always been. But I thought I'd wear her down and she thought she'd wear me down. After ten years the contest has been declared a draw.
It's obvious. She hasn't that much more time. Like I said, it's perfectly rational.

SHERRY. That's why she needs fifteen grand instead of ten. 'Cos she's going it alone.

PAUL. That's right. She's seen exactly the sort of place she wants. She's done the sums. It's very tight. She's made up her mind.

SHERRY. I haven't even thought. I'd pack and leave in an hour if I could and I haven't given a thought to where I'd go.

PAUL. Well. Perhaps it's time you did. How would you like to buy a flat with me and Howard?

SHERRY. Would I have to have childrent?

PAUL. Children do not figure in this particular deal.

SHERRY. That's something. A flat? You're crazy, with you and Howard? I haven't got any money, Paul, that's the whole point.

PAUL. Not any old flat. This flat.
    And you have got money. You're about to get x thousand pounds from Anthony Scott where x is a number between ten and fifteen.

SHERRY. But . . . if we buy this flat, then we can't be leaving it. And if we're not leaving it, then we won't be getting the money.

PAUL. Exactly. In this scenario, the money you would get from Scott would be theoretical money.

Pause. SHERRY *looks confused.*

PAUL. Scott phoned at seven a.m. yesterday. While he was out jogging. We had a lunchtime meeting. He's had to alter all his plans. Because of us. There'll be no central wall, no clusters of dinky flatlets. He just wants shot of the place. He's lined up buyers for the other four flats. As they are. He should worry. With the price boom, he'll still make two hundred grand. Just over a year, not bad. So. This flat is now valued at ninety-five, his figure. We can either take the forty grand between us to go. Or we can buy the flat at the knock-down price of fifty grand. See, he either gives us forty thousand in real money or forty-five thousand in theoretical money.

SHERRY. So you, me and Howard buy. What happens to Marion? Some of the theoretical money should be hers.

PAUL. Precisely. My plan is this: the three of us buy the flat for fifty. Seventeenish each. Then we pay Marion fifteen to go. And everyone's happy.

SHERRY. Marion gets fifteen grand?

PAUL. From you, me and Howard. Five each. It's a bit unfair, but it gets a result.

SHERRY. So what you're saying is instead of someone giving me a cheque for ten thousand pounds, you want me to give two other people cheques to the value of . . . twenty-one thousand pounds.

PAUL. Call it twenty-three with extras.

SHERRY. And you actually think this is an idea that should be seriously considered.

PAUL. Take the long term view. What would you do with ten grand? By the time you've bought some clothes, got pissed, had a holiday –

SHERRY. Twenty-three thousand? I haven't got twenty-three pence.

PAUL. The gap between the haves and the have-nots is increasing all the time. This may be the only chance you ever have to stop being a have-not. I'll get my accountant to beef up your earnings so you look good on paper. Then, all you'd have to do to pay the mortgage would be . . . to get more successful . . . or . . .

SHERRY. Or what?

PAUL. Nothing.

SHERRY. Or get a proper job.

PAUL. Or get a proper job. Nobody here is a chicken any more. That's for certain.

SHERRY *storms out.*

(*Shouting.*) Will you give the idea some thought?

Pause. PAUL *sits, muttering, pours a drink.* SHERRY *comes back.*

SHERRY. You know what this means don't you?

PAUL. What?

SHERRY. I would have to stay in my damp room.

PAUL. Ah.

SHERRY. All my clothes are getting damp.

PAUL. Well. That's because the flat belongs to the landlord. Once it belongs to us, we'll have a motive for improving it. Priority number one: the dampness in your room.

SHERRY. Or we could swap rooms.

PAUL. Or we could swap rooms.

SHERRY *goes to the door of* PAUL *and* MARION's *room, looks in.*

SHERRY. I've always liked this room.

PAUL. OK. If you buy a third, we'll swap rooms.

SHERRY. You want to stay here an awful lot, don't you?

Pause.

PAUL. You've got to have something constant in your life. At least I have. Those awful moments when everything changes. Leaving school. Moving house. Putting things in suitcases, I hate that. You have to fight for some kind of continuity. If you don't have the continuity you just . . . drift, you lose your grip . . .

A moment. MARION *comes on carrying four empty cardboard boxes.*

MARION. I got these from Sainsbury's. I think we should make a start on the pictures tonight. What are you doing Sherry?

SHERRY. I was just looking at your room. It's really nice, isn't it?

Pause.

You'll be sorry to leave it.

MARION. Yes. (*To* PAUL.) The pictures in this big one, yes? And the others will do for books.

PAUL. You're early aren't you?

MARION. Jeremy and I are going to a conference in Reading tomorrow. We've got an early start.

The phone rings in the hall.

You could pack your old records, Sherry, you never play them any more.

MARION *goes off to answer the phone.*

PAUL. She doesn't mean it.

SHERRY. You don't have to make excuses for her.

PAUL. She just thinks it's the best way –

SHERRY. It freaks me out, you know. You've been going out with her for a whole decade.

PAUL. It freaks *you* out.

SHERRY. It can't just be babies. Can it?

PAUL. Well. I suppose it's never one thing.

SHERRY. No. I suppose not. I'm really sorry. Is it all right for me to say that?

PAUL. Yes. It's all right.

MARION *is back.*

MARION (*to* PAUL). It's Anthony, he wants to speak to you.

PAUL. You mean Scott?

MARION. Yes.

PAUL. Why does it always have to be me?

PAUL *goes off to the phone in bad humour.* MARION *is looking at the pictures.*

MARION. I can't remember who these belong to.

She takes one off the wall and examines it.

SHERRY. Are you and Paul getting on OK?

MARION. Famously. I suppose this is bound to be his.

SHERRY. All this uncertainty. The flat and the money and so on. I just feel there's an awful lot of stress around.

MARION. I think everyone's coping very well.

Pause.

SHERRY. Well. I actually don't think that. I tend to think more the opposite. I think we're all going crazy. And we're going crazy for a basic biological reason. We're animals. Animals need a place to live. Take that away or put it under threat, and they – that is we – begin to behave in all sorts of crazy ways. Have you tried talking to Howard lately? Unless you've got any small talk on the shift from a labour intensive to a capital intensive economy he doesn't want to know. Me? I'm not well, I'm really not. I couldn't even face doing my spot at the Queen's Head last Sunday. They had to pull me out at the last minute. I don't know if I can face it this week either. And you . . . used to be my best friend, and now you don't even tell me you're splitting up with Paul.

Pause. SHERRY *sits down, almost in tears.*

MARION. It's a mistake I suppose, really. You should either get married or split up. This going out together for years and years. I think we rather missed one another at some point. He was always so concerned that marriage and commitment meant losing your personal liberty, I got used to the idea. But I don't think I ever took it that seriously. I mean I assumed secretly

that one day he'd stop mucking around and say 'OK, this is it
for life.' But he didn't and I'm now short of time. So it had to
end. But . . . there are financial considerations. There's this
wonderful development, Battersea, just what I want. But I need
that extra five thousand see? And I shall get it.

SHERRY. Paul just suggested I should buy this flat with him and
Howard.

MARION. It would be sensible. You really ought to think of
buying somewhere.

SHERRY. I wouldn't mind doing a bit of travelling actually. I
think I'd rather do that.

PAUL *comes back in a state of anxiety.*

PAUL. I was called names on that phone.

MARION. What did he say?

PAUL. I was referred to in very unflattering terms.

MARION. Is he upset?

PAUL. Upset? No he's not *upset*. Upset is what you get when you
cut yourself shaving. This man is *murderous*.

MARION. Poor darling.

PAUL. I was called an obstructive fucker on that phone. 'You,' he
said 'are an obstructive fucker.' 'Not only are you screwing me
about. You are actively and deliberately getting in my way. And
on the basis of this evidence, I do not hesitate to call you an
obstructive fucker.'

MARION. Paul, what did he actually say?

PAUL. That *is* what he actually –

MARION. Did he come up with a new offer?

PAUL. Yes.

Pause.

He said it was his absolutely final offer. He said if we didn't
accept it, he would personally guarantee that we wouldn't
make, and I quote, a brass centime out of the deal. And he
means it.

MARION. So what's the offer.

Pause.

PAUL. There are actually two offers on the table. If we do not accept one of these in the next forty-eight hours, then we can consider ourselves at war with Anthony Scott and his attendant powers of darkness. Offer one: forty-five grand for vacant possession. This works out at eleven thousand two hundred and fifty each.

MARION. Shit.

She sits down suddenly.

PAUL. Offer two: he will sell us, all four of us or any combination permed from the four of us, this flat, market value estimated at ninety-five grand, for forty-eight thousand pounds, i.e. he's giving us forty-seven grand. So . . . That's it. Any takers?

Pause.

MARION. Sherry?

SHERRY. OK. I just want to say this.

Pause.

You asked me to think about buying a share. Well I've thought about it for a full five minutes. And it was misery. I'm a thousand overdrawn in the bank. I'm over the limit on my Access card, my Barclaycard. And I owe people money. I owe all of you money. And on top of that you want me to buy a flat. And yes, I *do* know the phone bill's due again and most of it's mine, and if we could just take the money, I could pay it all, everything, easily, right?

She rushes out. Pause

PAUL. I didn't know she had any credit cards, they must be out of their minds.

MARION. Yes.

MARION *is thinking rapidly.*

PAUL. So. She wants to go. You want to go. So we have to take the money. Unless Howard and I buy the flat. Which would be forty-eight thousand, plus we'd have to buy the two of you off at . . . twenty-two and a half . . . which means (*Shocked.*) seventy thousand plus. We'd have to find thirty-five thousand each, it just can't be . . . it just can't be done.

Pause. MARION *gets up, goes to the picture she's just taken down.*

MARION. We'll do it.

PAUL. What?

MARION. You've discussed the buying option with Howard, yes?

PAUL. Yes.

MARION. Behind my back.

PAUL. Well tentatively, you know.

MARION. I don't mind, it's a good idea.

PAUL. But Sherry won't –

MARION. Howard will though, yes?

PAUL. What?

MARION. Howard is theoretically in?

PAUL. Well he can raise a reasonable mortgage on his –

MARION. So we'll buy it then.

Pause.

PAUL. We?

MARION. You, me, Howard. We buy the flat for forty-eight, pay Sherry off for eleven two-fifty, call it sixty grand between the three of us. Easy peasy.

PAUL. Does this mean?

MARION. No, it doesn't mean. It's going to be an investment. You can move into Sherry's room. We'll renovate it first.

PAUL. Renovate.

MARION. The whole place. Starting with Sherry's room . . . *your* room. It'll be nice.

PAUL. But –

MARION. I'll put some money separately into a building fund. I've got a big cash bonus coming from Jeremy. We'll keep accounts and reckon up when we sell the place. All right?

PAUL. When did you work this out?

MARION. Just now.

MARION *puts the picture back on the wall.*

There. We're staying. It's what you wanted, isn't it?

She goes off.

MARION. (*off*). Sherry!

Blackout. In the darkness we hear Dire Straits singing 'Money for Nothing.'

Scene Four

October 1985. A Saturday morning, around eleven o'clock.

The room is a little emptier – all the cardboard boxes have gone.
HOWARD *is working at the table, attacking the typewriter with vigour.*

SHERRY *comes in. She's wearing a long white nightdress and drinking a mug of coffee. She stands watching* HOWARD. *Some moments.*

SHERRY. I've got such a lot to do.

HOWARD *continues to type, muttering to himself.*

I can't believe I'm really going.

HOWARD *as before.*

Have they gone out?

HOWARD. Down the building society.

SHERRY. Oh already?

HOWARD. It shuts at twelve.

SHERRY. For my money?

HOWARD *writes some more.*

Great.

She sips at her coffee.

I'll never get it all done.

HOWARD *types some more, then takes the page out of the typewriter and scans it.*

HOWARD. I don't think anybody else has noticed this.

SHERRY. What?

HOWARD. Well . . . historically, for hundreds of years, the British were self-sufficient in food. I mean, we ate what we grew. What happened with the industrial revolution changed all that. We swapped our pre-eminent position as an agricultural nation for dominance as a manufacturing nation, i.e. other nations grew our food for us and we paid for them with ready-made goods. But now it's changing again. For the first time in history, we are running a deficit on our manufacturing industries. So. Where is our wealth coming from?

SHERRY. From the building society.

HOWARD. Exactly! That is exactly the right answer!

SHERRY. Oh.

HOWARD. You are a paradigm of the British economy. You consume more than you produce. You are heavily in debt. But you have managed to keep yourself afloat by selling off your personal share of the national infrastructure – in your case, the right to dwell in a small damp room. Clever isn't it? You stop making new things, instead you tell the world that the things you've already made, the things your grandparents and great-grandparents made, are worth immeasurably more than they were originally. You tell the world over and over again until they start – literally – buying it.

SHERRY. I've always wanted to be a paradigm.

HOWARD. But there's one problem.

SHERRY. I thought there might be.

HOWARD. How long will it last? Once the world's evaluation of our infrastructure falls . . . so do we.

SHERRY. Christ.

HOWARD. And so do you.

A ring at the doorbell.

SHERRY. My money!

She rushes off to answer it. HOWARD *watches her doubtfully. He looks at what he's written. Screws the paper up and throws it on the floor. Inserts a fresh sheet. Pauses a moment, then begins writing again.*

SHERRY *comes in showing signals of distress. Behind her is* ANTHONY SCOTT.

HOWARD. Oh.

SCOTT. Ah.

SHERRY. It's . . . Mr Scott.

HOWARD. Yes.

SCOTT. Is the other chap not in, Paul?

HOWARD. Paul. No he's not, he's . . . out.

SHERRY. That's right, and so's Marion.

HOWARD. But they'll be back.

SHERRY. Yes they've just gone –

SCOTT. Small problem. Nothing earth-shattering. Got a prospective buyer. Ground floor flat. She's upstairs at the moment, having a bit of a prowl.

HOWARD. Oh.

SCOTT. I think she's serious. I should say she's a very serious buyer indeed. This is her second visit, she's got a bloody great laundry list of questions. One of them is about the garden.

SCOTT *goes over to the window and stares out.*

Such as it is.

Pause.

You have access, she has access. The point is this. Where does your bit stop and her bit start. Any views?

He turns towards SHERRY *and* HOWARD. *Both are anxious not to commit themselves to a point of view which may later be interpreted as a tactical error by* PAUL *or* MARION. *So both look blank.*

Difficult to get a view round here, I tend to find. Everyone has to go into a huddle for a fortnight before coming to a decision. How was it divided up before?

HOWARD. We have use of it. So do the upstairs flat.

SCOTT. But it's on two levels. A smallish bit down on your level. And a biggish bit up on her level.

HOWARD. Yes, but the precedent is both flats use the whole garden.

SCOTT. Well we can't have that. It's not a bloody safari park. It's a piece of property. It needs dividing up. Can I bring her down. Talk about it?

HOWARD. Yes, I don't see why not –

SHERRY. I must get dressed.

But she makes no move. SCOTT *looks at his watch.*

SCOTT. Look, I'll nip upstairs. Few points to go through with her. Then I'll bring her down. Paul will be back, you say?

HOWARD. Very soon.

SHERRY. Very, very soon.

SCOTT. OK then. A few mins. You have been forewarned.

He goes. SHERRY *flaps around, wondering whether to see him out or not. Eventually decides to. Pause. She comes back.* HOWARD *is staring out at the garden looking annoyed.*

HOWARD. Just when you think you've . . . suddenly something else . . .

SHERRY. What are you saying, Howard?

HOWARD. I want to be left in peace!

Pause. SHERRY *is impressed by this sudden outburst.*

I'm sorry. I don't mean you. I just mean there are so many hassles. All the legal stuff, getting the mortgage organised. Haggling with Scott. Fine, OK I can live with it for a few months. But it doesn't seem to stop. I mean, I'm trying to write a book about the British Economy. It's a brilliant book, I know it is. But every time I try to get it out of my brains and on to the paper, someone comes barging in telling me to . . . draw a line down the middle of the garden or something . . .

SHERRY *goes to him and cuddles him.*

What I used to like about this flat . . . was the people. I could have gone and bought a little broom cupboard in Neasden years ago. But I didn't because I liked it here. And now you're going. And Marion and Paul are splitting up. And all that's left is the flat. It's hard to work here any more. It's hard to find people to chat to. It's just a building, that's all. An investment.

SHERRY. You ought to find yourself a nice girl.

Suddenly PAUL *and* MARION *burst in, excited.* MARION *holds a large brown envelope.* PAUL *carries a tray on which are four glasses and a bottle of champagne.*

MARION. Oh look, a moving human scene.

PAUL. For Christ's sake, you two. You've been living in adjacent rooms for a decade, don't start getting it together now she's leaving.

SHERRY. We were just having an innocent, sentimental –

PAUL. Champagne time. We thought this event should not go uncelebrated.

He starts peeling the wrapping off the top of the bottle.

MARION (*brandishing envelope*). It's all here. Exactly as you wanted it.

SHERRY *catches their excitement.*

SHERRY. Quick, quick, let me see it.

MARION. No, you have to wait a moment.

PAUL. For the champagne, these things have to be done properly.

MARION. Where's your key?

SHERRY. My key?

MARION. Door key.

SHERRY. Oh.

She goes off to her room.

PAUL (*to* HOWARD). Hold a glass so I don't spill any.

HOWARD. I think we're going to have a problem with the garden –

PAUL. Not *now* –

MARION. We want to give Sherry a nice send-off –

PAUL. Not that she's going to get off the premises by midnight at the current rate of progress –

MARION. If she's not out by midnight, we could start charging her rent.

PAUL *laughs,* SHERRY *comes back holding a Yale.*

PAUL. Right, here we go.

PAUL opens the champagne and pours it into glasses held out and then distributed by HOWARD.

SHERRY. Who's paying for this?

MARION. What?

SHERRY. The champagne? Is it coming out of my money?

MARION. The syndicate is paying. Paul, Howard and me. We have just bought ourselves a slice of London.

SHERRY. Let me look at it, let me see the –

PAUL. Not yet!

He looks around.

Everyone has a glass? Yes. Now then.

Mock formal address.

Dearly beloved bretheren. We are gathered here today to mark the demise, from these rented premises of our dear sister Sherry St George, née Martin. History will ask but one question: Did she fall or was she pushed? I think the answer will come ringing back loud and clear: 'A bit of both.' God bless her and all who sail in her!

All drink, offering various toasts.

Now if you'd like to step forward.

SHERRY *does so.*

MARION. In exchange for your front door key, I hereby present you with a cheque for ten thousand pounds.

SHERRY *examines the cheque carefully.*

And an envelope full of twenty pound notes to the sum of one thousand, two hundred and fifty pounds.

HOWRD. They can't all be twenties –

PAUL. Sixty-two twenties and one ten.

SHERRY *takes the cheque and the envelope,* MARION *the key.*

MARION. It felt terrible walking down the street with it all –

SHERRY. I don't think I've ever seen so much money before and it's all mine.

HOWARD. Paul, there's something important –

PAUL. Wait a minute –

SHERRY opens the envelope. She lets the money fall out all over the floor, kneels down and runs her hands through it.

SHERRY. It's so lovely. It really is so beautiful.

A moment, they watch her with the money. Then SHERRY lets out a whoop. Goes off to hug MARION, then PAUL.

Thank you. Thank you.

She's quite tearful. She swigs some champagne down and gives HOWARD a half-hug.

I'm sorry I was a bit of a pain. I was so afraid we'd end up with nothing. You were great, all of you being so strong.

A thought strikes her.

Oh. I owe you all some of this. Paul.

She hands him a twenty pound note.

PAUL. Oh. Are you sure this is –

SHERRY. Marion.

She hands MARION a twenty pound note.

SHERRY. Howard.

She hands HOWARD three twenty pound notes. He is embarrassed, not wanting the others to know how much he's lent her.

MARION. This is too much, you only owe me –

SHERRY. No, it's not too much. It's too little, I know there's lots of things I haven't paid for over the years.

MARION. Sherry –

SHERRY. No, I won't hear a word of it. It's not too much, it isn't nearly enough. This champagne is heaven.

She gulps some more down, PAUL tops up her glass. SHERRY delves deeper into the pile of money.

PAUL. You're welcome.

SHERRY. No, I've decided, you're all to have some more. There's all sorts of things I've used over the years.

PAUL. Sherry, just steady, all right –

SHERRY. Washing up liquid, soap, all sorts of things.

She picks up three more twenty pound notes.

MARION. Please. Sherry, put it all back in the envelope.

SHERRY. TOILET ROLLS!!! Do you know the last time I bought a toilet roll? Have another one of these.

She proffers three more twenty pound notes.

PAUL. It's all OK. It's all absolutely –

SHERRY. Nineteen seventy-nine, that's when!! In Dieppe. It was Bastille Day and I had chronic diarrhoea –

MARION. You don't owe any of us anything –

SHERRY. Streaming! And I went into this whatsit . . . Monoprix and bought a roll and I thought, Christ, I had no idea it was so expensive –

A ring at the bell.

HOWARD. Christ!

She's on her feet, trying to force money on everyone.

HOWARD. It's Scott. He's got this woman upstairs.

PAUL. Really?

HOWARD. A buyer. It's about the garden, we've got to divide it up.

MARION. I don't get this.

HOWARD. Marion, just sort her out.

HOWARD *drags* PAUL *with him to the front door, explaining all the way.*

HOWARD. She's buying the ground floor flat. But she wants to know how much of the garden is hers and how much is . . .

SHERRY *is getting more tearful. She swigs some champagne.*

MARION. What's all this about Scott?

SHERRY *drinks some more.*

SHERRY. I'm going to miss you all so much. It's been such a long time. I only wish there'd been some way. If only we could have found a way. For me to stay, it would have been . . .

MARION, *peering down the corridor, has realised that* SCOTT *is the impending visitor.*

MARION. Listen, we must clear up all this money –

SHERRY. No, it's mine, leave it alone.

MARION. Sherry, it's Scott, he's coming up the corridor now –

SHERRY. I like it. I like feeling it.

She pushes MARION *away.*

Leave it.

MARION *freezes, unable to make up her mind what to do.*

I wish I didn't have to go.

She reaches for the champagne bottle.

SHERRY. I really wish that.

PAUL *comes in followed by* SCOTT. HOWARD *brings up the rear.*

They all pause in the doorway, transfixed by the sight of SHERRY, *kneeling in a pile of twenty pound notes in her nightie, tears streaming down her face, clutching the champagne bottle.*

They're throwing me out!!!

SCOTT. Well they're having more success than I ever did.

MARION. It's all right, she's just a little –

SCOTT. Now, I mentioned when I was down earlier –

HOWARD. Yes, well they've only just come in, so I've not had time to –

SHERRY. There's a woman in the garden staring at me. (*To garden.*) Fuck off!!!

SCOTT. Ah yes, that's the prospective buyer. Claire Kinross, the Honourable Claire Kinross.

HOWARD. Oh Christ.

SHERRY *starts to struggle up on to a chair so she can abuse* CLAIRE *through the top of the window.*

SHERRY. That's our garden you know, you can't just wander round it like it was Brent Cross shopping centre –

SCOTT (*to* PAUL). Yes well, the thing is, the garden.

SHERRY. They hate me! They've always hated me. And now they're buying me off. That's how you really show you hate someone. By giving them piles of money. It's the biggest fucking insult in the world.

Pause. All stare at SHERRY.

PAUL. The best way, actually, into the garden is through this door here.

He makes for his and MARION's *bedroom door.*

He's through the door. SCOTT *follows him.* HOWARD *flaps.*

HOWARD. Do something with her.

He follows the others out into the garden. MARION *stares at* SHERRY.

MARION. Sherry, will you please sit on that chair, please.

SHERRY *immediately goes to sit at the table, among* HOWARD's *papers.*

Give me the bottle.

She gives MARION *the bottle.* MARION *puts it on the mantelpiece, then starts clearing up the money into the brown envelope.* SHERRY *watches her.*

SHERRY. There's something so . . . admirable about you. There always has been. You are so contained. People look at you, they admire you. You should have done better for yourself, you've got so much . . . class, so much cool. I've sat and admired your cool for hours at a stretch. At University there were all these dozens of men. Following you around. They used to plan their day around the possibility of catching a glimpse of your cool. Money would change hands for library seats affording a good view of you. It wasn't lust, it was a fascination with the outer limits of cool. I loved being your best friend. But I always wanted you to say it. I wanted you to say: 'Sherry, you're my best friend.' But I knew you wouldn't. If you'd said that, it wouldn't have been cool.

MARION *has the money in the envelope. She looks at* SHERRY.

MARION. Sherry . . .

Pause.

I think it would be a good idea if you took this money into your room and got dressed.

SHERRY. Yes. I've got such a lot to do. I've got to pack all the rest of my things and clear out of my room. And write all those cheques. Phone calls, must phone my mum. Load all my stuff on to the van by three o'clock for Paul to drive to my auntie's. Pick up my travellers' cheques and currency from American Express, get to the airport by . . . when do I have to be at the –

MARION. Nine o'clock –

SHERRY. Nine o'clock, right. And I shall get on the plane and drink lots and fall asleep watching the film. Then wake up in San Francisco.

MARION. Yes. You're glad you're going, aren't you?

SHERRY. I'm going to love it, I'm going to absolutely adore it. I used to say, when I was a little girl: 'I'm going to go round the world.' And now I really am.

MARION. Yes. Please get dressed, or you'll be behind schedule.

SHERRY *stands.*

SHERRY. I'm sorry about just now. It was handing in my key that did it. It suddenly hit me that I was leaving.

MARION *is looking out of the window.*

MARION. I think they're going to come back in.

SHERRY. I must . . . I don't want them to see me.

MARION. Just put some old jeans on, for the packing. I'll come and help you in a minute.

SHERRY. Yes.

She heads for the door. MARION *brandishes the envelope.*

MARION. Sherry. Take your money.

SHERRY *(taking it)*. Oh yes.

MARION. Put it under your pillow for now, right?

SHERRY. Pillow. Right. Yes.

She goes. MARION *looks out at the garden. Does some hasty tidying up. Quickly adjusts her own appearance.*

HOWARD *comes in, then* PAUL, *talking to* SCOTT.

MARION. Is it all right?

SCOTT. I've suggested a dividing line. When you've talked it over, you can telephone my lawyers.

He smiles.

(*To* PAUL.) So. Quick decision on this one, please. If need be, make a drawing and bike it round to me. Then we'll be ready to exchange on Wednesday, all right?

PAUL. Yes, fine.

SCOTT *looks around.*

SCOTT. Big flat. You got it bloody cheap. One of these, identical, just round the corner, went the other day for a hundred. So you're well in.

PAUL. Well, we're quite pleased.

SCOTT. I should say.

He makes to go, then turns for a moment.

Oh just one last thing. (*Pleasantly.*) You're bastards. You're a bunch of grasping, capitalist bastards. Congratulations. Wasn't too difficult, was it?

He goes. HOWARD *sits, looks at his notes.*

HOWARD. It's not real wealth, that's the point. There's no substance to it.

SHERRY *comes in. She's still in her nightie.*

SHERRY. Marion. Did I take that money or did I leave it here?

MARION. You put it under your pillow.

SHERRY. Pillow, of course.

She goes to the champagne bottle, drinks.

I've got such a lot to do.

Blackout.

ACT TWO

Scene One

May 1986. We hear Paul Simon's 'You can call me Al'.

The room is now completely bare. The carpet has been taken up and every single object removed. A huge dust cloth covers the floor. Early afternoon. A hot day.

For several moments nothing happens at all. Then for the first time in the play, the French windows open. In fact, they fly open at the combined push of PAUL *and* HOWARD *who come in from the garden carrying between them a large plastic dustbin full of rubble.*

PAUL *is wearing only a pair of cut-off jeans.* HOWARD *a tee-shirt and a pair of old trousers. Both look tired and dirty. After a few stumbling paces towards the corridor with the dustbin of rubble, it becomes clear that* HOWARD *can't carry it any further. They come to a halt in the middle of the room.*

HOWARD. No, no, no, no, just leave –

PAUL. Don't, not like that –

HOWARD. Down! Put it –

PAUL. For fuck's sake!

They stop and breathe heavily.

You can't just –

HOWARD. Yes, I know –

PAUL. Well, if you know then –

HOWARD. Yes, yes, all right yes.

They breathe some more.

HOWARD. Silly bastard.

PAUL. What?

HOWARD. Him, not you. He's filled it too full. Silly bastard.

Pause. PAUL *goes to the French windows and calls out.*

PAUL. Stewart! You are the subject of some criticism here.

HOWARD *is sitting on the floor, completely exhausted.*

(*Off.*) A section of the workforce is refusing to co-operate with the new norms.

PAUL *turns back to* HOWARD, *surveying him.* STEWART *comes on. He's around forty, strong, bearded. He wears old jeans, no shirt and carries a pickaxe. He stands in the doorway, looking at* HOWARD.

STEWART. What's up?

HOWARD. There's too much rubble in the dustbin.

STEWART. Too much? How can there be too much?

HOWARD *looks at him, suddenly animated.*

HOWARD. You chip it out with the pickaxe, right? And shovel it in the bin, right? And we walk it down the corridor and through to the skip, right? But if you put too much in the bin, we can't carry it. It doesn't get to the skip. It stays here in the middle of the floor.

STEWART. I thought you were supposed to be working-class, Howard.

HOWARD. I am not *supposed* to be working-class, I *am* working-class.

STEWART. The whole point of the working-class is that they should be able to work.

HOWARD. It is *too heavy*!!

STEWART *puts the pick down.*

STEWART. Paul?

He motions PAUL *to the bin. They pick it up with relative ease, and take it out of the door and down the corridor.*

HOWARD *sits there, defeated. He's at the end of his tether, trying hard not to burst into tears.*

HOWARD. I just . . . want it . . . to stop . . .

He reaches into his pocket for a cigarette. Lights it, smokes it, trying to pull himself together. A pause.

MARION *comes in, very smartly dressed. She carries a bag which obviously contains an exciting new clothes purchase.*

MARION. Hello.

She goes to the French windows and looks out.

You boys. You do have your fun and games.

She turns and looks at HOWARD.

MARION. Is Paul annoyed with me?

HOWARD. What?

MARION. He just passed me in the corridor without saying hello.

HOWARD. Was he carrying two and a half hundredweight of shite at the time?

MARION. Yes.

HOWARD. I wouldn't take it personally then.

Pause.

MARION. Are you all right?

HOWARD. No.

Pause.

I don't think I can take it any more. Let's do the flat up ourselves, let's save money. OK, I'll do that, I'm on the bus. Why pay a load of cowboys ten grand to excavate our half of the garden when we can do it ourselves for five hundred quid? These guys, they're not clever, they're not especially skilled, all you're paying for is hard physical labour.

Pause.

Well personally, I think they deserve it, all that money. I think hard physical labour *should* carry high rewards. I tell you one thing, I remember now why I stuck at my books when I was a lad. Anything to avoid looking like me dad did after a double shift at the shipyard. I worked one day there, Christmas Vac, 1971. Couldn't stand up the next day. Physically, could not stand up, get out of bed, anything. That's how I got my first. Fear of hard physical labour. And now here I am, doing this. I'm not practical enough to be the foreman, and I'm not fit enough to do the donkey work. This, this is what I've been trying to get away from all my life. I just want to be in a quiet room, surrounded by books, writing. Yesterday I took the top off a bottle of Tippex to remind me of the smell. It was beautiful.

Pause. HOWARD *is moved,* MARION *embarrassed by this confidence.* MARION *makes a move to touch him, then changes her mind.*

STEWART *comes back, carrying the empty bin.*

STEWART. Sorry about that Howard, you were right. I scraped my shin dragging the bugger up the steps.

He claps HOWARD *matily round the shoulder.*

Must not get carried away. Must not get carried away.

He takes the bin out into the garden.

PAUL *comes in carrying a postcard.*

PAUL. Second post. (*To* MARION, *mock surprise.*) Oh hello. Guess who it's from.

MARION. It isn't!

She snatches the postcard.

PAUL. It is.

MARION. From Sherry, wonderful, Paraguay!

PAUL. Well yes, the picture on the front is Paraguay.

HOWARD (*looking over* MARION's *shoulder*). But the postmark is Senegal.

MARION. Oh yes. (*She reads.*) 'Here I am in Burundi.'

STEWART *comes in. He stands in the doorway with his pick.*

'The most amazing things keep happening to me. Everywhere there is poverty, but mingled with the picturesque. It all seems a long time ago, the flat and everything. Money lasts longer here and it is truly a better existence. But I'll be back in the autumn. Love to you all, Sherry.' Well.

STEWART. So now you know. They live better over there.

PAUL. In Burundi.

HOWARD. Or Senegal or Paraguay.

MARION. It's not exactly . . .

HOWARD. Packed with those clinching details which are the hallmark of the great foreign correspondent.

MARION. Quite.

STEWART. Synchronicity, this is the thing.

They look at him blankly.

Synchronicity. A child is dying in Burundi. Say it's three o'clock in the afternoon. At exactly the same moment, an armed mob storms the gates of the President's palace in Paraguay and a couple in Senegal are screwing in blissful delirium on the damp earth of the rain forest. All these events are connected. A shift in a molecule here, a nudge of an atom there, and the child is dead, the dictator on the scrap heap of history and the couple totally shagged out and wondering what to do for the rest of the afternoon. It's like working in your garden. I swing the pickaxe and a shudder runs through the earth's core. Somewhere in Papua New Guina, a child is born.

He goes back into the garden with the pickaxe.

MARION. Is he all right?

PAUL. He used to be a DJ on Radio Caroline in the Sixties.

HOWARD. Although I don't think the current situation in Paraguay is nearly as dynamic as he suggested. I mean is it really possible that –

He stops, realises he's boring them. Goes into the garden.

PAUL *and* MARION *look at each other. A pause.*

MARION. Hello.

PAUL. Been out?

MARION. Yes.

PAUL. Long time.

MARION. Not really, I just got in very late last night and had to get into the office early this morning.

PAUL. On a Saturday?

MARION. Got the new launch coming up in ten days time. It isn't a doss there any more. I had to proof read the leaflets.

PAUL. Funny, we got up at half six. Didn't hear you.

MARION. Quiet as a mouse, me.

She stares him out, daring him to disbelieve it.

PAUL. I went into your room. You weren't there. You weren't there at midnight. Or seven in the morning, or any time in between. I know you were with Jeremy.

MARION. All right, I was with Jeremy.

PAUL. We're not meant to be a couple any more. You don't have to buy a dress from Next on the way back to make me think you've been out shopping.

MARION. If we're not meant to be a couple, how come you're going into my room at all hours checking up?

Pause. They both sit.

It's not working. We're still living together so it feels as if we're still . . . together. But we're not. Everything's changed and yet . . . everything still goes on the same.

PAUL. Well I'm sorry, but we decided on a course of action and we can't change our minds now.

MARION. I'm not talking about changing our minds, I'm talking about my feelings –

PAUL. Feelings don't come into it. We bought the flat together and while we're halfway through the building work we won't be able to sell it. And of course, since we can't afford to pay the ludicrous prices charged by so-called professional builders, we have to do it ourselves. So it's slow, very slow, but there it is. We've just got to lump it.

MARION. I hate the whole fucking business. Separate bedrooms. It takes me an hour to fall asleep every night. At least an hour. I don't know what your life is like any more. After all those years. I don't know what you're doing, where you go. I get jealous, with or without cause I don't know, I've no idea if you get jealous –

PAUL. Of course I get jealous, why d'you think I check up on you. I'd guessed about Jeremy, you knew I'd guessed.

MARION. Talk about being out of practice. I had been so monumentally faithful to you. It took me three months to realise that he wasn't just impressed by my new found industry. In the old days, when I was just mooching round the office clocking up the minimum, he wasn't interested. As soon as I started putting in every waking hour I would catch him staring at my legs. Same legs. Only industry is sexy to Jeremy. Adrenalin, power, all that go-for-it mentality. We're making so much money, you wouldn't believe. Just a little hole in the corner operation a few years back, then suddenly, wammo, you identify a gap in the market, you square up the state of the art technology with consumer demand and then you work and work and work till you're there. Our service, what we provide is actually brilliant, no hype, no bullshit. And to be absolutely honest, I love it, I adore it. It's only when I stop . . . come back here . . . stare at the Bob Dylan poster on the loo door . . .

HOWARD *and* STEWART *stagger through with another bin of rubble. They macho this up as much as possible.*

PAUL. So what do you want to do?

MARION. Well. I don't see it would be a disadvantage to sell in the current state. You need three things – location, quantity and quality. Well we've got the first two. The quality is something a buyer could work on. The potential's here, that's the important thing.

PAUL. You want to move in with Jeremy. That's what you're saying –

MARION. I'm not saying that. I don't know. Maybe. All I'm saying is I can't stand *this*. I could get a place on my own, you and Howard could chip in together. Everyone would be happy. Or at least, no one would be downright bloody miserable.

PAUL. I have to see this through. The building. It's the one thing I've concentrated on to keep me sane. I can't just throw it over now. After the garden, we're doing the damp in my room. Comes from that old sink. Take the sink out, dig up the rotten floorboards, burn them. Then dig down, improve the circulation of air underneath, replace the joists and the boards and there you are. Stewart's got a mate who deals in pine, we can do the whole job for a hundred quid. It's satisfying me, don't you see that?

MARION. And the music biz?

PAUL. That piece on the new Paul Simon album. *Q Magazine* want an expanded version.

MARION. Thank Christ for Paul Simon. You'd be sunk if you had to write about someone new, eh?

STEWART *comes on.*

STEWART. You know those four pieces of timber we need for the supports?

PAUL. The three be two?

STEWART. The three be two. Well, we only need three of them now.

HOWARD *comes on. He carries an estate agent's 'For Sale' sign mounted on a seven foot length of three by two.*

HOWARD. Seven foot of three be two.

STEWART. It suddenly fell away from the property it was advertising.

HOWARD. Straight into our honest hands.

STEWART. This is my point about synchronicity, you see. You need a piece of wood, you don't go out and buy it. You wait for *it* to come to *you*.

MARION. Is that . . . I mean isn't that theft?

HOWARD. From estate agents? No, no, you see, if all property is theft, then who is more culpable?

STEWART *goes off into the garden, leaving the estate agent's sign on the floor.*

HOWARD. It's quite a profound idea really. The advertisement for the property actually becomes *part* of the property.

He follows STEWART *out.*

A case of the sign as signifier becoming the signified.

PAUL. See, Howie's cheered up already, it doesn't take much does it?

MARION. Is that a warning to make me buck up?

PAUL. It would help. The morale of the troops.

MARION. You find out I've been screwing my boss and all you're worried about is the morale of the troops. You can't summon a full committee meeting of flat members to deal with this problem.

STEWART *comes in.*

STEWART. She's making peculiar noises.

PAUL. I'm sorry.

STEWART. That very rich, very titled lady who has purchased the flat above yours. She's making noises which indicate displeasure about our excavations.

PAUL. Oh give me a break.

STEWART. I think maybe a personal intervention –

PAUL *is already on his way out.* STEWART *takes the opportunity to rest.*

They are doing very well, those boys. Do you know, they've transported nearly two tons of London clay down that corridor by purely manual means. If my calculations are correct, this is the equivalent of carrying an average-sized man from here to Surbiton and back. (*Thinks.*) Yes Surbiton. And they have learned a fundamental truth about life, namely that the whole of the building trade is one enormous rip-off. No special skills are required. You've just got to be prepared to get you hands dirty. Any human being of moderate intelligence can build a home from scratch. I've built two myself, one in County Cork, one in Brittany. They're still standing.

It's a primitive urge, the yearning to place one stone on top of another. But you make an awful lot more money out of it than you do flogging away at the old nine to five.

MARION. What does she want?

STEWART. The rich bitch?

MARION. Claire.

STEWART. A territorial dispute. You can't blame her. With land at a hundred quid per square foot, I'd be jumpy if someone started tunnelling in my backyard.

MARION. Do you enjoy all this?

STEWART. The labouring game? There's a certain satisfaction, yes.

MARION. What sort of satisfaction?

STEWART. My woman just walked out on me. It's a natural cycle. A woman walks out on me, I do some building work to take my mind off it. Eventually I end with a new house or a renovated flat. There you are, a single man living in semi-palatial circumstances. For some reason, this combination of factors is sensationally attractive to women. Before you know where you are, a woman has moved in. Things go very well, then less well, then rather badly. Eventually she walks out and to stop being depressed you sell up, buy a ruin and start to renovate it. Then, before you know where you are, etcetera. That's why I'm working here. Doing up someone else's place means I won't be tempted to lure a woman back to the luxury pad which will eventually emerge from the ruins. In this way I will be delivered from the cycle and will be able to do something sensible with my life. You've done well out of this place, what did you buy it for?

MARION. Forty-eight.

STEWART. Be worth a hundred and twenty now, more when we've built the patio.

PAUL *comes in, angry, followed by* HOWARD.

PAUL. The nerve of these people. Her family own half of Cornwall and she starts belly-aching about two square foot of London clay.

STEWART. What's the problem?

PAUL. There is now no problem. I sorted her out. She says 'We agreed the dividing line between your property and mine should be three point five metres away from the back wall. Why are you excavating to a line four point five metres from the back wall.'

MARION. Doesn't she have a point?

PAUL. I had to spell it out to her: 'We are building a retaining wall. What will it be retaining? Several tons of earth. In order to prevent the weight of the earth pressing directly on to the wall and pushing it over, we have to start digging further back, *then* build the wall, *then* fill in the gap with loose rubble.'

STEWART. That was telling her.

PAUL. She went very quiet, I can tell you. Don't they teach them anything at Bedales?

HOWARD. Mind you, we should have asked her permission. To dig on her land, you know.

PAUL. She's never here. Anyway she's getting the benefit of our work. She's getting a free irrigation system. It really pisses me off.

HOWARD *indicates to* STEWART *that they should get back to work.* HOWARD *goes out into the garden.*

STEWART. The earth. The pitiless earth.

He follows HOWARD *out.*

PAUL. This used to be an interesting area. Now it's full of people like her.

MARION. Why do you have to talk about her like that?

PAUL. What?

MARION. Claire. I had a chat with her the other day. I like her. You should see what she's doing to her flat. She's got taste.

PAUL. She's got money.

MARION. It's not a sin to be rich. She was *born* rich, she can't help it. At least she has the grace to wear her wealth with a certain degree of style –

STEWART *and* HOWARD *come through with another bin of rubble.*

STEWART. Did I say Surbiton? I think I meant Winchester.

They go out.

PAUL. You want to put it on the market, don't you? And move in with Jeremy. Does he want children?

MARION. No.

PAUL. Oh. Doesn't that rather . . .

MARION. No.

PAUL. Have you changed your mind?

MARION. Did I say I wanted to move in with Jeremy?

PAUL. No.

MARION. Did I say I wanted Jeremy at all?

PAUL. You said you wanted children.

MARION. And no one ever changes their mind. Everything stays true for ever.

She goes towards her bedroom door. She opens it and goes in, leaving the door open. PAUL stares at the open door.

Paul.

PAUL. I . . . I have to work.

MARION. Stewart can cope. It stops him from being unhappy.

PAUL stands for a moment. He hears STEWART and HOWARD approaching. He goes into MARION's bedroom and shuts the door.

Some moments. HOWARD comes in. He carries two more estate agent's signs. He flings them on to the floor.

HOWARD. Blue collar crime. You get a taste for it.

STEWART comes in with another estate agent's sign and the empty bin.

HOWARD (*into garden*). Paul!

STEWART throws the sign down on the floor.

STEWART. And there's your four supports. Completely gratis and for nothing. See what I mean. It's the pagan philosophy, what the Anglo-Saxons called 'wyrd'. Fate. Don't go out searching for what you want. Stay put, send your message out along the web and what you want will come to you. Wyrd. The web of Wyrd.

Blackout. In the darkness we hear The Communards singing 'Don't Leave me this Way'.

Scene Two

November 1986. Early evening.
The room is still bare, but there are new curtains and a handsome wooden floor. In the middle of the floor is a newly delivered carpet, large enough to cover about two thirds of the floor. It's wrapped in thick brown paper. To one side is a sleeping bag and a rucksack, an oasis of mess in the cool order.

HOWARD is sitting on the rolled up carpet smoking a cigarette. He wears a heavy overcoat. Next to him is a black hold-all. SHERRY, in her nightdress, is pacing around.

SHERRY. So we get on the boat at Bilbao, about five thousand of us. Wedged. We're not talking sardines, we're talking mashed tuna. With no edible oil. There's these four nuns, they get so squashed, people start thinking they're newspapers. And in the middle of all this mayhem, I suddenly think 'I'm going back. I'm going back, after thirteen months to that funny little island.' And just at that point I'm hit by this giant wave of nausea. And I'm nowhere near the side of the boat. And it's too packed to make it to the rail. I reach for a newspaper, it turns out to be a nun. It's a huge crisis, I can't hold it back any longer. I try to smile and think of England. Only the more I think of England, the more I want to be sick. Then suddenly it happens. This Swede. Or maybe he's a Lapp. Or a Finn. One of that lot who have arrows going through their vowels, he comes up to me, these enormous blue eyes, real icy blue, the genuine boring holes through your retina jobs, he comes up to me and says: 'Do you believe in hypnotism?' At this stage, I'm prepared to believe in anything that'll stop me embossing the nearest habit with last night's dinner, so I say –

HOWARD. Sherry –

SHERRY. 'Of course I believe in hypnotism' – what?

HOWARD. It's so good to see you. Only –

SHERRY. Yes?

HOWARD. Like I've only just come back from a weekend in Govan which might not seem a very big deal, but –

SHERRY. Oh God, yes, Marion said –

HOWARD. No, no –

SHERRY. About your dad, they both told me last night, it's so selfish of me –

HOWARD. It's no big deal.

SHERRY. Just forgot in the heat of the –

HOWARD. It was three months ago now. It's all right, life goes on, he's better off out of it, it's just my mum. She's got nothing to do all day. I mean, I'm there, what, three days, she's following me round the house all the time like a lost thing. Emptied me ashtray three times during the same fag, I swear it. What can you do? There's only two people left on the estate she knows, she gets lost in the daft shopping centre . . .

SHERRY. I'm really sorry.

She hugs him, he's embarrassed.

HOWARD. Get off! Look, this carpet. Did it just walk in or what? what?

SHERRY. Oh no it was delivered. Couple of hours ago. I was dead impressed. Both the guys on the van had Eton accents.

HOWARD. But you're sure it was for here?

SHERRY. The chit's got Marion's name on it.

HOWARD. Only I didn't know about it. Should be a communal decision spending money.

SHERRY. Never mind money. Tell me about you. Your love life.

HOWARD. Usual, you know, who's got the time?

SHERRY. Well, almost everybody in my experience.

HOWARD. I've been working on the book. That and all the bastard DIY. Keeps you busy. Resigned all me NATFHE commitments, Labour Party never sees me.

SHERRY. It's not good for you.

HOWARD. It's the deal though, eh. When the time comes to look after number one, there's not a lot of room for anything else in your life.

SHERRY. Did your really do this floor, it's wonderful.

HOWARD. Well, I helped like. Paul and his mate Stewart, they were the gaffers. Paul's got very canny at it. And dead particular too, finicky you know.

SHERRY. The patio looks brilliant.

HOWARD. Nearly killed me. And I'm dreading the kitchen. Paul's been making drawings, studying the plumbing, visiting building centres. We'll be months at it.

SHERRY. He seems happy.

HOWARD. Yeah. Only . . .

Pause.

He doesn't spend any time on his work. Doesn't seem interested. Knocks off the articles and interviews in a few minutes, then spends a whole day fiddling around with a bit of wiring. Reckons it's a better way of making money. Never has any cash these days.

The front door shuts.

SHERRY. It's lovely to see you. Paul and Marion are they . . .

HOWARD. What?

SHERRY. Well, sort of . . .

HOWARD. Don't ask me, I only live here. Honestly I couldn't tell you if –

PAUL and MARION come in. MARION wears a very expensive coat. PAUL carries a small cardboard box.

MARION. Howard. Was it OK?

She kisses him lightly on the cheek. PAUL claps him round the shoulder.

HOWARD. Yeah, all right, you know. Got in about four hours ago, haven't got me coat off yet.

PAUL. Highlights of the world tour, takes a while.

SHERRY. Wait till I get the slides.

MARION. Oh it's arrived.

All look at the carpet.

PAUL. What is it?

MARION. Well what does it look like?

PAUL. I didn't think we'd made any decision about –

MARION. Have you got a knife?

PAUL reaches in his pocket and produces a complex Swiss Army knife.

When you see this, you'll be completely stunned.

HOWARD. When you look at the quality of their weaponry, it's amazing the Swiss Army don't have a better historical record.

PAUL has started cutting through the cords. Everyone gathers around to nudge and coax the carpet into position.

MARION. Sherry, I think your things are going to be slightly in the way.

SHERRY. Oh yes, sorry. I'll . . .

She pushes her sleeping bag and travel effects against the wall.

It's a dead comfortable floor, I slept really well.

PAUL. Marion, if you stand on the paper, Howard and I will roll it out . . .

MARION. Right, got it.

PAUL (*to* SHERRY). Out the way.

They unroll the carpet. It's sumptuous. All are stunned into silence.

HOWARD. Big, isn't it?

SHERRY. They've got bigger ones in India. Like this, but bigger, I saw them.

MARION. I'm so pleased. I think it's exactly right.

PAUL. Um, look, I didn't think we'd made any decision about . . .

MARION. And I think you'll find we can get away with very minimal dressing of the rest of the room. This makes such a simple bold statement. And then a fun thing somewhere . . . here, to take the edge off the severity. I know. That plant in my room.

SHERRY. Yes.

MARION. I'll get it, see how it looks.

MARION *goes out. A silence.* PAUL *sees the delivery docket on the mantelpiece, picks it up, reads it.*

PAUL. Howie, remember that carpet warehouse in the Harrow Road we went to.

HOWARD. Oh aye, we brought back some swatches.

PAUL. D'you think this one's better?

HOWARD. Better? Well of course its better.

PAUL. How much better?

HOWARD *catches his drift.*

HOWARD. How much?

PAUL. I'm asking you.

HOWARD. Don't piss around. How much did it cost?

PAUL. Two thousand six hundred and eighty-seven.

HOWARD. Pounds?

PAUL. Pounds.

A pause. Then HOWARD *goes to* PAUL, *snatches the docket from him and examines it.*

HOWARD. Two six eight seven. That's the delivery number.

PAUL. Well why's it got a squiggle with two lines going through it in front of it?

HOWARD. Because it means pounds. I'm an economist, that means pounds. Two thousand six hundred and eighty-seven. For a carpet.

SHERRY. It's just a big rug really.

PAUL. Now, tell me how much you like it.

HOWARD. I love it, I want to die on it.

MARION *is back with the plant. She stands it in a corner.*

MARION. There. That's the sort of thing.

PAUL. Erm, we were wondering . . .

MARION. This is my purchase. You can enjoy the benefits of it. I was very depressed by the swatches you brought back from the Harrow Road. And I was talking to Claire and we went out and bought it. Claire's right, she says money spent on the best is never wasted.

SHERRY. Well it certainly . . . I mean it brings out what you've done with the rest of the room so well.

MARION. The other thing is the kitchen. I was thinking perhaps we ought to pay some men to come in and do it. I mean, it's not like the rest of the house. You can't go for months without a kitchen can you? If I don't have somewhere I can cook, I go crazy. The people who did Claire's are very good, and not unreasonable. Five thousand or something. And it would be done in a fortnight. We could all go away and when we came back it would be done.

PAUL. But I've ordered the wood for the units. I measured it all up. There's all this wood coming.

MARION. Well it's just wood.

She goes out.

PAUL (*gesturing to the cardboard box he's holding*). I bought this junction box today. I've planned where the lights go. (*To* HOWARD.) Did you know about this?

HOWARD. She's been making muttering noises. About how long it's all been taking. I didn't know she would –

PAUL. Paying good money. To other people. For things we could do ourselves.

SHERRY. Well. I suppose she's right in a way. A good kitchen . . . is a good kitchen, isn't it?

PAUL. My kitchen would be a good kitchen. What she'll get is . . . some bunch of cowboys sticking in standard units. Quick grown steam-dried pine. Where's the individuality in that? Where's the pride?

HOWARD. Come on Paul. We've flogged ourselves to death on this the last eighteen months. All right, we've saved money, but look what it's cost us. The energy we've spent on it. Which should have gone into other things. Look at my work. Look at *your* work for Christ's sake. There's a stack of unplayed records on your desk you should have reviewed. Records some people would kill for, you get them free and you haven't even broken them out of the cellophane. What's that about, man?

PAUL *sits down suddenly, says nothing.*

SHERRY. This flat. It must be worth quite a bit now, eh?

HOWARD. I suppose.

SHERRY. I mean, that eleven thousand I took. What would that be worth? If I'd done what you did?

HOWARD. I dunno. It's a bit complex. I mean there's a lot of factors.

SHERRY. No there aren't. You must have some idea what the flat's worth.

HOWARD. Well it's, I mean if you take –

PAUL. Twenty-five thousand. If you'd done what we did. Instead of your eleven grand two fifty. Twenty-five thousand pounds.

SHERRY. Oh.

MARION *brings in a new drinks cabinet. She sets it down.*

This Scandinavian hypnotist I met on the crossing. He was really nice. He bought me dinner on the boat. And the train fare to London. All I had left was a few pesetas, you see. Seventeen pesetas. That's all I had left out of eleven thousand pounds. I didn't know how I was going to make it back. So it was great that he turned up. I mean, I slept with him. In his cabin. But it was still nice of him. He was an OK Swede. Finn.

Pause.

HOWARD. Well yeah, but you've been round the world. Really thoroughly, not just the obvious places. Not many people have done that. Burundi and places. That's worth spending a lot of money on. You can't put a price on that.

SHERRY. Burundi?

HOWARD. You sent us a card from Burundi.

Pause.

SHERRY. Oh yes . . . Burundi. Yes everyone was really nice there.

HOWARD. You did the adventurous thing. We were boring just . . . staying here.

SHERRY *stands.*

SHERRY. Is it all right if I go and have a bath. I haven't had a bath for an awful long time.

She grabs some things and goes out hurriedly.

HOWARD. Christ, Paul. You shouldn't have said that, about the money we've made.

PAUL. I think I'd like some discussion about this kitchen business.

MARION. Well of course.

PAUL. I want to do the kitchen myself. It's the thing I've been really looking foward to. And I know I can do it well. And I want to be given the chance.

MARION. And how long will it take you? Six months? A year?

PAUL. I don't know!

Pause.

MARION. What do you think, Howard?

HOWARD. Well. Suppose we look at this as a hypothesis, this getting builders in. We've done the patio. We ripped out all the damp in Paul's room. We transformed the bathroom. Put in central heating. Decorated Marion's room, the corridor. Now, if we accept what Marion's putting forward, getting builders in, that's the kitchen done. With the carpet down in here it means . . . well it means we've finished, doesn't it? It actually means we've finished.

PAUL. What about your room?

HOWARD. It'll do.

Pause.

It's over Paul. We've done it. We can go back to, you know, normal life.

PAUL. What about the money? I can't afford five grand. I can't even afford a third of five grand.

MARION. I've made arrangements. We account for everything in the accounting book. I pay real money to the builders and get theoretical credits from you two against the time when we come to sell.

MARION *goes to* PAUL, *touches him tenderly.*

Paul, be reasonable, it's got to be like this.

PAUL *looks at them both.*

PAUL. You've set this up between you, haven't you?

HOWARD. What?

PAUL. Behind my back.

HOWARD. First I've heard of it, man.

PAUL. I'm going to have to think very carefully about this. I'm going to have consider my position.

HOWARD. Accept it. It's over. Don't you feel relieved?

PAUL. Look at what we've done. Look at what I've done. Bought a flat in a Victorian house in a London conservation area for peanuts. At the start of a property boom. And renovated it. Myself. Eighteen months ago I couldn't hammer a nail in straight. That is an achievement, all that. And now. At the very end, she's trying to take it away from me, trying to cheat me of it.

Pause.

HOWARD. Come on Paul. You know, you've been fantastic. We both admire that. Can't you just relax and enjoy living here.

PAUL. No. I don't think I can.

HOWARD. Well Marion's made up her mind, I've made up my mind.

MARION. You're outvoted. You don't have an option.

She goes.

PAUL. Yes I do. I can invoke the lease.

HOWARD. You what?

PAUL. The lease. Tenants in Common. When one party wants to sell, everyone has to sell.

HOWARD. Sell?

PAUL. Sell, yes. I want to sell my share of the flat.

HOWARD. What? You're out of your mind. Haven't you noticed it's just got pleasant to live here. You don't take in a lungful of brickdust with your first morning fag. You don't find yourself halfway through a slash suddenly realising some dickhead's moved the bog. We're living in *luxury* and you want to *sell*.

PAUL. I was going to wait till we'd done the kitchen. Next summer, maybe autumn. But if it's going to be in a sellable state in a couple of months, OK.

HOWARD. OK what?

PAUL. Just . . . we can all make arrangements.

HOWARD. Is this Ruth's idea?

PAUL. What?

HOWARD. Has it got serious?

PAUL. Christ, Howie.

HOWARD. I need to know, man, I'm in the fucking middle. A few months back I thought you were getting on with Marion again. I mean nobody actually tells me what's going on.

PAUL. Yeah. Well we did. Me and Marion.

Pause

Just once. Well a few times. Nostalgia. It wasn't significant.

HOWARD. Does she think it wasn't significant?

PAUL. It was nothing. But Ruth. It's hard to persuade her I'm still living with my ex-girlfriend and it's completely innocent.

HOWARD. I can see her point.

PAUL. I get a lot of pressure. So all right. I'll sell up, at least it'll sort that part of my life out.

HOWARD. Well where are you going to live? Doss down in her little cubby hole in Whitechapel?

PAUL. Possibly.

HOWARD. Get married?

PAUL. Well it's a bit early for –

HOWRD. What then?

Pause

PAUL. Well there's an idea I had at the back of my mind.

HOWARD. Oh yeah?

PAUL. I was going to suggest it for next year. You wouldn't . . . you wouldn't fancy buying a house with me and Stewart would you?

Pause.

See my share of this place would be what . . . forty-five. It's not a lot to play with. But with your share it's up to ninety. And Stewart's not happy, problems with his new woman. He's looking to sell. Pool it all, you're looking at a hundred and fifty K. It's a different league. There's still bits of Islington up for grabs, even some areas near Docklands. For that sort of money you could get hold of a good size Victorian house, three-storey, double-fronted. Need a bit doing to it, but in the long run you'd be looking at a very sizeable –

HOWARD. Need what?

PAUL. Need . . . need a bit doing to it.

HOWARD. No.

PAUL. Stewart and I would do most of the work. Your bedroom first, it would be quick.

HOWARD. No. I do not want to see another bag of cement as long as I live. I do not want to carry twenty foot lengths of knocked off timber along the street at the dead of night. I have sold my *Guardian* offer toolkit. Definitely no.

PAUL. Well what d'you want to do then. Because I'm selling. Which means you have to as well. And what can you do with your share? Forty grand'll get you fuck all in London. What you want to do, go back to Glasgow?

MARION *comes in carrying bottles to put in the drinks cupboard.*

MARION. I gave her a mugful of gin. It seems to be taking effect.

PAUL *(quickly)*. I agree.

MARION *puts the bottles down.*

I think you're right. I think it's sensible. Let's get it done quickly.

MARION. You've changed your mind.

PAUL. Yes.

MARION. I think that's good. I really do.

She goes towards him to kiss him, but something stops her in her tracks.

PAUL. And then as soon as the kitchen's done I want to sell. Because I don't like living here any more.

MARION. Paul, You were the one who wanted to stay. All along. We only stayed because you insisted. Now you want to go. What's that about?

PAUL. Well. There's someone else in my life.

HOWARD. I think I'll just . . . see if Sherry's OK.

He goes.

MARION. So. It's to be Ruth. Ruth in Whitechapel isn't that right?

PAUL. I . . .

Pause.

MARION. You don't have to apologise I'm not your wife. It's just . . . don't let us go around telling everyone what good *friends* we are when we don't even give each other the basic information. I bet she's got long hair.

PAUL. She has got long hair, yes.

MARION. She has got long hair yes, what a breakthrough.

PAUL. I met her at a Style Council concert. Hammersmith Odeon, upstairs in the bar. It was truly horrible, everyone posing around, trying to look soulful. I was sticking my mike under people's noses trying to get some vox pops. Most of them refused because it wasn't television and their clothes wouldn't come over. Eventually I got round to her and she just said: 'I hate all these crappy people'. I felt refreshed, I really did. I thought to myself, I don't have to stay here, I can be somewhere else with this girl. It was a moment of enlightenment. We went for a pizza. It was great.

SHERRY *comes on wearing an old dressing gown of* HOWARD*'s. She's drinking gin from a coffee mug.*

SHERRY. Do you know the thing I discovered, the thing I *really* found out? The world is in a much better state than you'd expect. A much better state than you're led to believe.

HOWARD *appears in the doorway, too late to stop* SHERRY.

I mean, when you watch the news on television, you get so depressed, it's all wars and people blowing each other up, but when you actually get out there, in among it, it's not . . . you know . . . not such an awful planet after all. As planets go. I'm sorry, were you talking?

MARION. Just you know, passing the time.

HOWARD. Um, Sherry, I think your bath –

SHERRY. Oh God, I'd forgotten I put it on. Paul darling, you haven't got a clean towel have you, mine's in the wash.

PAUL *goes out.* SHERRY *follows him and* HOWARD *tries to.*

MARION. Howard.

HOWARD *stops and turns.*

MARION. Paul . . . hasn't offered you any sort of deal has he?

HOWARD. He was talking. About maybe him and Stewart buying a place and me chipping in.

MARION. What about this Ruth?

HOWARD. She's still a student, she hasn't got any money.

MARIN. But she'd live there as well.

HOWARD. I don't know, it's just an idea that's floating round.

MARION. Is she nice?

HOWARD. Only met her once. Good looking lass, doesn't say a lot.

MARION. Bit boring, eh?

HOWARD. I didn't say that.

MARION. No. It's a relief for me that she's like that. There's no contest or anything. Only for his sake I wish she'd been someone more . . . you know challenging.

HOWARD. Yeah.

MARION. So he's serious. About selling up.

HOWARD. I think he is, yes.

MARION *considers.*

MARION. It's stupid to sell this place now. The boom's not stopping. The German banker on the top floor's selling, according to Claire, and he's gone on the market at a hundred and seventy-five. And he'll get it. OK, he's got planning permission to develop another storey, but even so, we can't be far behind.

HOWARD. No.

MARION. Do you want to buy a house with Paul?

HOWARD. I don't know.

Pause.

It's all wrong. People in the South. Us. Making a fortune out of flogging properties to each other. Who are we making a fortune from, that's the point? My mum's still in the same house she's been living in for the last forty years. That's not appreciating at twenty per cent a year, that's for sure.

Pause.

He wants to buy somewhere and do it up. He's got the bug. I just don't want to live in all that rubble and disruption again.

MARION. Then don't. Stay here. You keep your third. And I'll buy out Paul.

HOWARD. Buy him out? You're talking about finding an extra forty-five grand.

MARION. I can jack up my mortgage. I can borrow from Jeremy. And I can borrow from Claire.

Pause.

HOWARD. Christ.

MARION. Remember all that hassle we had with Scott for a few thousand. All you have to do is sit in your room in this nice centrally-heated flat, and by this time next year you'll be worth another ten grand. You get the best of both worlds. It'll be quiet, you'll be able to write your book. No DIY. I work such long hours these days you'll have the place to yourself most of the time. You can use my word processor. And all the time you're getting richer. Now what's wrong with that? Mmmm?

PAUL *comes back on.*

PAUL. She's pissed already, I can't believe it.

MARION. If you want to go, Paul, that's fine, I'll buy your share. As long as Howard doesn't want to go as well.

PAUL. Christ.

MARION. Make a decision, Howard.

Pause.

HOWARD. I just . . . I'm fed up with all the disruption. I don't want to move and start all over again. That's the reason I'm going to stay. That's the only reason.

He goes out quickly. PAUL *goes to the french windows, peers out.*

PAUL. I still can't believe we dug all that out, you know. It was six big skips. Full of rubble.

MARION *holds him.*

MARION. This is what you want isn't it?

PAUL. Yeah. Yeah.

SHERRY *bursts in wearing only a bath towel and carrying a bottle of gin.*

SHERRY. Before I have my bath, I just want to say that I regret nothing. I am Edith Piaf. Got that?

Blackout. In the darkness we hear The Beastie Boys singing 'Fight for the Right (to Party)'.

Scene Three

May 1987. Evening.

The transformation of the room is now complete. It looks cool, refined and uncluttered – a few well-chosen objects in a big, open space.

STEWART *is lying on the floor, face up, head towards the back wall, fiddling with a radiator pipe.*

The french windows are open. PAUL *and* HOWARD *are standing outside.* HOWARD *is holding a large brown envelope,* PAUL *a lengthy document word-processed on to A4. This is the manuscript of* HOWARD's *book.*

STEWART *is under the impression that* PAUL *and* HOWARD *are in the room.*

STEWART. The argument that over one hundred and sixty thousand old people, all of them owner-occupiers, are projected to die in London in the course of 1988 and that, in consequence, an equal number of propeties will come plonking on to the market, flooding demand and bringing the price of property down is at first sight a compelling one.

Pause.

After all, Howard, everyone has a granny somewhere, and the mad stampede to get away, at all costs from said granny when she was a good deal younger and more socially useful than she is now, was a major factor in the property boom in the first place. So when Granny finally hands in her dinner pail, wouldn't one expect the nearest and dearest, doubtless a bunch of grasping bastards to a man, woman and child, to flog off the ancestral pile to the highest bidder and stuff the takings under their mattresses?

PAUL *and* HOWARD *come in.*

PAUL *(stuffing the manuscript in the envelope)*. . . . and all the stuff about the city is great, the money markets –

STEWART. Not so.

PAUL *and* HOWARD *stare at* STEWART.

The argument makes the fundamental error of over-estimating the ability of human beings to live in any kind of harmony with one another. The same impulse that caused son to abandon mother in the first place, i.e. the feeling that he couldn't stand the bitch, now impels him to leave his wife since he can now no longer stand that bitch either. So he returns to his now grannyless home with his new found doxy, leaving wife number one with her toy-boy in the house he's sweated away his life to buy. The number of available properties on the market remains constant.

He sits up, wiping his hands.

So there you are. Just a compression joint. All it needed was a quick tighten up. Now, where did I put the bathroom?

He wanders off to wash his hands. HOWARD *looks at* PAUL *anxiously.*

HOWARD. But, I mean, overall . . . do you reckon it's any good?

PAUL. It's great, of course it's good. I've just got one . . .

HOWARD. Yeah?

PAUL. The title.

HOWARD. *The Myth of Recovery*. Do you not like that?

PAUL. *The Myth of Recovery*. You see, I think it's a bit chancy.

HOWARD. What d'you mean?

PAUL. Well. Just supposing. Supposing the economic recovery isn't a myth, supposing there's some substance to it –

HOWARD. But it is a myth. The book proves it's a myth. The dependence on external factors like the valuation of the dollar and the price of commodities and the short term buoyancy engendered by nationalised industry sell-offs plus the end of the North Sea Oil bonanza means the so-called Thatcherite recovery could be wiped out tomorrow if –

PAUL. But from a publisher's point of view. I mean it's saying something people don't want to hear and it's sort of . . . speculative. I think that's why you're having trouble getting it into print.

HOWARD. So once the recovery has been clearly exposed as a fraud, it might get published.

PAUL. Yes, I suppose.

HOWRD. Only then . . . nobody'll have any money to spend on books.

PAUL. It won't be that bad.

HOWARD. I think it will. That's my conclusion. We're about to hit the downwave of a sixty year cycle. Prices, wages, it's all going to start falling. (*Reads.*) 'People in the North who are poor now will stay poor or become poorer. People in the South who are credit rich, theoretically rich, will find that the dwindling value of the assets on which they've staked everything will be far exceeded by the outgoings which are still paying for those very assets.' So in *real terms* they will be poor too.

STEWART *has returned in time to pick up the drift.*

STEWART. Going to sell this place then, Howie?

HOWARD. You what?

STEWART. If I thought what you thought, I'd sell up. No point having a mortgage in a downwave. Sell up and rent somewhere, that's what you should do.

HOWARD. Ah not this place, this is *central* London, man, it'll keep its value –

STEWART. Special factors eh?

PAUL. *Historical* factors –

HOWARD. And we're still paying peanuts for it. At least I am.

PAUL (*standing*). Up for the seven fifty-eight Stewart? We're a bit outclassed here.

STEWART. All right, young man.

Everyone is now standing.

HOWARD. Bloody commuters, provincials.

PAUL. Nothing wrong with Greenwich, very fashionable.

HOWARD. Apart from the fact you're in Charlton –

PAUL. Charltonish. It's nearer Greenwich though.

HOWARD. Is it knackers!

PAUL. Oh listen. End of the month. At the Palladium. The

Searchers are playing their Silver Jubilee concert. D'you fancy coming?

PAUL *gets out his diary.*

HOWARD. You have to hand it to them –

PAUL. Twenty-five years on the road –

MARION *comes in. She is carrying some candles for a table arrangement.*

MARION. Oh.

PAUL. Just came by to pick up those tools.

MARION. Oh.

HOWARD. Stewart's fixed the leak.

STEWART. Compression joint.

PAUL. Only we've got to be off. The train. That concert, Howie, it's the thirty-first.

HOWARD. Put me down for it. Might be the last chance, you never know.

PAUL (*watching* MARION *arrange the candles*). Nice.

MARION. I've got some people coming round to dinner.

HOWARD. Oh. Didn't see anything in the oven. Is it a microwave job?

MARION. Having it delivered, silly.

STEWART. Delivered, what, a dinner party?

MARION. Three courses. A firm called Mr Sloane. Very good.

STEWART. I'll make a note of the number.

STEWART *goes, followed by* HOWARD. PAUL *stands watching* MARION.

MARION. I thought you were rushing off.

PAUL. I was just watching. Just for a moment.

MARION. Is it working out?

PAUL. It's pretty good, yes.

MARION. The three of you.

PAUL. Four. Stewart's new woman got a bit of cash out of her divorce so she bought a share. Makes it quite cheap.

MARION. And how long will it take you to do it up?

PAUL. Couple of years. Maybe three. But it'll be all our own work. We start on the central heating next week.

MARION. And the writing?

PAUL. Bits and pieces, you know. The music scene, you know, not a lot happening.

MARION. Michael Jackson? Prince?

PAUL. Not a lot happening.

MARION. And Ruth?

PAUL. Fine.

Pause.

MARION. Is it true?

PAUL. Yes. It's due in October.

MARION. And you're happy about that.

PAUL. One of those things. You can't plan them really.

MARION. No.

PAUL. The train.

He kisses her lightly on the cheek.

MARION. Telephone me. I'll take you to lunch sometime.

PAUL. Good. Yes. I've always liked lunch.

HOWARD *comes back.* PAUL *thumps him on the shoulder. Then goes.* MARION *looks at the room. Adjusts the lighting.*

HOWARD. Well.

MARION. These people who are coming tonight –

HOWARD. Yes. OK I'll keep out of the way.

MARION. There's bound to be some food left over if you want to eat late.

HOWARD. No. I'll go down the Hot Pot or something.

Pause.

MARION. I don't suppose I'll ever get to meet her.

HOWARD. Well, she's a bit shy. Maybe when the baby's born.

MARION. Why does he want to spend his life with someone who's shy? I just don't see that.

HOWARD. She's a nice kid.

Pause.

Sherry was on the box again. I got it on the video for you.

MARION. Oh.

HOWARD. Did this stand-up monologue about roll-on deodorants. Magic. Audience were pissing themselves.

MARION. Yes, she's doing so well.

The entryphone bleeps. MARION *goes towards it.*

Hello.

The entryphone crackles.

Yes, bring it through, will you.

She turns back to HOWARD.

The food, thank Christ. If the guests arrive before the supper, the artifice is ruined.

HOWARD. I'll get out of your way then.

Sees his manuscript on the table.

I'll take this. (*Riffles pages.*) Might do a bit of tinkering with the chapter about the money supply.

MARION. Great.

He goes, bashing the manuscript against his thigh.

Some moments. A uniformed DELIVERER *comes on, laden with bags.*

DELIVERER. Got yer scoff, lady, Gawd bless yer.

MARION *turns. The* DELIVERER *is* SHERRY.

MARION. Sherry. But –

SHERRY. I haven't let success go to my head. Yet. And it's a bit of steady money. Keeps me sober before I go onstage at ten.

MARION. I –

SHERRY. Couldn't resist it when I saw your name on the list. The starters are in this green bag. And the Salmis de Dinde à la Berrichonne's here. I'll put them in the kitchen on my way out. Do you want the gateau in the fridge?

MARION. Well, I suppose . . . yes.

SHERRY. And here's your aerosol.

MARION. Aerosol?

SHERRY. It's a new touch. You waft it round the flat, it gives a general cooking smell.

She sprays some in the air.

SHERRY. Nice, eh, this is the Paysanne flavour.

MARION. You've only just missed Paul.

SHERRY. Oh. Shame. Still I see him a bit. He comes along and heckles me at the quiet venues. He's a good mate. Do you see him much?

MARION. A bit. I'm very busy at the moment.

SHERRY. Great. And happy?

MARION. It's really bizarre seeing you like this.

SHERRY. I'm happy. I'm having a great time. People point me out on the tube. Funny thing, though, if I've got this uniform on, nobody recognises me. Good, eh? Howard walked straight past me in the corridor.

MARION. I've seen you on the television. You've got very good. Much sharper.

SHERRY. After I came back. From the world tour. Things sort of fell into place for me. It all seemed so strange, this country. Cold, you know, emotionally cold. I just felt like grabbing hold of people and saying: 'Care. For fuck's sake, will you please care.' So I just put that feeling into my act.

MARION. And people laughed.

SHERRY. That's it. For the first time they laughed. Well better be off. Sign this. Next drop's in Cheyne Walk, can't keep them waiting.

MARION *signs the proffered chit.*

And this is your receipt madam. I'll give Howard a cuddle on the way out. Take care.

They embrace for a moment. SHERRY *makes to go.*

MARION. Sherry. Ring me.

SHERRY. Might well do. Or you could come and see me on the circuit. I'm better live.

She looks around.

Nice place you've got here.

She goes. MARION *sits. Opens the bag. Looks at the food. Stands. Pours a drink. Drinks. Looks around. Some moments.*

The end of 'Needles and Pins' fades in.

Lights fade. Music ends. Blackout.

End of play